WITHDRAWN

*Guide Library*

*Hillwood Museum*
*Washington, D.C.*

RUSSIA IN MY LIFE

# RUSSIA
# IN
# MY LIFE

THOMAS P. WHITNEY

*REYNAL & COMPANY / NEW YORK*

*To Julie*

# Contents

# List of Illustrations

(Between pages 148-149)

RUSSIA IN MY LIFE

# 1. *A Strange Language*

I stood in a cornfield in Coon Rapids, Iowa, on a day in September, 1959, and watched the astonishing scene unfolding before me.

Several score news photographers battled for position. They screamed, yelled and pushed each other and the American and Russian police and security officers who were trying to hold them back. Behind them were dozens of struggling reporters—attempting to peer past the massed photographers and security agents and see what was going on. Down the rows of corn upon us there advanced an enormous wicked-looking corn chopper. Mounted policemen started to ride down on the photographers and someone quickly set up the cry: "Look out! The Cossacks are coming!"

Immediately in front of me my friend Roswell Garst, wealthy farmer, shouted and gesticulated at the photographers to get them to move back. Then, when they did not heed him, he pulled up a big stalk of corn by the roots and started to fling it at them, but, overcome by his own momentum, he ended up on his behind on the black earth of his own corn patch.

Next to me, in a dapper beige suit adorned with a solitary golden Soviet government decoration, there stood Nikita Sergeyevich Khrushchev, Premier of the Soviet Union, cause of all this melee. Bemused by the spectacle, he watched quietly. He and I started to discuss in Russian the quality of Mr. Garst's corn. I was working as a reporter for the *Washington Post*—and that was my exclusive interview for the day.

But while we stood there, Khrushchev and I, with that pitched battle taking place in front of us, I could not help marveling at the fate that had deposited me in the center of that fantastic picture.

How could it be that I, who came from a home in Toledo, Ohio, in which no word of Russian was ever spoken, who had for the first twenty years of my life hardly the slightest interest in Russia or the Soviet Union, who had never had the least aspiration to become a reporter or diplomat or foreign correspondent, got myself involved in this?

Not in the most fanciful dreams of my youth had I pictured myself exchanging chit-chat with a Soviet dictator in an Iowa cornfield. And so much else in this same tenor had happened to me that I had never expected.

I had never thought I might fall off a speeding trolleybus in front of the Kremlin at one A.M. in the morning, nor that I might cause a holocaust in the scientific world of a great country by an attempt to investigate a cancer cure.

Nor had I ever foreseen that I might be invited by a Soviet agent to inspect uranium samples in a Moscow hotel room, nor that I would introduce lawn mowers to the startled natives of a Moscow suburb, nor that I would be on the scene when the brass of the Soviet Army—and a future United States President—were told of the end of World War II by an American Ambassador, nor that I would make an orange and white Siberian cat named Charley one of the companions of my life, nor that I would be one of half a dozen Americans invited to attend the greatest—and most felicitous—funeral of the century.

In particular, I never dreamed I might lose my heart in the "Gorky Park of Culture and Rest"—nor that my romance would become a subject of great-power negotiation. All of this—and more—happened because I decided one fine day to study the Russian language and Russian history.

I am far from Russia right now. I am writing these lines in the study of my New England farmhouse. But even here Russia manages still to surround me. There are half a dozen Russian dolls upon my mantel. That Siberian cat, Charley, now fourteen years old, is vigorously washing himself on my bed. Russian newspapers and magazines are piled along one side of my room. Russian books fill my bookcase. Next to my phonograph is a record album entitled "Moscow After Dark" by a girl named Yulya, who has played more than a passing role in my life. On the desk in front of me is a photograph clipped from the front page of the *New York Times* of a short while ago showing four of America's leading diplomats, all of them men who have occupied the post of American Ambassador to the Soviet Union, all of them former bosses of mine, conferring in the White House with the President.

And here I am, glancing now and then out of the window at the rolling hills of Connecticut, and writing a book about Russia.

\*    \*    \*    \*    \*

I remember vividly how the idea of my studying Russian history was conceived.

It was late winter in 1937. I had just had my twentieth birthday and was a senior at Amherst College. In four months I would graduate. In the fall, I had decided, I would enter graduate work at Columbia in European history, planning to go into university teaching. I stood in the office of Professor Charles W. Cole, one of my advisors. We were discussing where I should go for graduate work and in what area to specialize. In a corner at a small desk sat Cole's assistant, Fred Barghoorn, his nose buried in a Russian text. Fred had just completed several years of graduate work at Harvard.

"Why don't you specialize on Russia like Fred?" asked Cole. "It's an important field and one sadly neglected."

I left Cole's office pondering this. Russia! Here, it seemed to me, was a challenge. During my college work I had read several works on the Soviet Union and Russian history. They had left me curious— but unsatisfied. In those years every book on the USSR seemed to be either violently pro-Communist or violently anti-Communist. In them, Soviet Russia was either paradise or hell. They left unanswered, it seemed to me, most of the important questions one could ask about such a revolutionary scheme.

What were the origins of the cataclysm in Russia? And what did it foreshadow for the West? Here were questions worth study.

I talked it over with another of my advisors, Professor Lawrence B. Packard. He was excited. He told me how he had spent a short time in Russia—in Vladivostok with the American forces during the Russian civil war. His brief stay had left him eternally curious.

"Certainly, study Russia," Professor Packard told me. "It is a fascinating field. You'll have to learn the language and it's not easy. But it will be worth it."

I kept thinking over this idea.

In early May I was in the Amherst Chapel building looking at the bulletin board where the dean posted notices of scholarships and the like. I read:

"Intensive Russian Course . . . University of California Summer School in Berkeley . . . Professor George Patrick . . . Apply for scholarships for full tuition . . . Ten weeks . . ."

This drove itself into my awareness. I reacted. I read more closely. Here perhaps was a way of getting a headstart in the language before going to graduate school in the fall at Columbia. I jotted down notes and wrote to Professor Patrick in Berkeley that evening.

In the mail a week later I received two communications. One came from Professor Patrick. Yes, he could offer me a scholarship for the Russian course at the University of California. My heart jumped. Then I opened the other letter and my heart jumped again. The manager of a professional baseball team in Vermont offered me a job as pitcher. He had seen me play while scouting college teams—and he liked my style.

I put the two letters on the table in front of me and scratched my head. Which? I loved baseball, and always wanted to play as a pro— even if only one summer. And if I once got started, who knows? That was one of my most treasured boyhood dreams . . . But if I did not take the opportunity to learn Russian it seemed unlikely I would ever specialize in Russian history. If I were serious about this Russian thing I should go to Berkeley. Again I scratched my head. This was a hard decision. All day long I could think of nothing else. Finally late that night instead of studying I went for a long walk—pondering.

At two A.M. in the morning I came home with mind made up. The die was cast—for Russian. A few weeks later I sat on the porch of the Connecticut farmhouse where my family spent vacations and chatted with mother. These were the days preceding graduation and my bag was already packed for the trip West. Father drove into the yard from a trip to town. He walked up and handed me the *New York Times*. I scanned the headlines and read: "Tukhachevsky and Other Red Army Leaders Shot for Treason."

For months the press had been carrying reports on executions and disappearances of Soviet officials. This was the boom year of Stalin's great purge. But this latest development, the wiping out of the leadership of the Soviet army, was the purge's nadir. It was one of the most dismal days of Russia's history. A fine omen for the beginning of Russian studies!

A few days later I looked down from the window of the little Boeing airliner in which I was traveling at an altitude of 5,000 feet over the cornfields of central Iowa and considered the paradox that to study Russian I was traveling not toward Moscow but away from it—with great speed.

*     *     *     *     *

I sat relaxed in the midsummer morning heat in the classroom on the University of California campus and watched George Patrick at work in front of the class of a dozen students. I was fascinated. He was like an orchestra leader. He talked with his hands as effectively as with his vocal chords. The way he swung his right arm down in an arc to indicate the proper place for an accent was unforgettable. And the fervor with which he devoted himself to the propagation of Russian was fantastic. With him, teaching was not so much a job as a mission.

I have been fortunate to know a number of talented teachers, and George Z. Patrick stands out among them for his ability in communicating and for the deep affection he inspired. He was as Russian as troikas or samovars, despite his Irish-sounding name. He headed the team of three teachers that pummeled us in relays all summer long for five hours of class a day, five days a week, for ten weeks, giving us no rest from the terrors of Russian till it was coming out of our ears— and our mouths. For every hour of class I suppose we were spending another two hours sweating over homework in the afternoons and nights. This called itself an intensive course and it was.

That first Russian class of mine was devoted to the tongue-twisting letters of the Russian—more properly, the Cyrillic—alphabet. We had in front of us a Russian grammar which was almost the only one on the market. In those days nobody but a few lunatics studied Russian. This curious grammar must have been designed to meet the needs of British commercial travelers at about the turn of the century. It contained copious advice on the conduct of commercial correspondence and nothing on how to understand Soviet newspapers.

One phrase I learned during my first lesson I still remember.

"Oo-muy-vahl'-nuy yash'-cheek"—this term intrigued us all. After we had wrapped our mouths around it lusciously several times, savoring its flavor, Patrick explained that literally translated it meant a "washing box"—a wash basin.

For a week every sentence we constructed contained that omnipresent "washing box." Then with accumulation of new vocabulary the term got lost. But not in *my* mind! I waited to be able to put this term to use. When I got to Russia, I imagined, the porter would show me to my hotel room and I would ask where the "washing box" was located. He would stare with surprise—astounded that any foreigner should know such an occult term.

As it happens I am still waiting to find an occasion to use the phrase "oo-muy-vahl'-nuy yash'-cheek." When I did get to Russia I found that in the Hotel Metropole a wash basin was called a "taz" or a "tazik." Much simpler but so much less satisfying!

How interesting to me was that strange language! I never had so much pure enjoyment from learning as during the summer session at Berkeley that year. Part of this, no doubt, was because of the friendships I struck up with kindred souls. Some of it was a flaming spirit induced by the injection of doses of Russian soul along with the language into our hides. The carefree atmosphere of Berkeley played its role too. It was all magical!

Ralph Collins and I used to devise curious ways of studying Russian to satisfy our interest in the methodology of learning and also, I suppose, because we were lazy. Afternoon after afternoon we lounged in the sun at the pool in Strawberry Canyon and, instead of doing the lessons assigned, fired words at each other in our system of vocabulary drill. I ended the summer with a better knowledge of Russian vocabulary—and a more careless knowledge of Russian grammar—than anyone else in the course.

Ralph found a lonely Russian chicken rancher for us to talk Russian to. He had been in California since 1918—but could not speak English yet. As he said to us sadly, "You don't have to talk English to chickens."

He had come to Berkeley in 1937 to try to pick up a smattering of the language of his adopted country so as to be able to talk to his neighbors out there in the valley where he had his farm on which he lived by himself. Ralph and I offered to trade English chit-chat for Russian chit-chat with him. He was a voluble fellow and the two of us came out far ahead on the deal. He was so glad at last to have some one to speak to in any language!

One cannot learn Russian without coming into contact with Russian —and Communist—politics. This was as new to me as the language. Even in the radical thirties there were not many Communists at Phillips Exeter Academy or Amherst College where I had gotten my schooling. Things were different in Berkeley. Our little class had, so to speak, its Communist cell whose core consisted of a charming, talented couple who had decided the time had come to learn their real mother tongue. They did not try to organize the class and conducted themselves circumspectly. Their indignation, however, was frequently aroused by one of our teachers, a rotund, lovely little old Russian lady who never lost an opportunity to take a dig at the Bolshevik devils.

I used to overhear whispered imprecations in the hallway during intermissions: "reactionary," "white guard," "Menshevik" and others. Generally speaking, however, we non-Communist students managed to live in pleasant peaceful coexistence with the extreme left wing.

Peaceful coexistence, however, never applied to Trotskyites, as I discovered. Ralph took me one day to visit cousins of his in San Francisco. They were a pair who had spent years in Soviet Russia and returned dedicated anti-Stalinists. They were conducting agitation among bay area workers and had to contend with the well-organized Stalinists among the longshoremen and other left wing unions. On their wall hung the goateed portrait of old Lev Davidovich Trotsky himself. For the first time I came into contact with an atmosphere of conspiracy. They talked in whispers, convinced that the walls had ears. They told of surprising things—of being spied on, of slander campaigns conducted against them, of comrades beaten or even killed. It was all so very unreal. We walked out of their tenement into the bright San Francisco sun and it all seemed unbelievable.

Ralph and I one day shortly after marched up to the Soviet Consulate to inquire about visas to go to Moscow to study Russian. This was a rather unrealistic scheme we had been cooking up. We were ushered into an office furnished in a style I would now recognize as "Soviet bureaucratic" and waited a long time until a nervous young lady came out. We got a cold shoulder. No, no visas were being given to Russian language students. Please go away, she seemed to be saying. And so we did.

The weeks went by swiftly and the tempo of the intensive language instruction increased. The teachers demanded more and more. Patrick forced us to stand up and talk. Patrick sent us to the blackboard and made us write. Patrick stood up in front of us and delivered lectures to us in Russian—when we had had just five weeks of the language. And he made us understand. We absorbed declensions, conjugations, aspects, prepositions—in enormous doses. The alphabet which had once seemed so abstruse became second nature. We learned. We never had time to forget. Patrick kept pounding, pounding, pounding. As the weeks went by I found I could begin to express myself—haltingly —in my new tongue of which I had not known one word a month before. I talked and talked. I used every possible occasion to speak in Russian. I made mistakes and mistakes by the mouthful. My pronunciation was atrocious and my grammar impossible. But I kept talking Russian—and I have never stopped.

*    *    *    *    *

Learning Russian was an experience. At the time I studied it few Americans were interested in it. This gave the feeling of exploring the unknown. Nowadays studying Russian has become a fad. There are many Americans, including some in grade school, learning Russian. Still most Westerners still think of Russian as a particularly difficult subject. It is unfortunate it has this fearful reputation. Russian is not really an extremely difficult language to acquire. It is not easy. But the question is partly how thorough a knowledge one requires. If one *must* master it to the very end it can be a life work, for it is complex, with many irregularities, rich in vocabulary with fine shades of meaning. But, other than a linguist, who is there that needs a complete and perfect knowledge? A fair fluency in speaking and the ability to read the papers and most literature without a dictionary can be picked up rather quickly. Russian in my opinion is not more difficult than German.

Any language written—like Russian—in an alien alphabet looks difficult till one learns the alphabet. The Cyrillic alphabet is actually an aid to learning Russian. It is phonetic and effectively represents the sounds of the language.

Russian is an Indo-European language and closely kin to all the other major European languages including Latin, Greek, French, English, German and the rest, and to such other Indo-European tongues as Sanskrit and Persian. The word for mother in Russian is "mat," for brother "brat," for sister "syestra." There are thousands of Russian words close in their roots to words in English and other Indo-European languages. One who knows several European languages such as French, German and English starts with a large Russian vocabulary. Russian is not so distant in any sense from English as Hebrew or Arabic, Chinese or Japanese, Hungarian or Turkish or any other language from outside the Indo-European group.

There are some difficult points. Russian is an inflected language like German, Latin or Greek. The case endings are sufficiently elaborate to be bothersome. The accent is irregular and frequently shifts with conjugation or declension and can therefore be learned only by ear and experience. The most difficult thing about Russian is its verb system. What it amounts to is that Russian verbs are very confusing to an American.

One of the pleasant things about Russian is the fact that a foreigner does not have to speak Russian without mistakes to be understood— and appreciated. Whereas English-speaking peoples are often inclined to ridicule cruelly those who speak with accents and make errors in grammar, Russians, linguistically speaking, are hospitable. They like a foreigner who is making an effort to learn Russian. They make him or her feel that they take this effort as a personal compliment to themselves.

I should be sorry, however, if anything I have said about not having to learn Russian letter-perfect were to be taken as a justification of sloppiness in study and use of Russian. Russian is a beautiful, richly poetic language. It will reward bounteously those who work at acquiring it, who savor its bright colors, who appreciate it and love it.

On a day in late August 1937, I bade goodby fondly and sadly to Professor Patrick and Berkeley. In ten weeks he had given me much— a foundation on which I could build further by my own efforts. More than this, he had opened a window into a world which was new. I had much left to learn, of course, before I could actually read or speak Russian with even modest fluency. But I had made a beginning.

# 2.     *Education for What?*

On a day in mid-September, 1937, I sat in an office in Fayer-weather Hall at Columbia University and talked with a tall, spare, bald and dignified gentleman in a black suit who looked to be in his late fifties but was actually, I am sure, younger. This was Professor Geroid Tanquary Robinson, specialist in Russian history of Columbia University and authority on the role of the peasants in Russian history. Robinson was regarded with awe approaching terror by students in graduate history at Columbia, including some who had squirmed under his questioning in fatal oral examinations. I was nervous myself— for I was asking him to become my sponsor during graduate work, which would make him the arbiter of my destiny for at least three years during which I struggled toward a doctorate.

As things worked out it was for seven years that Robinson was the dominant personality in my career. During all that period there was never an occasion when on receiving from him a small, neatly-inscribed envelope containing usually a one-line note beginning with the carefully and precisely handwritten salutation, "My dear Whitney," that I opened and read it without trepidation. Geroid T. Robinson is a man of parts and he has left his imprint on everyone who ever worked under him. In his somewhat dry, stiff, demanding and totally dedicated way he is as remarkable a teacher as the effervescent, affectionate and dedicated George Z. Patrick was in his.

Robinson was telling me about his visit to the Soviet Union that summer and about how pessimistic he was about the possibilities for

Western scholars to do work and research in Russia. As a person who had studied in Russia during better times he was able to make comparisons. In 1937 the great purge was raging. He had found that men whom he had known well had disappeared. Others still at their posts refused him appointments. There was an atmosphere of universal fear of the foreigner. Robinson's conclusions: With the purge continuing and the danger of war rising, American students of Russian affairs would have to be prepared to face the situation of having perforce to study Russia from a long distance away. This was discouraging, though I had already begun to sense this. For the time being I should have to be content with musty pages rather than living people.

And the pages were musty. During this conversation Robinson told me he wanted me to participate in a new special seminar which the History Department had set up as an experiment. Instead of concentrating on one country and one period under one professor, like other seminars, this would take an institution—slavery and serfdom—and study it through all its length and breadth under four talented scholars specializing in Ancient Times, Latin America, North America and Russia. The four professors would choose for this course exceptional students and outside specialists would be invited to attend. It promised to be interesting.

Along with myself Robinson picked as his other student for this seminar my friend, Bill Armstrong, whom I had met at Berkeley. Robinson put us to work looking over source materials. One of us would take as an object of study a Russian province from the plains region in the south where one type of serfdom prevailed, and the other would take a forest province in the north. Bill ended up with Vologda Province in the north, and I got Ryazan, about one hundred miles southeast of Moscow, divided between plains and forest by the Oka River.

I was shocked to find I would have to do *all* my research in Russian. After all, George Patrick's talents notwithstanding, I had had only ten weeks of Russian. My vocabulary was small. I had other responsibilities than the Slavery Seminar. How great a portion of my time could I devote to puzzling out painfully Russian source materials on serfdom in Ryazan Province?

As it turned out for not quite half a year I devoted nearly 100 percent of my time to just that. I did it because I felt I had to succeed in this initial project or fail in the whole plan of becoming a specialist on Russian history.

One particular book was a foundation stone of my study. It consisted of hundreds of pages of archive materials. There were statistics, cases, suits and the like from the files of government agencies in Ryazan Province dating from the first half of the 19th century. The information was fascinating—once one had read it. To read it was excruciatingly difficult.

The pages were immense. The type face was foggy. The paper was yellowed. The language was that of peasants and bureaucrats of more than a century ago—crops, rotation systems, articles of clothing and food, barnyard subjects. Many of the words were not to be found in my dictionary. There were meanings I had to guess. It was tough sledding. At first by dint of a work day lasting from dawn till midnight I could read three or four pages, taking notes. This went on week after week. I did nothing else except read this book for two and a half months. I neglected all other work totally. I wore my Russian dictionary ragged, leafing it over and over. Every morning I awoke with a splitting headache. My eyes continually smarted. As I went along my speed increased a bit. I got up to five or six pages a day by the end of a week or so. In a month's time I was completing nearly ten pages in a day of sixteen hours. Finally I finished with a spurt, having upped my capacity to twenty pages a day. I went through some other materials. Things still seemed to come hard. I was so slow in reading that I despaired of being ready to make my seminar report at the end of January as planned. But I continued to work away.

It was the second week in December. I had started a new book, telling about the evil doings of a lusty old serf-owning type by the name of Lev Izmailov from Zaraisk County in the extreme Northwest of the province. This character spent his time thinking up cruel punishments for his male serfs and prurient ways of amusing himself with the females. It was a good story as these things go, but as I looked at the four hundred and fifty pages of additional reading my heart sank. This would take me two months. Maybe more, because the book was available only in the New York Public Library and had to be read during library hours. How could I get it done? Yet I needed it. I started. Miracle of miracles, I shall never forget it! I breezed through the whole book in one glorious week, averaging ninety pages a day. I could hardly believe it. Just for fun I picked up another book and started reading something having nothing to do with serfdom. I read one hundred pages the first day. I still do not understand the mechanism of mind vs. language that made this happen so suddenly, but that was the way it was. When I went home for Christmas that year I could properly celebrate. The time that had elapsed between the day I first learned a word of Russian and the day that I found I could read fluently was exactly six months.

\* \* \* \* \*

Once I made my seminar report I could begin to catch up with my neglected course work. But I was not too busy to continue my immersion in the entrancing field of Russian culture begun in Berkeley. I read Russian novels and plays, some in the original, some in translation. I went to every new Soviet motion picture that came to town— and there were good ones. Some, like *Peter the First* with Nikolai Cherkasov in the lead, I must have seen four or five times. I read Soviet and emigre Russian newspapers. I visited the Russian bookstore, ate often at the Russian Tea Room on 57th Street. Most importantly I went out of my way to meet Russians and I always jabbered with them in Russian. They were patient, listening to me desecrating their tongue, and I took advantage of their patience. I was managing to live part of my life in a sort of Russian world of my own creation.

Summer vacation came and was welcome. I spent the hot months at quiet family residences in Connecticut and Ohio, doing reading in preparation for the oral examinations for the doctorate. Away from the university I could sit back and take stock of just where I was headed. What I saw was this: I had set out to become an historian, to take up a career in university teaching. My models were Professors Cole and Packard of Amherst, both great teachers. The Russian idea had come because one had to have a field of specialization. So I had gone ahead and learned Russian, done a seminar report in the Russian area, written a Master's essay expanding it, and completed one full year of graduate school. This was fine. I was fulfilling the plan I had set. The trouble was something had happened in the meanwhile. I had become more interested in Russia and less in more general history. So far as Russia was concerned, I was more interested in contemporary Russia and less in the past. I wanted to know all about the entire spectrum of Soviet life—economics, politics, foreign affairs, culture, sociology, even sports, religion and the like.

What I really wanted to do was to specialize on contemporary Russia. I would have liked to cross all faculty lines, take courses in Russian literature, the Soviet economy, the language, Soviet foreign policy; on Communism, and, of course, also on Russian history. And I wanted to be able to earn a degree at it and to get a job to put to use this specialty.

I wanted a lot. Nowadays this seems like a reasonable aspiration. I wanted to become a regional specialist at a time when there were none.

At such a university as Columbia there were courses not only in Russian history but in the language, the literature, the Soviet economy, the ideology of Marxism and the like. But, though the course program and the personnel were on hand, it was not practical to cross departmental lines. There was no provision for a specialization cutting across such lines on a regional basis. There was no cooperation between faculty members who would be involved and there were hostilities which made it inadvisable to attempt this.

There was no Russian Institute at Columbia, no Russian Research Center at Harvard, nor any of the other centers of regional studies that have sprung up at universities throughout the country. These were created as a direct result of experience during World War II when it became apparent that regional specialization was a vital need.

There were almost no jobs for regional specialists. The China Service in the State Department and the Department's modest training program for Russian-language officers were instances of regional specialization but they were exceptions.

But if there were no jobs for regional specialists there were almost no openings for historians in general. These were bleak years. Able students with degrees lingered for years around graduate departments waiting for job openings. There was no assurance of any employment.

I settled down to my reading for the oral examinations in a mood of despair. When I got a degree I might be unable to get a job and if I did the chances were better than even that it would be one which gave no opportunity to put to use my interest in contemporary Russia.

Just what was I getting educated for?

*     *     *     *     *

When I returned to Columbia in the fall of 1938 I got an important break. I found Professor Robinson helpful. He pointed out to me the possibility, through use of new regulations, of narrowing my major and minor subjects considerably.

I set myself a plan for reading that makes me shudder. My list of books that I decided I must read before oral examinations came to around three hundred volumes in the East European field alone plus another four dozen in Western European economic history. Some were long works of a thousand pages. A fair number were in Russian. I allotted myself a year to read all of them.

I read and sometimes reread Klyuchevsky, Pokrovsky, Platonov, pages from Soloviev and the other outstanding Russian historians. By all odds the greatest of them all is Vasily Klyuchevsky. I found him a revelation. I had familiarized myself, of course, with his famous *Course in Russian History* in five volumes. I returned and returned to this work. It was fascinating reading, particularly in the original Russian. He managed to communicate the majestic sweep of the history of his enormous country.

Who can forget that wonderful lecture of Klyuchevsky in which he tells of the burden on fifteenth- and sixteenth-century Russia of the vital defense line against the steppe nomads.

"Thus step by step," he wrote, "the steppe was won from the brigands. During the sixteenth century from year to year thousands of the border population were lost to the country, and tens of thousands of the best people of the nation fought on the southern border to protect from captivity and ruin the inhabitants of the central districts. If one can picture to oneself how much time and material and spiritual forces perished in this monotonous and crude, tortuous pursuit of the sly steppe beast of prey, hardly is there one who will ask what the people of Eastern Europe were doing when Western Europe attained its successes in industry and trade, in social life, in science and the arts."

In Klyuchevsky the immediacy of Russian history struck one. Here is how he writes of Ivan, the Terrible: "Stubbornly familiarizing himself with his favorite texts and endlessly thinking about them, Ivan gradually and unnoticeably created for himself from them an ideal world into which he retreated like Moses into his mountain, in order to rest from everyday fears and disappointments. With love he viewed those ancient elect and anointed of God—Moses, Saul, David, Solomon. But in these images he, as in a mirror, tried to see himself, his own sovereign figure, to catch in them a reflection of his brilliance or to transfer to himself the reflection of their light and grandeur. It is understandable that he fell in love with himself, that his own person in such a reflection seemed to him to be illuminated with gleam and majesty such as his ancestors had not sensed in themselves, ordinary Moscow princes. Ivan IV was the first of the Muscovite sovereigns who felt vitally and saw in himself a king in the real biblical sense, an anointed of God. This was for him a political discovery, and from that time his royal 'I' became for him an object of divine worship. He became sacred unto himself and in his thoughts created a whole gospel of political self-adulation in the form of a learned theory of his royal power . . ."

If one changes just a few words in this passage is this not an effective description of the attitude of Stalin toward his power? So often in Klyuchevsky a passage, taken in isolation, could be taken as referring to contemporary Russia.

Klyuchevsky and the other Russian historians whom I studied were good only up to the middle of the eighteenth century—and then they thinned out. My concern was with the nineteenth and twentieth centuries. For this period the standard of historical works was low. The political sensitivities of the regimes, before and after the revolution, were such as to inhibit objective work and to lead Russian historians to devote themselves principally to earlier and less touchy periods. I was making rapid progress in my reading. It looked as if I could complete it by the end of the summer. I began to look forward to taking my orals in early October.

The end of that fateful summer of 1939 approached. To keep at my work I tried to keep from listening to the news bulletins. But who could? Things appeared blacker. The denouement came—I listened to the announcer tell of a pact between Russia and Nazi Germany—Ribbentrop flying to Moscow—The swastika waving over the Kremlin—A sweeping pact signed. A Nazi-Soviet Alliance. What a combination! The green light for World War II. Then it came. Invasion of Poland. That tired voice of Chamberlain's announcing Britain's declaration of war. The partition of Poland. What a nightmare! And yet I managed to continue my reading.

As I began to complete my reading schedule I realized that reading was not enough. I started asking myself the questions my examiners might ask me and I could not answer them. I had read scores of thousands of pages. I had filled a file case with notes. But I had not integrated my knowledge. This was no course examination I faced in which one night's cramming could cover the ground. This was an examination on everything I had done.

I had read too much but studied not enough. I was desperate. I postponed my examinations till December. I sat down and did what I should have done months before. I started making a list of all the significant questions I could be asked—and then to dig the answers out of my notes. By the time I was through I suppose I must have had a list of about two thousand questions. The process of researching the answers brought my knowledge together.

On a bleak gray day in December I sat in a room in Fayerweather Hall in front of a panel of five professors headed by Carlton J. H. Hayes, including my own sponsor, Professor Robinson. For two hours they fired questions at me. As things got going I felt more at ease. By the end I was sure it was going all right.

I left in a daze. Those two hours in the examination room were the test of success or failure of two and a half years of graduate work. I didn't even want to think about it. I went out with friends. I don't remember whether or not I got drunk. If I didn't, I should have.

A few days later the grade was posted—"Excellent."

And that as it turned out was the climax of my graduate work. There remained between me and the Doctor's degree the writing of a dissertation and its formal defense. But this, as things turned out in my life, is something I never completed.

But I have never regretted my work in Russian history. I could not have chosen a more appropriate and firmer foundation.

\* \* \* \* \*

Time and time again in my work in Soviet studies when faced with a puzzling development I have gone back over the study of Russian history I did while preparing for my oral examinations. I have tried to see whether I could not find somewhere in history an explanation of the particular riddle in front of me. Time and again Russian history gave me an answer.

One example can perhaps illustrate this. During the onset of the Cold War in 1946 and 1947 some of us in the American Embassy in Moscow were puzzled to find rationale in the way Stalin's government dealt with foreign diplomats. The system of annoying surveillance, supervision of activities, tight restrictions on movements, cut-off in relations between diplomats and Soviet citizens, a contemptuous attitude by authorities, and just plain unwillingness to deal at all, did not seem to have a logic. It appeared to go beyond the needs of security and to hinder realization of important aims by the government. It seemed designed to antagonize every foreigner coming to Moscow on diplomatic assignment.

Why? We asked ourselves repeatedly. We never found anything in the texts of Marxism-Leninism to justify this behavior. Then we turned to Russian history. George Kennan turned up a passage from Klyuchevsky on the treatment of foreigners in Muscovy in the fifteenth century. It was a remarkable passage. John Patton Davies, then First Secretary, called me to his office and without telling me the source, read it to me aloud. "What do you think of that?" he asked me.

"An excellent description of our situation," I replied. "Is that from a new book on the Soviet Union?"

Then he told me to which times it referred. Here was light on a vital aspect of modern affairs out of a history book. What we could learn was that we were dealing with more than a caprice of totalitarian, Communist dictatorship. The scheme of surveillance over the foreigner within the gates and supervision of his activities was a recurring phenomenon in Russian history. It was not to be regarded as logical behavior but rather as a phobia or psychosis which, even if not rational, did have an actual basis in efforts by foreigners to meddle in Russian affairs. Once our situation was viewed in this light it became more comprehensible, though hardly any easier to live with.

Russian history is an indispensable basis for trying to understand the Soviet Union of today. The USSR proclaims itself a socialist country founded upon Marxist-Leninist ideology. So it is. That is only half the story. It is insufficient merely to understand Marxism-Leninism to understand the Soviet Union. If the USSR is a socialist country founded on the ideology of Marxism-Leninism it is also a supra-national state based upon Russia. And it is the creation, heir, continuer, of Russian history.

In examining Soviet policy there is always the question of where Marxist-Leninist "internationalism" ends and Russian nationalism—and imperialism—begins. There is rarely, of course, any pat answer. To the extent that these diverse elements can be sorted out it is knowledge of Russian history that facilitates the process.

I learned many lessons from Russian history, but there are some that stand out above the rest. For example:

Never in Russian history has there been permitted to develop any effective system of autonomous local self-government. The beginnings that once existed—as for example the city-state democracy of Great Novgorod—were ruthlessly wiped out by the tsars of Muscovy as they expanded their power.

The only experiment in modern times in development of local self-government was the *zemstvo* reform of Alexander II in the nineteenth century, which bore great promise but which was hurriedly emasculated by Alexander II's successors.

And so today, just as one hundred or two hundred years ago, the local governments of Russia depend on the central political authority for the appointment of chief executives, for revenues allotted, for lines of policy.

The effect this fact has on the daily life of Russians is enormous. In vital areas of local concern Russians are accustomed to depend on initiative from the center. One of the results has been that much that should get done locally does not get done because the center never gets around to ordering it done. Another result is that the central authority has much too much to do. A third effect is that because of the absence of power in localities the power of the center must be great to deal effectively with the affairs within its responsibility. Here one sees a kind of vicious circle. The powers of the central government must be great because there is no effective local self-government. And the existence of such enormous power in the center acts to inhibit growth of local self-government because the center is fearful of giving away power. This applies today, too.

The Soviet government is not unaware of this dilemma. The most interesting effort to deal with it is the recent economic reform of 1957, reorganizing most of the economy from a branch of economic effort basis onto a regional basis. One cannot say this reform begins to touch on the heart of the problem, however.

If absence of local self-government is one of the constants of Russian history another is absence of rule of law.

Hardly ever in all Russian history have laws been superior to the rulers. Never in Russian history to the present has Russia had an effective, impartial system of laws, courts and justice. All the sovereigns of Russia have tended to regard themselves as above the law.

They have tended to keep courts subordinate to the government administrative machinery. Nothing has exercised a more pernicious effect on Russian life.

But of all the impressions which remain from my intensive study of Russian history I suppose the most vivid are two aspects of Russian life not well enough appreciated in the West.

The first is that touched on in one of its aspects by Klyuchevsky—the never-ending struggle of the Russian people in the fifteenth and sixteenth centuries against the incursions of nomads into the steppe lands being settled by Russians. The word here is *never-ending struggle*. And this summarizes much of Russian history. Never-ending struggle against nomads, against more modern states from the West, against the forces of nature so formidable in the North and East of the Russian land. Some nations have been more fortunate than others in their geographical position and political and technological heritage, a fact of which Russians are acutely conscious. Some nations have had to struggle harder than others to preserve their existence. One need hardly elevate the hardships inflicted by history and geography on Russians into a special merit belonging to them, as Russian chauvinists are wont to do. It is nevertheless true that, if gold medals are to be passed out to nations for the suffering they have borne to preserve their independence and carve out of a hostile wilderness a fertile land, the Russian people are entitled to one. Russia's never-ending struggle has had its fruits in the form of some qualities of Russian people—patience, fortitude, willingness to accept sacrifice, great energy. These play their role in international affairs today.

Another vivid impression which recurs to me constantly is that Russia of the late nineteenth and early twentieth centuries was by no means such a backward country in culture, science and economic development as many Westerners seem to think. The Russian culture that has had such tremendous influence in the West is primarily pre-revolutionary culture. The basic cultural capital on which the Soviet Union has been living for more than forty years is pre-revolutionary Russian culture. It was pre-revolutionary Russia that spawned such greats as Tolstoi, Dostoyevsky, Chekhov, Tchaikowsky and others. They created for the Russian audience of their time, a cultured, perceptive, advanced audience. Even in economic development one cannot call pre-revolutionary Russia a backward country, even if it was behind Britain, Germany, France and the United States in its state of industrial maturity. Pre-revolutionary Russia seemed backward to Western European contemporaries in considerable part because of political backwardness which contrasted so starkly with Russia's cultural flowering and economic growth. If one puts Russia of 1860 to 1913 against the background of the world as a whole one must conclude that Russia of that time was in some respects behind Western Europe, but in other respects advanced. Russia stood out as a country and culture of very great promise. The Soviet government did not inherit an economic and cultural wasteland.

\*       \*       \*       \*       \*

A bright Sunday morning in June 1941. I lay half-awake in the large bed enjoying being alive. Through the window came the twitter of birds and the sounds of the nearby village. I stretched out luxuriantly. My father was moving around in the dining room below me. I thought about things and reviewed my life since I had come to the end of my schooling. I had completed a year of college teaching and was to return in September for another year. I had taught courses in Economics, Sociology, Political Science and European History. Organizing my work had kept me busy indeed. It was a satisfaction to have a job of my own but there was one keen regret. During that year I had gotten a long way away from my specialty—Russia.

A sound came from below. My father was calling me.

"Tom, have you heard the news? Come on down."

I threw on my robe and descended.

"Hitler has invaded Russia," my father told me.

I jumped—yet the news did not come exactly as a surprise. For weeks the papers had been buzzing with rumors of German troop concentrations on the Eastern Front. I had felt all along that Germany and Russia must sooner or later come to blows. And now it had happened. I tried to picture that flaming battle line a thousand miles long and more!

On a day in late August that same summer I was working on my new apartment at college trying to get it in shape. The telephone rang. "This is Geroid T. Robinson," said a familiar voice through the receiver, sounding a long way away from me.

# 3.     *Washington in Wartime*

I listened to him. It all became a bit mixed up . . . War work . . .
Washington . . . Can't discuss it on the telephone . . . You are
badly needed . . . Work in your field—on Russia . . . Research
. . . I urge you to come . . . Intelligence . . . Meet me tomorrow
morning at eleven A.M. . . . Apex Building . . . Constitution and
Pennsylvania Avenues . . .

I was still confused later that same day as I rode the train from New
York to Washington, D.C. But it seemed pretty obvious that my teaching career had come to an abrupt end.

\*     \*     \*     \*     \*

On a torrid September morning I disembarked from my train at the
Washington, D.C. Union Station and emerged from its cavernous
waiting room into the daylight to see squarely in front of me the white
dome of the Capitol. I stood for a moment, suitcase in hand, looking
at it, and then got in a taxi and proceeded a few short blocks to the
large triangle-shaped building at the junction of Constitution and
Pennsylvania Avenues. I entered, found a receptionist, asked for Professor Robinson and was asked in hushed tones to wait. As I sat there
I watched professorial-looking men going in and out of some sort of
inner sanctum down the hall. They seemed to be wearing some sort
of badge on their jackets and displayed these to an armed guard on
entering or leaving. It seemed to me they all had a furtive air. I was
impressed. I waited with expectation.

Finally I was ushered in. The receptionist accompanied me, holding a temporary pass permitting me to enter. Robinson occupied a desk in an office in which one other official had his head bent over papers laid out in front of him. Robinson talked to me in a low voice. I was not to tell anyone what he talked about, he said. It was all "confidential." In fact, however, he told me little more than he had already told me on the telephone. It would be war work. It would consist of special research on Soviet affairs. He could not disclose anything beyond this. I would be directed by an organization known as the "Coordinator of Information" headed by William J. Donovan. But I would be nominally a staff member of the Library of Congress, would be carried on their payroll, and would work in the new library annex across the street from its famous old building. The pay would be modest. I must report as soon as possible. He could give me a week to wind up my affairs at college, move my personal effects to Washington, and find a place to live.

Robinson escorted me out of the building personally. On the way down the hall he invited me to stop with him at the men's room. I busied myself about the usual business conducted in such places and presumed he was doing the same. But when I turned about I was astonished to see that with a slightly embarrassed air this exceedingly dignified Virginia gentleman was tearing into small bits sheets of paper on which there were notes. He then carefully dropped them into the toilet bowl and flushed them down, watching to be sure none remained.

*"That,"* he remarked to me with emphasis, "is one way to be sure that no one reads things he is not supposed to."

I walked out of the building overwhelmed with this atmosphere of secrecy.

On the train that evening I considered Robinson's proposal. I knew almost nothing about the job. I was buying a pig in a poke. I had great faith in Robinson but I had the impression he didn't know much about the prospects himself. I was taking a chance. The prospect of "secret government work" was intriguing. Yet, there was something else more important for the long run. If I accepted Robinson's offer I would at last have the chance to devote my energies to my area of professional specialization.

I called Robinson the next morning and told him I would accept.

*        *        *        *        *

It was one A.M. on an October morning. The ceiling of the small dark green room in the upper reaches of the Library of Congress Annex was obscured by a cloud of cigarette smoke. Two portable typewriters were banging away. Across the desk sat Professor Robinson with a big red pencil editing sheets as they were handed to him, then clipping them and pasting them together again to form a rough draft. I rubbed my eyes wearily and searched the Soviet statistical handbook in front of me again for some figures.

Besides Robinson and myself there were present S. Kuznets, an American statistician of Russian origin, a friend named Harold Weinstein, who was another of Robinson's students and an expert on Ukrainian nationalism, and a tall and jovial geographer named John Morrison. We were a motley, disreputable-looking crew. Bleary-eyed, shirts open at the collar, jackets off, unshaven, unkempt, tired and puzzled we worked away.

The report we were turning out had as many footnotes as a doctoral dissertation but was hardly so remote from current life. From up on the summit somewhere we had been asked for a report on Russian capabilities for staying in the war. These were the worst days of the conflict for the Soviet Union. Moscow was in mortal danger. And some of the richest industrial and agricultural regions of the country had been lost to the invader. The report had to be ready by dawn when it must be delivered. A secretary was waiting to type it. Someone had a rubber stamp marked "Top Secret" and kept stamping pages as they emerged into the draft of the report. It struck me as amusing that conclusions we were drawing from books of published statistics should immediately become classified information.

By three A.M. Robinson had edited the last page. He crossed off the last sentence and rewrote it meticulously in his precise penciled handwriting and looked up at us:

"Well, I guess you can go home now and get some sleep. We've done the best we could. Thanks for sticking with it."

Not one of us was proud of that first report on Soviet capabilities. It was sketchy. Our statistical information was elementary and had enormous gaps. We were in some cases making mere guesses. None of us had much idea at that time of the economics of war. The only information we had to work with was that in published material—and the Russians had cut off all significant statistical material from publication in 1937—four years before.

What could we base ourselves on? Just a few figures and some educated guesses. To make such guesses we had to abandon ingrained academic prejudices and take a flight right out into the wild blue yonder. The only real justification we had was that our guesses were needed and we had the right to assume we knew as much or more about it, though that was little, as whoever would be called on to make the guesses if we did not.

\* \* \* \* \*

By the time our little task force had completed its first report on Soviet capabilities for staying in the war I had been working in Washington all of three weeks. But, because of the daily accretion of new staff members to the newly-born organization of which I was a member, I already felt a veteran. In a way I was. I had a badge with my picture, a desk, a typewriter. I even had a telephone and was listed in the directory—a classified document. I had an apartment. I had acquired rudiments of knowledge of where to find things.

I had also begun to dig into my field and to look into the information on various aspects of Soviet activity available in government agencies in Washington. And in this I had commenced to make a momentous discovery. Robinson had, no doubt, discovered it for himself long before. That was perhaps the reason for his sense of urgency. It came as a great shock.

The solemn, unsavory fact was that the state of knowledge of the United States government about the Soviet Union, including that available on the topmost levels, was not just lamentable. It was disastrous. Accurate information on the USSR was nonexistent in Washington.

To cite one example, it was common knowledge in Washington that when Germany invaded Russia in June, the situation evaluations the White House had received had underestimated Soviet capabilities of staying in the war to a fantastic degree. It was said this was what had opened the President's eyes to the absence of effective United States intelligence and led him to call on Donovan to set up our new agency.

During the late months of 1941 I made a systematic effort to find out as much as possible about activities outside our organization in the collection and processing of information on the USSR in the government.

I found that nowhere—except for our small, still rudimentary group —was there any organization or group capable of attempting to answer in an objective and thorough way the numerous geographical, economic, political and other questions bound to arise for the United States government as the war continued and spread.

The total effort in gathering and analysis of information on Russia on the part of all United States government agencies combined was insignificant, this at a time when the USSR held the crucial role in the war. Of course, one could not take the total effort of all agencies combined, because they all worked in their own corners without cooperation.

What was there? In the Department of Agriculture there was one experienced specialist engaged in a continuing study of the Soviet food situation. In the Department of Commerce there was an affable official who was doing his best all by himself to keep up with the developments in the entire Soviet economy. On the army side in Military Intelligence there was a room in one of the World War I temporary buildings on Constitution Avenue devoted to Soviet affairs. Out of a dozen people, or so, including secretaries in it then there were two—both reserve officers taken from academic life—who knew the language and qualified as specialists on Russia. On the Navy side there was an office in Naval Intelligence which had, so far as I could discover, just one officer qualified as a specialist on Russia. He was also a reserve officer from academic life.

The State Department had a Russian desk headed by a leading diplomat closely familiar with Soviet affairs out of long experience. One of his staff members was an academically-trained specialist on Russia. But this desk was overworked and only equipped to handle diplomatic business with Russia. It had neither the staff nor space nor facilities to gather or process basic information on the USSR.

The American Embassy in Moscow was incapable of furnishing Washington with information of significance on Russia other than that concerning day-to-day relations. The Embassy had begun the war by burning nearly all its files, by sending out of the country a large portion of its staff, and by busying itself with various programs of evacuation of the Embassy. This was at a time, of course, when information on Russia had acquired more importance than it ever had. The Embassy's plans seemed to have been based on an estimate that the Germans would take Moscow within a few weeks of the date of their invasion. The sole officer of the American armed forces present in Moscow for the first months of the Russo-German conflict was the Military Attaché in the United States Embassy. He was presumably the source of the evaluations from Moscow of the military situation on the Eastern front cabled to Washington. He was an Army officer and had been in the advanced section of the same intensive Russian course class at Berkeley which I had attended four years before. He seemed a decent, friendly chap but not, one would judge, particularly brilliant. The impression is that he sadly underestimated Soviet staying power in the war. This was the state of American government information and intelligence on Russia on the eve of American entrance into World War II.

One of the tragic aspects of it was the fact that at one time in the State Department there had been a realization of the need for special study of Soviet affairs. A promising small-scale beginning had once been made to fill this need. In the late twenties and early thirties in United States diplomatic missions in Riga and Moscow a well-picked little group of young American career diplomatic officers, including several with special training in Russian, had been charged with systematic reporting on the Soviet scene. But this nucleus for study of Russia, which had compiled very useful reports in its time, had been dispersed by the time World War II set in.

I have sometimes wondered what the cost to the United States has been of the failure to have before World War II good and accurate information on the USSR and an adequate staff of regional specialists trained in the evaluation of Soviet affairs. I think it is quite incalculable—and astronomical. It can be measured in part by some of the grievously wrong decisions made during World War II and after. For these wrong decisions we will be paying for a long time to come.

*     *     *     *     *

It was an unseasonably hot day in early December. I sat at a desk in an office on the third floor of a gray stone building—a former hospital—located off 25th and E Streets N.W. I was working in Robinson's office on an urgent report. It was Sunday and I was by myself. Now and then I caught a whiff of malt from the brewery next door. I looked out at the Lincoln Memorial wishing I were outside instead of inside.

Robinson opened the door and briskly entered. There was an air of urgency about him. "Well, I suppose you've heard the news," he asked.

"What?" I asked.

"War!" he replied.

"How?" I gasped.

"The Japs bombed Pearl Harbor," he announced—and then gave me more details.

I could not concentrate any longer on my report. We talked for a while of what this meant and I went home. So it had finally happened! What would it bring to me, I wondered? Millions of other Americans were asking the same question that evening.

What it brought for the short run soon became apparent. Our work load, already heavy, increased. Working evenings and weekends now became routine.

Donovan's organization acquired new personnel even more swiftly. Its East European Section, as our group was called, carried on a search for qualified specialists. I pored through questionnaires sent to universities all over the country. Suddenly, regional specialists, many unable to get jobs in their fields previously, were in great demand. And this applied particularly to specialists on Russia.

Before Pearl Harbor the East European Section had half a dozen specialists. In the next two years the USSR Division of the Branch of Research and Analysis of the Office of Strategic Services (OSS)—which is what it became—grew to include perhaps two score of Russian specialists.

It was a setup which defied conventions. Civilians worked alongside military. A man might be drafted or commissioned and be back at his own desk shortly after—the difference being uniform and pay. Sometimes non-coms supervised work of commissioned officers. We found most of our people in universities.

I found myself studying strange and interesting subjects. For two months I was an expert on icebreakers in northern ports of Russia. This came up in connection with a monumental report on wartime transport routes into the USSR.

For four months I became an expert on Soviet synthetic rubber. This resulted from my pointing out to higher authorities—at a time when building a synthetic rubber industry had become crucial for the war effort—that the Soviets had more experience in synthetic rubber than any country. I was assigned to write a report. I had to become a chemist to make head and tail of the technical literature which I read for this report. It was a pretty good report, covering economics and technology, and it helped get the government to send an American delegation to the USSR to learn more about Russian experience.

The more continuous work I was engaged in was an estimate of Soviet capabilities in the war, in particular, of the economic-technological base for the effort at the front. Periodic reports on this were sent by our division to the Joint Chiefs of Staff.

This was difficult and vital work. Estimates of what would happen in Russia were a key matter for all Western military calculations. The Soviet government never gave its allies any economic or military information on the USSR throughout the war. The Soviets likewise kept most economic information, except very fragmentary data usually in the form of percentages, out of the controlled press. The situation changed as the front moved East or back West again, so that continual revisions were necessary in all estimates.

My friend, Irving Rudd, was, for example, engaged in study of the Soviet steel position. He did what had never been done before by any government agency. He located every blast furnace, open hearth furnace and rolling mill in the USSR. With these data he could estimate steel production at any given time.

I also developed a technique for my own work. My field was armaments. Nothing was published on it. There was virtually nothing to work with—until I made a discovery by careful reading of the press. Soviet newspapers used to brag about the work done by defense factories. They were sometimes identified by the name of the director, sometimes by their number, all secret defense factories being numbered. By cross checking steadily all papers one could sometimes get the following results: *Pravda* might report that X factory, directed by Comrade Popov, had fulfilled its production plan for May on the 25th. *Izvestia* might report that the X factory directed by Comrade Popov had produced ten planes over plan in May. By putting the two references together one could therefore gather that from May 25 and June 1 Popov's factory had produced ten planes. On this basis one could get a very rough idea of a possible monthly rate. Through similar cross-checking elsewhere one could find that Comrade Popov was the Director of, let's say, Factory Number 121 located in Sverdlovsk which produced, say, MIG fighter planes.

I worked out other techniques, too. Taken all in all they resulted in at least a beginning in objective estimates of production of planes, tanks, trucks, etc. As time went on I developed new sources of information and new approaches. This work occupied as much as a year and a half or more of my two and a half years in Washington. It was a new kind of education—a venture into a field in which I had no experience and into the process of developing new methods to attack difficult problems.

\*    \*    \*    \*    \*

I learned many lessons in the course of this type of study. One, I suppose, stands out above the others. It has been reaffirmed time and time again since in my further study. I can illustrate it with an example taken from the work of our group in OSS during the war.

Irving Rudd, a Russian-born American businessman, worked up his estimates of Soviet steel production with skill. His research was exhaustive. Early in 1943 he submitted his estimates of Soviet steel production in 1943. I have forgotten his exact figures, but let us say, for this discussion, that he predicted an output of nine million tons plus or minus five-hundred thousand tons.

His estimates went in for combination into a comprehensive comparison of Soviet and German military-economic capabilities. Irving was called on the carpet. Some able economists subjected him to a grilling. His estimates, he was told, *must* be underestimating seriously what the Russians had. It was pointed out to him that the Germans, with steel resources several times larger than he estimated Soviet steel resources, were barely holding their own. Reports indicated Soviet ammunition expenditure was high, Soviet firepower heavy, that the amounts of steel the Soviets were throwing into frontline operations were large. How could such a situation be fitted into Irving's steel estimates? It was suggested that Soviet production of steel might have to be half again larger than Irving's estimates to account for the state of affairs. Go back, he was told, and reexamine the estimates and find out what was wrong with them.

Irving defended his estimates vigorously, but he told them he would reexamine the study. He did. He returned to the discussion more convinced than ever he was right. He could concede, he said, perhaps a million tons on the upside at the most. This he did not want to do, but it was possible, though highly unlikely as he saw it. The higher-ups were forced in the end to accept Irving's estimates, revised slightly upwards but far below figures they had in mind.

The argument never did get really settled in wartime. By the time the actual figures came out through Soviet official sources the war had long since been over, the OSS dissolved, and the individuals involved dispersed. The payoff was that, as it turned out, Irving's original estimates of Soviet steel were not too low, but slightly on the high side. The moral to be derived is not that Irving's critics were fools. They were able men, acting in good faith on their best judgment based on experience.

As a generalization what I would say is this:

The results which the Soviet government gets in critical areas are sometimes greater than one would expect on the basis of the over-all material resources available to it and judged by the experience of other non-Communist nations. In the illustration of the steel estimates, what it came down to was this, the Soviets were bringing to bear at decisive areas of the front greater firepower and weight of arms per ton of steel at their disposal than the Nazis. The Russians were steel-starved and the Germans had enough but *where it counted* the Russians delivered enough.

This concept is applicable outside wartime economics. Thus, competent Americans underestimated Soviet ability to develop nuclear weapons. Thus, competent American specialists underestimated the pace of Soviet rocketry. This underestimation of the USSR goes on right now, despite all that has happened in recent years. One could cite more than a few examples.

The main element in this, as I see it, is not wishful thinking by Westerners about the Soviet Union, though there is still plenty of this around, it is a simple lack of understanding among Westerners, including technical experts and even social scientists, of how the Soviet economic and political machinery operates and their capabilities for concentration on major objectives. The key word here is *concentration*.

The economic-political organization of the USSR gives the national leadership the power to concentrate an extraordinarily large proportion of total resources, material, fiscal and human, on key goals. And the psychology of government is such as to lead to concentration of enormous resources on such key goals.

This is in contrast with the United States. In peacetime America, national leadership lacks power to concentrate more than a small proportion, relatively, of resources on key objectives. And more than this, political tradition and psychology run counter to the selection in peacetime of key objectives in any positive sense. This can be illustrated in a dozen different ways, some obvious, others not yet apparent. The crux is that the superiority of the United States over the USSR in gross production levels or material resources owned may conceal an inferiority where things really count in terms of national survival.

\*    \*    \*    \*    \*

On a tired day in the fall of 1943 I completed my latest report on the Soviet aircraft industry. I was weary but satisfied. I took the draft to Robinson's office and returned to my own desk.

I leaned back and thought. Would I be doing just this the rest of the war? It was very interesting work but there was a point of diminishing returns. Here I was—a specialist on Soviet affairs. But I had never been in the Soviet Union. How could one be considered a specialist on a country unless one had lived there? It was apparent to me that the only way to get to know Russia was to go to Russia. But it was not so easy in wartime. Would I ever make it? The answer came suddenly.

January 18, 1944, I sat in an office in the OSS, lit with large fluorescent lamps, talking with a tall, handsome Colonel with a large shock of snow-white hair. He had come to the point immediately.

"How would you feel about going to the Soviet Union?" he asked.

I guess my face told my reaction.

"Well now, it's not certain," he continued. "Don't get your hopes up. But I would say there is a good chance."

He was just back from Moscow, where he had accompanied General Donovan. There had been high-level conferences with Soviet officials, he explained, but they had nothing to do with my assignment. Only later I found that Donovan's talks were concerned with a proposed exchange of wartime intelligence on the common enemy—Nazi Germany—and that Donovan had met directly with Russia's police head, Lavrenty Beria.

The Colonel said he was interviewing me because, while Donovan was in Moscow, Ambassador Averell Harriman had asked him whether he knew of a young Soviet affairs specialist who could come to the Embassy to get things moving in a study of the Soviet economy —a field in which Harriman found the Embassy weak.

This was the post for which I was being considered. It was not an

OSS job. I would transfer to the State Department—but it would be an opportunity to get some useful work started.

"Be ready to go at any time," Colonel Haskell told me as the interview came to an end. I left the room in a daze.

Ten weeks later I was still in a daze. It was April and springtime. I sat at a desk in the East European Division of the State Department in its grandiose ancient building next to the White House.

I went over the preparations for my imminent departure. I had worked hard to get ready. I had cleared the hurdles in near record time, and now it seemed that nearly everything had been completed. I had made the transfer to the Department. My passport with the precious Soviet visa was in my hands. My steamer trunk was en route to Moscow via the Pacific. My necessities to go with me by air were packed and I had been home to bid goodbye to my parents. I had had conferences with various officials in the Department, OSS, and elsewhere, who were interested in my mission. I waited for word on transportation.

Next to me at one of the spare desks in the division there was a man bent over a department report who looked to be in his mid-thirties. Who was he, I wondered? I had seen him there the previous day. He seemed to know his way around the department very well, I had noted, but he was on the shy side. I was hesitant to introduce myself, so diffident was his air.

And then I heard one of the secretaries calling him to the telephone: "Mr. Kennan . . ."

Kennan! The name immediately rang a bell. This, I concluded, must be George Kennan. I had heard him mentioned by the people in Washington who knew most about Russia and his opinions were always cited with respect, even with awe. A little later we were formally introduced and he asked with some interest about the work I intended to do in the Moscow Embassy in the USSR.

"Mr. Whitney . . ." The secretary told me I was wanted in the office of the head of the division and I went in. Sitting behind his desk in the corner was Charles E. Bohlen. It was he who had acted as the President's aide and translator at the Teheran Conference and at other top-level meetings. As I had had occasion to observe, he possessed a nimble mind, a deep knowledge of Soviet affairs, and a keen sense of humor.

Bohlen looked at me with a smile and asked, "Well, are you ready to go?"

I hardly had time to nod a yes when he went on. "I've just had a call from the Navy. You're to report to American Export Airlines in New York. They'll get you off. Be sure to get your travel orders."

He got up from behind his desk and, with a smile in which I thought I detected amusement and a touch of that sardonic pity the experienced old-timer reserves for the utter neophyte, he said, holding out his hand in a farewell clasp, "Good luck. You wanted to get to Moscow. I hope you like it."

April 18, 1944. It was gray and misty as the little flying boat taxied out from the loading ramp at the La Guardia Marine Terminal into the murk of the East River. I looked around me. It seemed a frail craft for a flight across the ocean. I sat beside Bob Tucker, a friend who was going with me to the Moscow Embassy. We grinned, but the grins were on the weak side. The motors roared. The flying boat speeded up and began to lift up in the water. At last we were airborne. I looked down behind me to see New York disappearing in the distance.

May 7, not quite three weeks later, Bob and I stood on the balcony of the home of our friend, the Norwegian Consul in Teheran, and looked into the darkness at the Persian garden beneath us. Of the garden itself we could see little. But there was the high stone wall around it in shadows. There were the slim poplars which lined it, standing straight and tall with their leaves rustling in the soft breeze off the high mountain range to the north of the city. Over it was the large May moon. All about us the dogs were barking—nearby, then in the distance, then from the other direction, then nearby again, back and forth. Bob exclaimed with feeling, "Can you believe that this is all real, that we have come this far?"

"What I cannot believe," I answered with a sharp laugh, "is that that talkative head of the Intourist office is going to put us on that Soviet plane tomorrow morning as he promised."

"Maybe he will and maybe he won't," came the voice of our generous host, the Consul, from behind us, "But right now at any rate I would suggest you might like dinner."

"Just think," commented Bob, as we turned to go inside, "perhaps tomorrow night at this time we'll be in Moscow."

# 4. Introduction to the USSR

May 8, 1944. That day is in my books forever. It was the day of my arrival in the Soviet Union.

Bob Tucker and I stood in rapt attention in the big customs shed—a vacated hangar—at the desolate Baku Airport. We watched the goings-on with intense interest. An attractive blonde Russian woman of about thirty was arguing vociferously with the inspector. We gathered she was returning to Moscow after a stay in Iran with her husband, a Soviet official. Her baggage was out on the floor, suitcases and boxes all opened and their contents poured out and exposed. There was a lot to look at. The total must have come to some seven hundred pounds. She had a wide selection of merchandise ranging from a fascinating collection of intimate female apparel to huge cheeses and sacks of sugar. But she seemed to have specialized in the acquisition of ladies footwear. There were four dozen pairs of women's shoes. They were a chief cause of controversy. The argument concerned what she could keep and what duty she would pay. Finally it was settled. She sputtered but acquiesced. She was allowed to take it all—for a price. So she paid her duty and repacked her booty.

A few hours later our Soviet-built DC-3 skimmed beneath a low thick cloud cover at an altitude of 200 feet, not far above the tree-tops. Our pilots seemed to be following the course of a railroad leading to Moscow which we were approaching. Bob and I craned our necks to look at the forested landscape below. Spring had not yet come and things seemed desolate. In ravines drifts of snow lay unmelted. We could see now and then little villages of small log huts thatched with straw.

The plane was filled with a buzz of conversation. After a full day of flying everyone knew everyone. A motley group of passengers we were too. A young army officer, Lieutenant Kadetov, a veteran of Stalingrad, had acted as our guide to the battlefields of the lower Volga in the early afternoon. Pointing down he had shown us where his unit had entrenched itself in the lengthy struggle. A Soviet diplomat stationed in Italy asked us about acquaintances from the American diplomatic service. There was a Soviet agronomist, author of numerous books, who had been on duty in Iran and was returning home with sacks of wheat. In the backmost seat sat a disreputable-appearing character, some kind of nondescript foreigner, who had confided to me that all of his baggage consisted of Iranian vodka. I had the impression he may have been sampling it en route. There was warmth and excitement in the air and I could not help being impressed at the easy fellowship that prevailed in this largely Russian-American group thrown together by chance in an airplane for one day.

The pilot dipped the nose of the plane steeply and literally dived right down onto the apron of Moscow Central Airport. The plane door opened and the cold damp wind of Moscow blew into our cozy and friendly midst. Suddenly, abruptly, things chilled. Our Russian fellow-passengers seemed to freeze perceptibly under our eyes with the recollection of where they were. We disembarked. Bob and I stood shivering. The change from the 100 degree heat of Teheran to the 50 degrees of the unseasonable cold spell lying over the capital was almost too much to bear. We looked about us hurriedly and spotted a decidedly American visage approaching.

We rode through the streets of Moscow in the American station wagon. Bob and I were busy looking out the windows at the buildings lining famous Gorky Street down which we were riding and at the Russians trudging along the sidewalks. In the gray light of the twilight of the cloudy day things seemed colorless, cold and drab. The people, still wrapped in their winter clothes, looked stolid and serious with nary a smile to be seen for blocks. The store windows seemed empty and the building façades decrepit. The monotony sank icily into our hearts. Such a sunless, gray day was an unfair introduction to Moscow —and yet it had its element of truth.

There was another element of truth that we glimpsed. After three weeks in the Middle East we had returned, we discovered, to Europe. If Moscow was less colorful, noisy and sunny than Teheran and Cairo it was also cleaner. There were no beggars with fetid sores on the street corners, no open sewers along the gutters of the streets.

An imposing neo-classical building of gray stone loomed behind an elaborate cast-iron fence and we drove into the driveway. This was the Ambassador's official home—Spaso House, as it was called. He was not in Moscow we had learned earlier. The servants showed us to a corner room where we were to stay until hotel rooms became available.

By the time we had eaten and unpacked a bit it was nearly eleven. We looked out of the window. There was total darkness for there was still a blackout. We could see nothing except vague shadows but the temptation to take our first walk was too much. Mike, the Russian telephone operator downstairs, looked at us as if he thought we were crazy to go anywhere without a car—but he gave us instructions how to find the main thoroughfare nearby—the Arbat. We walked out past the uniformed militiamen—police guards—at the gate and around the little square in front of the residence. A few hundred feet further, past the shadowy silhouette of the abandoned church which gave Spaso-Peskovsky—Our Saviour of the Sands—Street its name, we came to the Arbat. On the corner we stood pondering the fact that our feet stood on a Russian sidewalk on Joseph Stalin's well-known route to and from the Kremlin, but our reveries were brief. We were approached by a Soviet militiaman.

"What are you doing standing here, citizens?"

"We are looking," I replied in Russian, a bit surprised to be challenged.

"Nelzya!" he replied abruptly—"It's not permitted!" And he waved us on.

Bob turned to look at me as we walked back to Spaso House. I could almost see his broad grin in the dark. We had arrived.

*     *     *     *     *

Six weeks later. It was a night in late June. I sat up in bed in my room in the Savoy Hotel and thought over the happenings since I had arrived in Moscow May 8. In some respects I was pleased with the way things had gone and in other respects dissatisfied. Of one thing I was certain. My first weeks in Russia had been perhaps the most vivid weeks of my life. They were filled with new impressions piling on one another. I had seen much and learned much.

At the same time in my work at the Embassy there was much that was quite unsatisfactory. Even though there had been a promise of improvement there seemed to be a good deal of uncertainty. I was not sure things would develop so that I could do useful reporting on Soviet affairs.

I went to Moscow with a mission, one, as it had been represented to me, of usefulness to the government. I was to inaugurate a program of reporting on the Soviet economy to help fill in a gap in the information from Russia. The Ambassador had requested me for this work. Both the OSS and the State Department had devoted appreciable effort to getting me to Moscow fast in response to this request.

Furthermore, I knew how desperate was the need in Washington for first-hand objective reporting on economics. There was a crying demand for first-hand information on Russia. The fact was, as everyone in intelligence in Washington knew, that the competent, professionally qualified observers of Soviet affairs among the one hundred and fifty or so official Americans in Moscow at the time could be numbered on the fingers of two hands, maybe even one.

It was with a sense of urgency, therefore, that I proceeded to the American Embassy on Mokhovaya Street across from the Kremlin on May 9 to start work. After waiting for a half-hour or so I was ushered into the office of the American diplomat, Embassy Counselor Max Hamilton, who was then in charge of the Embassy under Ambassador Harriman. He chatted with me for fifteen minutes or so. I had some letters for him which I had brought from Washington, he understood. Where were they? I explained that by some mistake in the Department I had been issued instead of a diplomatic passport a special passport which did not provide diplomatic immunity for the bearer. I had had, up to Teheran, a batch of letters including some for him. But since I did not have a diplomatic passport the Russians would have confiscated any letters on me. So I had left the letters with the Courier Office of the Embassy in Teheran. They would be brought in by one of the next couriers. Max seemed to become disturbed as he listened. Shortly afterward he dismissed me abruptly.

About my work, my desk and other such? I just managed to get in the question at the end of the interview. Oh yes, that. He didn't know much about my work or why I had been sent anyway. I detected a peevish tone. Go and see so-and-so, he said. He was the Commercial Attaché. He would look after my work.

Only later the word filtered through to me. It seemed the question of mail was a very sore point with Max. There hadn't been any for weeks. It was said he had been in a temper for days. Then I came. I had had in my hands precious letters to him, and I had surrendered them to the Courier Office in Teheran. The thought was nearly unbearable. When he sent me out of the office he dictated, as I learned, a blistering telegram on the question of mail. I was deep in his special doghouse, because he felt, possibly correctly, I had not stressed sufficiently in Teheran the importance of his mail.

All this I did not learn for some time. My reaction was to be taken aback at the marked lack of interest in my work. I had never heard of the Commercial Attaché, but I went upstairs to see him. He was pleasant and kind—a sincere, hard working officer. He was also even more vague about my assignment than the counselor. He did not know very much about Russia or the Soviet economy, nor much Russian either, as he admitted, but he was studying hard. He had served long years in Commercial Attaché work, a specific foreign service branch intended to be of assistance to American firms doing business abroad. He was thinking, I judged, of his job in Russia in much the same terms. He seemed to be unhappy that there were no American businessmen, except for a few fur buyers, engaged in trade with Russia.

He showed me his section. He had a small cubicle and a larger office across the hall in which there were four people. Two were middle-aged Soviet citizens engaged in combing from Russian newspapers bits of economic information which they translated. Another was a pleasantly good-humored young man, an American typist, who had been in the Embassy for three years. The fourth was a clerk by the name of Ed Ames who struck me after hardly ten minutes of conversation, as a superior individual who alone seemed to have any idea of the purposes of wartime economic reporting—and the technical know-how. Except for Ed the whole show was unimpressive.

The Commercial Attaché called me into his cubicle and said he presumed I would be working under him. He assigned me one immediate task. I looked over the sheet he had handed me. It was a routine circular request from the Department of Commerce asking all missions for estimates of the current cotton crop in their area.

My God, I thought to myself, was it for such drivel I had come to

Moscow? Washington had, as I knew, good estimates of Russian cotton prospects. That the United States Embassy in wartime should be occupying itself with replying to routine circulars giving unneeded information for trivial purposes seemed to me to be monstrous. But I did a brief report. It didn't take long.

"Patience! Patience!" I said to myself as I lay in bed trying to go to sleep after that first day at the Embassy. "The Ambassador will be back, and he certainly knows why he wanted you. At any rate you are in Russia and no one, not the Counselor or anyone else, can stop you from getting out to see it for yourself."

During the next several weeks I did keep my patience. I also kept my mouth shut and my ears open at the Embassy. I raised no troublesome questions, did what I was asked to do politely without seeking assignments, and talked at length to all the Americans inside and outside the Embassy with whom I had connections.

I suppose it was Ed Ames, the clerk in the Economic Section, who gave me my greatest shock. "I have something here I would like to show you," he said to me one day shortly after my arrival. He pulled out of a drawer in the safe a sheaf of documents about two inches high.

"What are these?" I asked.

"They are reports I have written on a half dozen different subjects," he replied.

"I wonder why I didn't see them in Washington," I said, leafing them through.

"Because they have never left the Embassy," Ed replied with a sardonic smile.

"Why not?" I asked. Their titles were interesting and intriguing. They were the sort of thing needed in Washington.

"That," he said, "is a long story." He told it to me. Ed was a Harvard graduate, a young economist who had studied Russian in an intensive course, and then taken a job with the Department to get to Moscow where he hoped to put both economics and his Russian to use. In the Embassy, however, he had received little encouragement of his wish to do economic reporting. He had been held at routine tasks during office hours—but had on his own initiative, on his own time, undertaken to write reports based on observation and research. However, when he submitted a pair of them he found reluctance in the Embassy to take responsibility. There was no one willing to pass judgment on them. As a result the Counselor had been unwilling to let them be sent.

"So," commented Ed, "I have continued to write reports. But I keep them right here in this drawer in the safe waiting till there will be someone bold enough to sign them and send them to Washington."

It seemed hard to believe but there were Ed's reports. I read them. They were good. They reported new information. Still I was not convinced that there could be a partial blockade against economic reporting. I had to find out for myself.

A week or so after, I myself wrote two lengthy reports. Ensconced at the Savoy Hotel I had begun to make the acquaintance of fellow foreigners living there. There were some American engineers, most of them sent there to help the Russians build four huge oil refineries to produce aviation gasoline. The equipment was being sent from America. Four parties of engineers were in the field at far-flung locations—Kuibyshev on the Volga, Orsk in the Southern Urals, Gurev and Krasnovodsk on the Caspian. They were living among Russians and working with them. Every so often they came to Moscow to the Savoy. These men were a gold mine of precious first-hand economic information. They knew about labor conditions, the state of nutrition, construction methods, material shortages, transportation and a dozen other subjects in the distant provinces where they worked. Since almost no other Americans were permitted to travel in wartime in the Soviet Union, these engineers were unique as a source.

After talking to a dozen of them I wrote up their observations under various relevant headings. I got two reports typed and ready for initialling and sent them to the Embassy. I was proud. My pride was premature. My reports never left the Embassy. They caused quite a to-do. I shall not recite the tale. It is too complicated. Suffice to say that Ed's description of the situation was correct.

And yet as I looked at the Embassy I saw that in other fields than economics there was excellent work done. Francis Stevens, for instance, a talented career officer, with a command of Russian and a knowledge of Soviet politics, was turning out able analyses of Soviet foreign policy. Fred Barghoorn—the same scholar present at Amherst seven years before when Professor Cole proposed that I specialize on Russia—was writing good studies of Soviet internal policy. There were some exceptionally able men on the Embassy staff. These things and the fact the Ambassador was apparently himself conscious of the problem gave me cause to hope.

In the meantime there was plenty to be done. There I was in Moscow, a throbbing metropolis. Around me were live Russians. Information about the Soviet Union was no longer something to be culled from newspapers but something to be seen and experienced. For the first time I was myself an observer there on the spot. I had the training and the energy to do something about it.

Always when Americans had talked to me of Russia after living there, they had told me of things they could *not* do. They could *not* travel as they pleased. They could *not* have Russian friends. They could *not* get official information. They could *not* study in educational institutions. These and a hundred other things.

When I went to Russia it was with a determination not to worry about the things I could *not* do but to do the things I could do. I was sure there would be plenty. And, as I had already found in my few weeks in Moscow, there were. I could go for a walk in the park. And so I did. I walked in a dozen different parks and I watched what Russians were doing there.

I could go to the theater. And I did go, night after night. I could hear the living language spoken from the stage, spoken beside me between the acts. I could go out in the intermissions and walk around with Russians in the endlessly-moving circle in the theater foyer. I could often discuss the play with whoever happened to be sitting beside me—a Russian. I could ride the suburban trains into the countryside outside Moscow. I could feel the crush of the Russian crowd at close quarters. I could look out the train windows and see all sorts of things.

I could go into stores. I could listen to public lectures. I could wander into courtrooms spotted around the town and listen to the evidence and the sentence. I could browse in bookstores. I could get out into the Collective Farm Markets and look at the merchandise being sold there. I could get in an Embassy car and take a ride to any distance up to sixty miles out of town, farther than that being forbidden to foreigners, but sixty miles are a lot of miles and there was a lot to see within that circle. I could go for a swim at the public beach on the Moscow River. I could go and eat a meal and drink a drink in the newly-opened, expensive "Commercial"—in other words unrationed—restaurants. There was much to do and I tried to do all of it.

Most important, of course, I could talk with Russians. I did not find that they ran away from me when they found I was an American, as some people had predicted they might. On the contrary most of them were interested in talking to an American and immediately plied me with dozens of questions. Every question told me something about them, their knowledge of the world, their attitudes and aspirations.

I had gone a long way in my first six weeks in the Soviet Union toward steeping myself in Soviet life. I had learned much that could not be found in even the wisest of books.

In early June, Ambassador Harriman returned to his Moscow post. I was overjoyed. At last I could hear from him directly. Some days after his arrival he called for me. I was ushered into his study. He greeted me with a smile and asked me how things were going. I told him briefly of my problems. He cut me short after I had given most of the picture.

"I'm going to ask you to be patient for a little while longer, Tom," he said. "A new Counselor—this is between us—is coming next month. Perhaps you've met him. It's George Kennan."

I must have jumped a little with inward glee, for the Ambassador immediately added, "I think things will be different after he arrives. He'll be directly in charge of your work."

I went home very pleased. At the end of the first week in July Kennan arrived and took charge, under Harriman, of the Embassy. He called me to his office one morning and chatted for a half hour or so. He had already seen reports which had been submitted by me. He liked them.

"How would you like to work by yourself directly under me for a while longer?" he asked. "I'll see that you get secretarial assistance as you need it." I was overjoyed and I said so.

"Maybe by the end of the year," he said as I went out of his office, "you can take over the Economic Section. I have some ideas of my own how it should be organized and I want to tell you about them when I have time."

# 5. *Meeting Russians*

"What are Russians like?"

This was a question asked of me countless times by curious Americans before I went to Russia. It was a question I myself had asked dozens of times. And I had never received satisfying answers.

Russians were dull and spiritless, said some. Russians were gay and fascinating, said others. Russians were an oppressed, seething mass, said much anti-Soviet literature. Russians were cast in the prototype of the "new Soviet man"—a sort of Marxist-Leninist superman—said Soviet propaganda.

These answers sounded like the fabled replies in the anecdote of the six blind men asked to describe the elephant they had each touched in a different part. The elephant is a big and varied animal, and the Soviet Union a big and varied country, with a couple of hundred million inhabitants each with a claim to individuality. One could never comprehend all Soviet citizens within one generality. Yet there were things to be comprehended about Russians. There was a feel for the spirit of the people to be acquired by the assiduous foreign observer in their midst. I, at any rate, was determined to acquire this feel. During my first months in Moscow I made it my business to meet as many Soviet citizens as possible on whatever basis possible. I had all kinds of experiences. Three of them stand out for their particular vividness.

\*     \*     \*     \*     \*

Bob Tucker and I walked around Dzerzhinsky Square, glancing now and then at the massive, monotonous gray building on the other side of it. This was police headquarters—famous as the "Lyubyanka." We went past the Metro Station and crossed a thoroughfare. A bit further we turned down a small side street. It was between the Polytechnical Museum, on one side, a building designed in a sort of imitation Muscovy Baroque, and on the other side, the headquarters of the Communist Youth League—the Konsomols. Down on this side street about half way we found the door we wanted in a decrepit two-story building. Inside the rickety door we stopped and blinked. Only a few rays of light penetrated from a half boarded-over window. In a while our eyes became accustomed to the darkness and we managed to see the staircase. We climbed it—taking care not to stumble on its well-worn treads. At the top of the stairs a pungent smell of sour cabbage filled our nostrils—a most typical odor in Russian apartment buildings. At the end of a dark passageway we found the last door on the left and we knocked diffidently. We waited. Evidently we had been too diffident. So we knocked again—louder.

I went over in my mind's eye the course of events that had brought us to this particular doorway. One evening weeks before, Bob was at the Art Theater. During the long intermission he struck up a conversation with the young woman sitting next to him. They began by talking about the play. But when she found that he was an American, she was full of questions. The conversation went on after the play when Bob walked Dusya—that was her name, short for Avdotya—part of the way home.

"Could I see you again?" Dusya asked Bob. So they arranged to meet at the theater again.

When Bob met her in the lobby at the appointed time, she was taking off her shoes—relatively worn out ones—in which she had come to the theater and putting on her best shoes. This was a little wartime device of women, which one could see enacted in any theater cloakroom. Its intent was to save wear on best shoes which were irreplaceable.

So Bob made Dusya's acquaintance, and through Bob I met her. Dusya was a widow. Her husband had disappeared at the front. He was undoubtedly dead. She had never received an official notice, but this was ordinary. Dusya had been overcome with grief for months, but gradually had come to the realization that she had a life to live and a daughter to look after and must snap out of it.

The daughter was about nine. Dusya had to see that the child was looked after while she worked. She was a minor official in the chemical industry in the State Planning Commission and worked in the modern Council of Ministers Building, a block from the American Embassy. Her salary of nine hundred rubles a month was good as salaries for women ran—but in 1944 what with small rations, it did not go far. Dusya was having a tough time. She showed it. Despite her young years—about thirty—she looked worn.

One evening I met Dusya at the theater and she was excited.

"Are you and Robert free tomorrow evening? Could you come and visit? My brother's going to be there. He's well again. He's out of the hospital and he has two days leave before returning to the front. He wants to meet you. Can you come?"

She got all this out in almost one breath, with the words tumbling over each other.

"I'll have to ask Bob," I started to say. Then seeing her expression of disappointment I hurried. "Don't worry, we'll come."

And so we had. Our second knock was more effective. The door opened and we saw in front of us a fairly spacious room. It was early evening with plenty of daylight outside but things inside were rather dark. The windows were small and heavy curtains cut off most of the daylight. The room was furnished poorly. A pair of cots stood against the wall. There were two upholstered chairs, on the grimy side. In the center of the room there was a small table with a lamp hanging down from the ceiling over it with a large orange silk lampshade on it. In a corner there was a sort of a stand holding a hot plate on which Dusya did her cooking. On the walls, decorated with faded wallpaper, there were family photographs and a portrait of Stalin.

Beyond Dusya who had opened the door and welcomed us stood a tall, cadaverous looking man in army uniform smoking a Russian "papirosa"—cigarette with long paper mouthpiece.

He advanced on us rapidly with his hand outstretched.

"This is Alexei . . ." Dusya introduced him.

"My sister has written me all about you both," he declared in Russian quickly. "I told her I wanted to meet you and I am glad you could come. This is a big night for me. It is my last in Moscow for a long time. Tomorrow I leave for the front."

He hesitated.

"You know—maybe Dusya has told you—I've recovered from my fourth wound. I didn't think this time I would make it. But I did. And now I'm fit to fight. This is the second day with my family and friends here."

Bob and I felt flattered that this warrior would want to spend some of his limited time with us.

Then we looked at the table and gasped. We had not noticed before. There was spread out a feast—caviar, sour cream, cucumbers, herring, a bottle of Georgian wine, Moscow vodka, sardines, even tomatoes, items that I knew must have cost Dusya more than her whole month's wages.

Alexei motioned us to the table.

"Sit down," he said. "My sister has outdone herself. I appreciate it. I'm going to remember this evening for a long time out there."

He pointed West.

We sat down. We drank toasts to each other and to our countries. We stuffed ourselves with Dusya's priceless provender.

Alexei asked a few questions but mostly talked about himself. Out of what he had to say there emerged for Bob and myself a picture of the feelings of a Russian Communist.

His father, a foreman in a factory, was an Old Bolshevik—a member of the party from before the Revolution. All the family were Party members. Before the war he worked in the Ministry of Foreign Trade. They had sent him to Italy and he had spent several years there. He pulled out a snapshot of himself taken on a park bench in Milan. It didn't look like him. On the bench in the photo was a man of over two hundred and twenty pounds and before us a man of maybe one hundred and forty pounds.

"Ah, yes," he said, noticing our train of thought, "I used to weigh a lot more. They didn't give us much to eat in that hospital I just got out of. Sometimes I wondered which I was going to die of first—my wound or starvation."

His story of the hospital was a true horror and he told it without much emotion. No medicine. No food. Men dying like flies. He, a political officer and a Communist Party member, attempting to keep up morale in these conditions, himself near death, taking six months to recover from wounds which should have healed in six weeks. He shook his head sadly.

"In comparison with that hell-hole," he declared, "the front is heaven. There one can see the enemy."

Alexei looked like a man in his mid-fifties, his hospital experience had so aged him. Pale and thin, he looked as if he needed rest for a couple of months. But he was headed back for the front—and eager to go. I took out a pack of cigarettes, lit one and offered him one. He took it, examined it, then lit it nervously and pulled on it carefully.

"We make better cigarettes than these," he said challengingly. I let this pass.

He noticed Bob's cigarette lighter. "We used to make better lighters than that before the war in the Soviet Union," he said challengingly. I looked at him and could almost see the big chip on his shoulder. He was waiting for someone to contradict him.

And so it went all evening. Everything that America or the West made had been made—before the war—better in the Soviet Union.

Alexei asked how people lived in the United States, but no sooner had we begun to tell him than he brushed us aside and changed the direction of the conversation. What about unemployment? What about the Negro problem—race discrimination? Dusya interrupted to ask how women in America dress. Alexei interrupted our exposition. He gave us a speech on how well Russian people had lived before the war and how well they were going to live again after the war.

During this oration Alexei made some pretty outrageous claims for Soviet accomplishments which we knew to be outright falsehoods. And it was my impression that, had we called him on these lies, he would have been flagrantly insulted. We let them pass because we were fascinated with Alexei. Here was a real live Russian Communist. What was it that made him tick?

Alexei as he emerged in character was not stupid. He had had extensive experience in various types of work and his education and indoctrination had been thorough. This showed. He was able to talk with us about many different things. Unlike many Russians he had had the experience of being abroad. This had had its effect. He was not a provincial hayseed. He had been raised in the metropolis, the capital, and he had "seen the sights." But if he was not stupid, he was very limited in breadth and outlook. "The letter of the Law"—that was his point of view. The Party says, and therefore it is so. And if the Party were to declare, "The moon is made of green cheese," then Alexei would repeat faithfully, "The moon is made of green cheese." No generosity of spirit. A fanatic—without qualifications.

Yet he was not deprived of human qualities. He had burned with resentment as he told how his fellow patients at the hospital had died like flies. He was an angry man and one with sympathy for the sufferings of fellow-Russians.

But his sympathies were reserved for fellow-Communists. Alexei was a burning chauvinist and a dogmatic Communist. Of all the traits he displayed, the one that stood out the most was his fantastic sensitivity lest we, foreigners within the gates, should think badly of the Soviet Union and Communism. His aggressive assertiveness, his bold claims of accomplishments which did not exist, were a manifestation of a deep feeling of insecurity on the part of a Russian Communist faced with a pair of Americans.

And this was a feeling I encountered on other occasions in dealings with Russians. It is a rather general thing, I believe. Wrapped up in it, I suppose, are all sorts of primitive emotions: fierce pride, begrudging envy, fear, covetousness, yes, and a good dose of hate as well, all mixed up with a simultaneous admiration and desire to be friendly and well thought of. Most of all, perhaps, there is deep determination to outdo these foreigners, these Americans, these capitalists, and be *first* in the world.

The feelings of Russians toward foreigners and particularly toward Americans are very strong indeed and so little understood.

Now Dusya was different. She had not the slightest hesitancy in expressing her admiration for things Western. A party member she was and a loyal citizen, but she was also a woman who knew pretty things when she saw them.

The evening with Alexei and Dusya moved toward its end. I raised a toast to Alexei:

"Here's to your victorious return from the front."

He raised his little vodka glass to me after we had drunk that down and let it soak in.

"Here's to a better world once this war is over!"

Bob and I drank down that toast too. But as we wended our way home after goodbys I could not help consider the fact that Alexei's idea of a "better world" was in all probability something very different from my own. It was problematical whether there was any place for people like me in it. And whatever I did not know about Alexei I did know one thing—he would be prepared to fight for his idea of a "better world."

*    *    *    *    *

The little old man, in the rumpled gray tweed suit which looked as if he had slept in it for a week, winked at me from across the foreigners' dining room in the Savoy Hotel as I sat there munching steadfastly on a meal of something that looked like seaweed but which had been described to me by the waitress as sauerkraut.

I winked back. I had watched the old man for several weeks in this dining room as he chatted with his constant companion—a nervous Yugoslav diplomat who was trying to make up his mind whether to go over to Tito's partisans.

A round-faced Russian waitress put a glass of tea in front of me.

The little old man in the gray suit got up from his table slowly and with elaborate casualness meandered to mine. He and I were the only people in the dining room. I motioned him to the chair opposite. He sat down heavily.

"Davaite poznakomyemsya!" he said in Russian. "Let's get acquainted."

And then he said in somewhat halting English, "My name is Antonov."

"Mine is Whitney," I returned and then I switched to Russian. "Are you a Russian?"

Antonov was a typically Russian name but my question was relevant because Mr. Antonov was eating in the foreigners' dining room at the Savoy from which Russians were excluded.

"Yes," he answered, understanding the drift of my thought. "I am a Russian. I work for the Narkomindel—the Soviet foreign office—and they made arrangements for me in view of my poor health to eat here in the foreigners' dining room instead of out there."

He gestured in the general direction of the larger—and inferior—restaurant for Russians.

"What do you do in the Foreign Office?" I inquired. I had already observed that he could be found in the hotel dining room at almost any hour of the day.

"Well, as you can see, I'm an old man now and I worked for the Ministry of Foreign Affairs before the Revolution then after the Revolution too. But I am, what you say, retired . . . except that now and then they call me in to help on something special."

I thought I caught a glitter in his eye when he said this. Antonov did have a sense of humor.

"And what about you, Mr. Whitney? What kind of work do you do in the Embassy?" he asked with an innocent air.

"Oh, I'm an attaché and I work on economics most of the time." I told him. I wondered whether he had not received a pretty thorough briefing on me before he undertook to make my acquaintance.

"Ah," he said, turning the word over in his mouth several times, "Economics . . . economics . . . economics . . . that is a very interesting field."

He was a wizened little old chap with snow white hair. I suppose that he must have been in his early seventies, but age had not dimmed his faculties. I had observed before that he spoke with acumen and seemed alert behind a screen of relaxed and quiet demeanor.

If old Antonov had come over to engage me in conversation he must have something on his mind. I wondered what it could be. We kept chatting. And I waited for him to show his hand.

"I have a very pleasant hobby, Mr. Whitney." I heard him say out of the corner of my consciousness. "What kind of a hobby do you have?"

And then he went on monotonously,

"You know my hobby is collecting rocks—minerals—from all over the Soviet Union. I have a wonderful collection of rocks." He continued, "We here in Russia have tremendous ore deposits—of all kinds of things."

He waited a bit. I supposed I was to show some sort of interest. But I didn't. I just didn't care about rocks. Mr. Antonov's hobby bored me.

"Maybe you would like to see some of my collection . . ." There was a highly expectant air in the way he said this.

I was by this time looking for a way to bring the evening to an end and this seemed to be an opportunity. I manifested sudden interest. "Why, yes, Mr. Antonov. I would be most interested in seeing your mineral collection. Do you have it here?"

He jumped up with great alacrity. I followed him upstairs.

His hotel room was cozy and very luxurious. I was surprised and interested. Certainly he was really a mineralogist. All about the room there were displayed rock and ore samples. Some were undoubtedly unique. He was not joking when he told me about his hobby.

"Now here I have something very interesting," he said with a certain special tone in his voice.

"What is it?" I asked.

"This," he said with strange emphasis, "is uranium."

I said nothing. I knew what uranium was, of course. But it was no concern of mine.

"Look here," he said. "I have a very particular interest," and he underlined the word very, "in radioactive ores. I have taken many pictures of them—or rather I have let them take their own pictures."

I leafed through his photographs of radioactive ores. They did not interest me. Antonov seemed to think, obviously, that I ought to be interested. But I was not and I showed it.

Finally I put the sheaf of photographs down. We chatted a bit about routine subjects and I bade him goodnight. As I left I thought I detected a shade of disappointment in his look at me. Evidently there was something I was supposed to have done that I did not do.

That was in June of 1944. It was over a year later in August, 1945, that I read the announcement of the Hiroshima atom bomb. When I did, I kicked myself under my desk in the Embassy. "Why that bastard!" I exclaimed. But then I thought a bit more. After all, Mr. Antonov, like all the rest of us, was only doing his job.

\*     \*     \*     \*     \*

It was a Sunday evening in July, 1944. I sat in my hotel room at my typewriter ready to start a letter. I thought of the circumstances that led to that letter, of what it would mean to the person receiving it, and of the interesting day I had passed—running a family errand for a friend.

A few weeks before I had left America for the USSR I had had lunch with a friend of mine named George Ivanov. He was an American of Russian extraction and was well known among Russian specialists in wartime Washington. We had talked of my coming trip to the USSR. He gave me good advice. Before we parted he had taken a slip of paper and handed it to me. On it was a name and an address in Russian. "What is it?" I asked.

"I don't have the right to ask you," he said with a good deal of feeling. "But there is something I would like to have you do—if you can. My family is in Russia. I have not heard from them since the beginning of the war. I don't know whether they are dead or alive. I don't know whether they need help nor for that matter what kind and how I can give it. I don't even know whether it is safe to write. When you are in Moscow wait for a time until you get the feel of things. Decide whether you think a visit can cause them harm. If you think it won't, then when you have the time, drop out to see my sister, Maria, who lives with her husband, Misha, just outside Moscow."

"I'll do it if I can, George!" I told him. And I swore that I would carry out this errand if it seemed practical. And I had—that very day. So I began my letter to George. I told him the story of the whole long interesting day.

At the Kazan Station I had finally found the right train. It was so crowded that I had to find myself a place on the outside of the train in a precarious position between two cars—one foot on the coupling and the other on some sort of a metal lever which protruded. That was certainly something my insurance company never envisaged when it wrote my policy. Anyway I got to my destination—a small, typically dilapidated and run-down Moscow suburban settlement. Little shacks and houses lay all about, most of them made of logs with tin roofs, almost all of them with a potato garden in their courtyard and a fence around it, and a goat tethered in the yard. There were no street signs.

I asked questions of children. I had learned by experience that they usually know more than adults and that generally they were more willing to answer questions. By that method I finally got directed to the home of some relatives of George's sister's husband. In a sun porch in the rear of the home in which I found myself there sat a gray-haired middle-aged man with an open, likable face. Who was I, and why did I want to see Maria, he asked? I wasn't quite sure what to do, but decided to take a chance on telling him why I had come. The man heard me out and looked a little relieved and introduced himself as Maria's husband—the brother-in-law of my friend, George. He had been visiting his kinfolk and I had chanced in while he was still there. Yes, it was Misha of whom George had told me. I had found the family!

Misha at first had been much on guard as he had talked. I didn't blame him. But he had asked question after question, and I had told him about George, about George's work and friends, and about my connection with him. He soon realized I was telling the truth.

He insisted on taking me immediately to see Maria. We walked on over to their home. Maria met me with tears in her eyes. One of the children had run ahead of us to let her know that a friend of her brother was on the way. She had not heard from him for years.

Misha and Maria lived, as I had found, in a little one-story home of their own. It looked a bit run down but was neat, though frugally furnished, indoors. Maria was a Russian woman of over fifty who looked worn, worried and tired. She complained of headaches and weakness. The war had taken its toll of her as of millions of others in Russia.

I gave George the news of the family: Maria's and Misha's son, Boris, eighteen years old, was a Senior Lieutenant in the Red Air Force. He was at an officer's school. The family had not seen him for two years. Maria complained of being ill. She was extremely nervous, particularly because of Boris' dangerous profession. Misha was working at a factory in Moscow. I had not asked him where precisely because I had not wished to appear overly curious. He had remained in Moscow all during the siege of the city in late 1941. Maria had been evacuated to the Urals and returned home only after very difficult experiences. The son, Boris, had lived with Misha until he left Moscow for officers' school.

George's other sister, Raisa, had also been evacuated to the Urals with her children. She had returned to Moscow and was living with Maria. Her boys and her little girl as well were well-fed and active. They were chasing each other around the place while I was there and generally making a nuisance of themselves in the best tradition of childhood. One of them, Vanya, had taken it on himself to give me a lecture on the tactics of Field Marshall Kutuzov. Raisa herself appeared to be well—though her trials certainly had told on her nervous system. Her husband was an officer in a Guards Division, possessed the medal of the defense of Stalingrad and was due to receive the Order of the Red Star. Raisa had not seen him in over two years. When she had come back from the Urals she had lost most of her personal possessions through theft. She was hoping to move into her Moscow apartment in a month or so when it would be repaired.

The other sister, Galya, had remained in the Urals. She had with her both her son and husband. Her husband had been a partisan behind the German lines. He had been seriously wounded in the head and shoulder but had been successfully evacuated to safety behind Russian lines.

I wrote to George in my letter, "Your father also remains behind in the Urals."

I had to gulp when I typed this line in my letter. I am not a person to tell lies or soften bad news. The fact was that George's father was dead, a victim of the hardships of war. He had died far from home in the Urals. But Maria had begged me not to tell George. She had even exacted a promise I would not write the bad news to him. I had consented, but only at the price of agreement to let me inform George in person through a mutual acquaintance who was going to Washington.

The family had many stories of German atrocities. Many of their close friends had been killed. Whole families among acquaintances had been wiped out. While I was there at their home one of the neighborhood women had come to tell Maria she had just received the news her husband had been killed on the Leningrad front.

Misha, when he lived alone in Moscow during the siege, had had a bad time. He had worked long hours at the factory and then came home to do the housework. There had often been air raid alarms so that he sometimes had spent the entire night in an air raid trench.

Maria and Raisa had had hard times in the Urals. They had had at times to pay up to one hundred rubles a kilogram for potatoes in order to keep from starving. This was a fantastic price—equal to a week's wages for many Russian factory workers. As George well knew, this meant they had had to sell most of their precious clothing and other personal possessions to get food to keep alive. I was able to continue the letter, however, on a happier note.

By the time of my visit things seemed to be better. Raisa, Maria and the children were getting three hundred grams of bread and Misha six hundred and fifty a day. That made an average of about two-thirds of a pound per person in the family. In addition they got a separate small dry ration since Misha did not eat lunch at the factory canteen. All available space in their garden was sown to potatoes. But they still had to buy on the open market, principally potatoes, at around twenty-five rubles a kilogram, also a fantastic price, equivalent at the time to about three dollars a pound at the official exchange rate.

They insisted on entertaining me. I could hardly refuse without being impolite. They treated the news from George as the biggest event of the year. As the bearer, I was well feasted. We drank a toast to George—in Georgian wine. I hated to eat their precious food, but did so with the mental reservation that I would make it up to them.

I closed my letter to George. Then I sat back and thought. For a few hours I had been part of a Russian family. They were giving their all for victory. Like other Russian families they had suffered grievously from the war—a loved one lost, trouble, wounds, pain, anxiety, hunger, hardship. From June 22, 1941 on, it had been one long unending nightmare of hurt and sorrow. Yet they were surviving. They were continuing to put forth their utmost for their country. By June 1944 they were already recovering—though slowly—from the worst wounds of the war. They had, as I could feel in the infectious laugh of Misha, kept their sense of humor. And when an emissary from the long-lost brother in America appeared they could pull themselves together and even deliver a banquet for the occasion! Truly, I could only conclude that these were golden people and I felt that as long as such people represented the spirit of the nation, the future of the country, regardless of the political system, was secure. This at any rate was my feeling as I addressed the envelope that evening to my friend George who had done me a favor by making me his messenger and thereby giving me an introduction to a Soviet family in wartime—to its sorrows, its joys, and to its heroism.

\*     \*     \*     \*     \*

# 6.    *V. I. P. Trip*

We sat, the American Major-General and I, across a small table from each other in a peasant hut about thirty miles west of Moscow. In one corner of the room hung a religious Ikon. On the opposite wall was a photograph of Politburo member, Andrei Zhdanov. We munched sandwiches which Ambassador Harriman's Chinese cook had provided and sipped tea out of glasses which the lady of the house, who knew us not from Adam, put before us. We had been out for a ride and I had simply stopped the car at a likely looking cabin and asked the chauffeur to ask the owner whether we could come in to eat our meal. And she had consented. One could always count on Russian hospitality.

The American Major-General talked and I listened. He had been around and he knew how to tell a good anecdote. This was Public Works Administrator, Major-General Philip Fleming, a top-ranking American engineer who had bossed some of the biggest construction projects the world had seen.

Fleming had come to the Soviet Union at President Roosevelt's instructions. His mission was to investigate war devastation and reconstruction in the USSR, and to make a report to the President. I had been named as his aide and translator and this was a rewarding assignment. Out of it I got my first glimpse of provincial Russia.

\*    \*    \*    \*    \*

General Fleming and I stood at the very center of the Dnieper Dam at Zaporozhe in the Ukraine. We were the first Americans to be taken to see the dam after it had been retaken from the Germans.

We looked to the West where the sun was sinking over the steppes in a blaze of red glory. Just below us down the river was the famous Island of Hortitsa where once the Dnieper Cossacks had maintained their fortress center. The vast arc of the dam extended majestically on either side—but it was a sorry sight.

We were at the bottom of a big gap which the Germans, during retreat, had blown in the dam. Above us, where once an enormous reservoir had been accumulated behind the dam there was the Dnieper River, shallow over its rocky rapids just as it was before the dam was built. Below us the waters boiled through "bottom perforations" made at river level by the Russians themselves to let the water level behind the dam all the way down so that reconstruction could be carried out.

"All my life I've been building dams," said the man next to us who wore pince-nez. He had on a rumpled felt hat and a wrinkled tweed overcoat and looked more like a scholar than a great hydroelectric engineer. This was Chief Engineer Kandalov of Dnieprostroi—the organization rebuilding the dam and power station.

"It was right here I started," he said with some feeling. "What a terrible thing it is to build a great structure like this and then later to have to return to build it over again!"

He turned to Fleming. Fleming shook his head sadly. He understood. A few minutes later we got back in the jeep with Kandalov and proceeded.

An hour later we sat at a banquet table. Around it were a dozen and a half of the Communist élite of the Zaporozhe Region. Kandalov was at the head of the table. He stood, making a brief speech. There had been all the routine toasts between allies but Kandalov was striking a more original note.

"I speak," he said, "with feeling. We have here tonight American guests. It gives me a chance to make remarks I have long wanted to. I learned my profession here at Dnieprostroi a dozen years ago. I had Soviet teachers. They were great men. But the man who taught me and most of the rest of us here much of what we know was an American. I want to express gratitude to our guests. I want to toast the American who led us in building the Dnieper Dam—Hugh Cooper."

There was applause. Cooper had made a big impression. And I remembered this scene in years afterward when from 1947 on the Soviet propaganda machine tried to ridicule American scientific and technical accomplishments and claim every important invention for Russians.

The next day Fleming and I were up early. Three barefooted Ukrainian girls served us our breakfast of fried bologna and eggs. A jeep was at our door with a chauffeur.

Kandalov awaited us in his office, with photographs and drawings spread out all over his table. For an hour he lectured on the damage and how he planned repairs. Fleming began to ask technical questions. My abilities as a translator fell short. But the Russians soon recalled the English terminology and they and Fleming talked back and forth in a sort of engineers' lingua franca.

Then we went out to the dam and power house. We clambered about all day long. We watched the husky peasant girls who constituted the labor force carting away concrete debris in hand barrows after it had been broken into small enough chunks by sledge hammer.

It was pitiful to see the wreck of the powerhouse. The Wehrmacht demolition squads had left things in such a state that the Russians were tempted to abandon the site. The following days we spent in visits to nearby factories and cities. I shall never forget the shambles at the Zaporozhstal Steel Plant, one of the largest, most modern units of the steel industry. It was a mass of wreckage and tangled debris for acres and acres. Reconstruction was only starting. Astonishing was the thoroughness of German destruction of the city of New Zaporozhe. This modern town, consisting of four and six-story apartment houses, built in the thirties, was Russia's newest city. The Germans had vented terrible vengeance on it. Every apartment house in the town had been gutted or demolished. Our tour was a terrifying view of the vandalism of modern war.

But the most interesting thing of all to me was not this but our host Kandalov. I was getting an opportunity to see a Soviet executive engineer at work. He carried on his own work at the same time he showed us around. He gave orders on the spot in our presence—cleanly, neatly, precisely, without fuss or bluster. Though soft-spoken, he commanded great respect from subordinates who listened to him intently. He was dedicated to his job and knew his men backwards and forwards.

In long conversations with Fleming a different Kandalov appeared —the scientist. He was not merely a practical engineer but a competent theoretician. He was a master of the science of hydroelectrics. Mention a dam in Korea, Brazil, India, Africa, the Tennessee Valley, Armenia or Central Asia, and he could rattle off instantly its characteristics. He was familiar with every solution for a hydroelectric problem anywhere that had been devised and knew in what conditions it could be applied. His knowledge was encyclopedic. I remember how, with a small smile at the corner of his mouth, he declared "We engineers are the Pharaohs of today. The Pharaohs built pyramids to honor themselves which are useless. We engineers today build bigger pyramids than they which bring light to millions. By the time I die I hope to have built dams all over the Soviet Union."

As he spoke there was inspiration in his eye. It was appealing. But suddenly I, a young newcomer to the Soviet scene getting my first glimpse of such a person and aspect of the system, was struck by two big facts. The first was, of course, that Kandalov was competent, hardworking and dedicated. And the second, equally important, was that he was working without stint for the Soviet Union without, I am sure, questioning the political objectives of the system which he was serving.

*      *      *      *      *

"Most of the reconstruction carried on here in Stalino so far," said our rough-hewn host, "we have done by ourselves, without much help from Moscow."

He was a good-humored man with an air of tough self-assurance. His face was pleasant but hardly gentle and his eyes were narrow with a definitely Mongoloid cast. They twinkled as he talked. I judged him to be about forty. This was Alexander Ivanovich Struyev—Sasha to his intimates, Alexander Ivanovich to everyone else. He was Chairman of the Executive Committee of Stalino Region in the Soviet Donbas, center of Ukrainian coal-mining and steel-smelting. This put him in charge of the apparatus of government. He was outranked in the province only by the First Secretary of the Party, Leonid Melnikov.

Struyev was showing Fleming and me through the Stalin Steel Works. We had flown to Stalino that day from the Dnieper Dam and Struyev continued his talk as we tramped from one smoking blast furnace to another.

"We wire Moscow for this and that. But Moscow always says

'There's a war on and everything goes to the front. Get along as best you can.' So that is just what we do."

We stopped to watch molten iron flowing from one of the furnaces. In contrast to the steel plant in Zaporozhe, this was producing steel. It was working—one year after being recaptured—at about one-half prewar capacity.

"Do you have to worry about this steel plant too?" I asked Struyev. "I thought steel plants were the responsibility of the Ministry for Ferrous Metallurgy in Moscow."

"We have to worry about everything," he replied. "If the plant doesn't fulfill its plan Moscow calls us. If coal production slows down then we catch it from Moscow. If grain deliveries aren't on schedule Moscow calls us. Right now our biggest problem is grain deliveries. What a headache!"

"Who is 'us'?" asked General Fleming.

"Us is Leonid Grigorievich Melnikov, the First Secretary of the Party, and me. We have to watch everything."

"Are you a member of the Communist Party?" asked the General.

"I'm too young," retorted Struyev. "They won't let me in."

Two of his colleagues who were with us laughed uproariously. Struyev was a veteran leg-puller. As everyone knew, Struyev was the second most important man in the regional Party.

The Plant Director came out to meet us. His name was Pavel Andreyev. A tall, scholarly-looking chap, wearing high leather boots, a leather jacket and a cap, he accompanied us on our tour, showing us what he had succeeded in rebuilding and introducing us to all his workers and foremen. He seemed to know all his men by first name and patronymic.

As we went the rounds I noticed that Struyev and Andreyev had their heads close together repeatedly. It dawned on me that they were using our presence to conduct one of their regular tours of inspection.

"We must have more trucks," I heard Andreyev say.

"How many?" asked Struyev.

"Twenty," came the reply.

"Well, I know a repair shop which can rebuild ten for you which are not usable now. The other ten I'll find somewhere else, some from the town Council. But they don't have enough as it is."

"I'll be grateful," said Andreyev warmly.

"Save your gratitude," replied the political executive. "I'll be making requests of you."

We took our leave from Andreyev. Struyev continued on the tour of devastation and reconstruction in Stalino. There was plenty and Struyev was inexhaustible. By the time Fleming and I reached our guest house after dark we were nearing collapse but Struyev was fresh as a daisy. At the dinner table I could size him up a bit better. He was a solidly-built, physically fit, hard man of a little over average height with a thick head of dark hair which he combed back from his forehead. Under a dark woolen suit which fitted loosely and needed pressing he had on an embroidered Ukrainian shirt—no necktie. His features and head were large. And there was that omnipresent twinkle in his slightly slanted eyes.

Two days Fleming and I spent with Sasha Struyev. We got to know him and like him. We saw him in action at collective farms, coal mines, steel mills, the giant Zuyevo Electric Power Plant and other enterprises. He had an impressive knowledge of the economy, personnel and technology of his region. Most of all he seemed to have the touch for dealing effectively with the men in charge of factories, farms and mines. And they looked a tough lot. Coal miners and steel workers have never been noted for their daintiness. And Struyev was one of them. Like Nikita Khrushchev himself, whom he knew, he had emerged from the mines of Stalino.

Watching Struyev I began to understand the role of the Communist political executive in the provinces. In part he is a politician on familiar terms with everyone important in the region who knows how to get them to do what he wants. In part he is a trouble-shooter who spots bottlenecks and helps to break them by direct action as brutal as necessary. He is a hard-bitten straw boss accustomed to push things through by main force whenever Moscow demands.

The provincial Communist political leaders constitute Soviet power in person throughout the country. They give it much of its flavor. After all, Nikita Khrushchev is one of them. Though in a totalitarian system their position is different from that of politicians in a democracy, yet they are nevertheless professional politicians. Their special talent lies in dealing with people, and if they are tough, rude, crude and brutal, it is also a fact that the Soviet provinces in general are rude and crude and life in them is tough and brutal.

*    *    *    *    *

General Fleming soared away from the Stalino Airport on a brisk October morning at daybreak bound for Teheran and Washington. Back in Moscow a week later late at night in my hotel room I sat down to write him a letter to tell him the odyssey of my return. My letter began:

"I think you will be interested to hear of my trip to Moscow from Stalino. By the time I got back from the airport after seeing you off the accumulation of the champagne and vodka consumed the night before, plus my cold, plus the last flurry of vodka toasts at that early breakfast, plus my accumulated weariness, left me near collapse. I lay down to take a nap about nine-thirty A.M. and struggled out of bed at eleven. I pulled myself, by a supreme effort, into one piece, washed my face and remembered I had work left to do."

I interrupted the letter to recollect that little adventure. The "work left to do" was something the General knew about. When we visited the opera house in Stalino to see an operetta we found in the lobby a detailed exhibit reporting on reconstruction in Stalino, giving data on important plants and industries in this key area. This exhibit was a mine of information unavailable to the United States government. I determined to get back there, even if it landed me in jail. So when the General had departed and I had managed to arouse myself I sneaked down to the opera house with my little notebook. I was able to get inside and spent an hour and a half jotting down data. It was a major coup for me. I continued my letter: "We had lunch and went to the train at five-thirty P.M. Struyev accompanied us. At lunch the vodka was still flowing and there was still that insistence on downing toasts. I never want to see a glass of vodka again."

My companions for the train trip, as Fleming knew, were Captain Rubanov, Special Assistant to Minister of Foreign Trade Anastas Mikoyan, and Lucy Morozova, the jovial big blonde Intourist interpreter, both sent with us by Mikoyan to assist us on our trip.

I resumed: "The train was 'soft.' That is to say we had a small compartment for four with bunks which had mattresses. Lucy took one lower and I the other. The Captain had an upper. The other upper held our baggage. In between the bunks there were about eighteen inches in which there was a small folding table on which one could eat, play cards, lay out one's toilet articles or the like. This was a typical Russian train.

"The train went slowly through devastated areas including some in which hardly a hut was left. Scars of war were everywhere. It was a rough but interesting ride. We ate out of lunch boxes supplied in Stalino—bread, dried fish, vodka, tea and butter. Tomatoes and onions, along with honey, apples, hard-boiled eggs, and an occasional chicken, we bought from peasants along the way.

"Everyone on the train was in a buying fever. Prices for foodstuffs in the areas we passed through are lower than in Moscow and everyone aboard was engaged in filling cartons, sacks and suitcases with produce. Our passenger car began to bulge with booty at the seams like a freight wagon. Sacks, bundles and boxes were sticking out of every nook and corner.

"Lucy, the Captain and I also joined in food buying. The Captain proved by far the best. He got his produce for half the price we paid and always swiped the only container before we got it.

"I made the acquaintance of a leading Soviet lion tamer who traveled in our car and there was a railway man from Tula who insisted adamantly, with alcoholic hospitality, that I come home with him for the weekend.

"I found out all about 'samogon'—the bootleg variety of vodka. It was on sale openly at every stop. It is murky and fiery. Results are guaranteed—shortcut to oblivion. It was made from sugar beets. Pretty tough stuff!

"I could write a dissertation on sanitary facilities on the Soviet railway system. They are neither the cleanest nor the most modern in the world.

"After two days and six hours—to cover five hundred miles—we got back to Moscow—cold, damp, dark, crowded and gloomy. No one was there to meet us. Lucy and I left Rubanov with the baggage and went to look for porters and a phone. To use the phone we had to find a ten-copeck piece. Lucy canvassed one side and I the other of the station, where scores of people were huddled on benches and on the floor, spending the night. Finally she got two of these rare coins. I called the Embassy—no answer. She called the Ministry—with luck. I found two porters at long last and finally the Captain as well. He, wise man, knowing the problems of finding ten-copeck pieces and cars at midnight in wartime Moscow, stood patiently waiting for us to get some results.

"Back to my hotel and to bed at last. Home such as it is! But it was good."

I finished my letter to the General and sat back and thought about things. I had by then spent more than five months in the Soviet Union. I had come to Russia as an experienced student of Soviet affairs with six years of study and work behind me, but as an utter novice in my experience of the country. During my first five months in Russia, I had worked hard, gotten around a lot, seen and observed much. The extensive trip with General Fleming had come as sort of a culmination. It dawned on me that after these five months and this trip I was no longer a novice in my experience of Russia.

# 7.     *Yulya*

But here I find I have gotten ahead of myself in this narrative. It was ten weeks before I made the trip with General Fleming that an important event in my life took place.

Friday evening July 15. I had returned to the hotel after a long session at the Lenin Library. As I walked past the door to the large room at the head of the stairs on my floor I heard the warm and raucous sounds of a party. I sighed and went on down the hall. It was only after I had opened my door that I remembered that the American engineer, Jerry, occupant of the large room where the party was going on, had invited me to drop in on his gathering when I got home. So I went back, pushed open the door of Jerry's room, and was greeted heartily.

Liquor was flowing and the lights were bright. Whiskey mingled with vodka in the stomachs of a dozen or so diplomats, engineers and journalists present. "Those damned Russkies." was a phrase I heard several times floating through the air. Some of the outspoken engineers were discussing with other visitors their difficulties on their assignments in the interior of the Soviet Union. But at this party, as at other American parties in Moscow in 1944, when the Soviet-American alliance was at its wartime warmest, there were Russians present, as I could see. A hefty and bouncy blonde was joyfully tossing about her ample charms and her flaxen locks as she chanted at the top of her lungs "Jawn Jay Fitzgerald! Jawn Jay Fitzgerald!"

The name tickled her sense of rhythm, and John J. Fitzgerald, a jovial American engineer who truly bore this name, sat there, smiled, and looked pleased with himself. The blonde I had already met. She was a friendly person and a guest of Captain Smith of the American Mission, who had come to this party with several of his Russian and American acquaintances. Her name was Vera. I looked around and discovered there was other company.

In a corner in an armchair sat a small girl with dark brown hair and green-gray eyes and a small nose which seemed to have about it an air of healthy contempt for the goings-on. She was dressed in a black silk print dress decorated with bright orange, pink and yellow flowers. Her features were delicate and sensitive and her eyes were bright. She was interesting in an aristocratic way, and impressed me as a very unusual person. I watched her closely. She was engaged in conversation in Russian with an acquaintance of mine, a diplomat from the American Embassy—obviously about politics or philosophy. My friend was arguing with her and she was listening and replying with an elfin-like twinkle in her eye which made me sure she was pulling his leg.

"Who is she?" I asked of Vera.

"Who? Oh, that's Yulya—Julie," she said. "She is my good friend and sings on the stage in the same group as I. Tonight she was sad, so I told her to come along. Maybe she could forget her sadness." And then she added quickly: "Yulya ochen talantlivaya—i ochen temperamentnaya."

"Julie is very talented and very temperamental." I had put down three drinks in rapid succession and I was belligerent enough to be rude. I decided to invade that serious conversation between my friend and Yulya. I might lose a friend, but who knows, it might be worth it. I barged in and without introducing myself I sat on the floor beside Julie's chair. As my friend waxed eloquent I interjected rather rude remarks. I got precisely the result I wanted. He grew angry and got up and left us.

Julie did not bother to look at me. Staring at the ceiling she listened without comment to my now polite effort to engage her in conversation—and finally said something sufficiently indicative of how she felt, "Mne skuchno!" Which is to say, "I'm bored."

Then she got up and left me, just like that. She went to her friend Vera and told her she would like to go home. Then she waited at the opposite side of the room for Vera. I had struck out. Yet I was smitten with interest in this cool girl and determined to get to know her. I took Vera aside to ask her to patch things up for me with her friend Julie.

"Well, well, Tomochka!" she said, addressing me by the Russified diminutive of my name. "So you haven't done so well! Why don't you give me a ring at six o'clock tomorrow afternoon? We'll see." She gave me the number. I took it down. Then I went back to my room, chagrined and ashamed.

The next day at six I phoned Vera. She answered the telephone and I started to discuss the whole thing with her but she interrupted me and said:

"Just a minute . . ." She put down the receiver and a few seconds later a different voice came on the line. It said,

"Nu chto?"—"Well, what?"

I jumped. This was Julie. I recognized her expressive voice. She heard out my apologies. After I finished there was a pause. As seconds passed I became certain that, so far as Julie was concerned, I had had it. But I heard her say,

"Well, so tell me something about yourself."

That was the beginning of a fifteen minute conversation. It was the first of successive telephone conversations every day at the same time. We chatted. We exchanged small talk. She told me a bit about herself. I told her about myself. Fascinating originality, startling self-assurance, and striking frankness of self-expression emerged through her telephone remarks. I became more and more intrigued. But Julie refused to meet me, despite my pleas. This went on for well over a week. Finally on a Saturday night she said suddenly to me,

"Be at the subway station at the Gorky Park of Culture and Rest tomorrow morning at ten-thirty. Wait on the sidewalk. I may be able to come."

*    *    *    *    *

It was a bright, chilly Sunday morning at the end of July. I stood in front of the subway station on Crimean Square and scanned the hordes of Muscovites in their Sunday best, which in wartime was pretty shabby, pouring from underground into the sunlight and making their way across the Crimean Bridge to the park across the river. I had been there fifteen minutes. I paced back and forth and looked at my watch. Would she come? This was my first meeting with any

Russian girl in whom I had any interest other than sociological. And, if I guessed right about Julie, she was incalculable. But I continued to watch eagerly the faces in the crowd.

Suddenly I saw her. She had seen me and was approaching. Small, bright and delicate, she stood out from the crowd of typically stolid, heavy-set, squat, drab Russians like an Oriental poppy in a field of grass. Again she was wearing that black silk print dress with its pattern of orange, pink and yellow tropical flowers. Up she came to me with a swinging quick walk.

"I had begun to think you weren't coming," I declared when I was able to speak.

"I didn't know whether I was," she retorted. And then she continued, with a laugh, "What I really wanted to do, Tomochka, was to give you a little test—to see if you would wait for me."

I waited to see what was coming next.

"Well, why are we standing here?" she asked.

"What would you like to do?" I returned.

"Maybe you would feel like taking me for a walk in the park?" she commented.

So we set out strolling across the bridge, stopping to lean on the railing and stare down at the waters of the muddy Moscow River below. As we walked along she looked at me and laughed. I grinned back.

"What are you laughing about?" I asked.

"You Americans are so funny!" she said. "Take your suit. It's such a bright color. No Russian would be seen in a suit that bright." And then she hesitated: "But I like it. It's so different."

We came to the park. We walked along the paths like ten thousand other Muscovites that day and enjoyed the sun. We were passing a flower bed. Julie stopped. She pointed her finger at a red zinnia in the very middle of the enormous, carefully-cultivated bed, and exclaimed in a languid tone "Ya eto khochu." In other words: "I want that."

"What?" I stammered.

"Ya eto khochu!" she demanded.

I looked at her in panic. Did she really want that red zinnia? My God! This was originality all right, but originality that might land me in a police station! I pictured the headline in *Pravda*: "American Diplomat Caught in Vandalism in Gorky Park!" Nevertheless, I was damned if I let myself be nonplussed by this wisp—very well-shaped wisp—of a Russian girl. I looked about. There stood one of those omnipresent militiamen, one hundred or one hundred and fifty feet away. He was looking at the sky, with his back turned. Suddenly I leaped into the flower bed, step after step, to its center, bent down and picked the red zinnia. Then I turned and leapt back to Julie.

"Vot, Mademoiselle, vash tsvetochek!"—"Here, Mademoiselle, is your flower!" I presented it with a flourish. Only then did I look at her.

She looked amazed. Her mouth was open, but transformed itself into a smile as she accepted her posy. I realized she had not expected me to go into the flower bed. Her question was rhetorical—intended evidently to start a conversation. But now there was something different in her eyes. Was it admiration?

We walked on through the park slowly and talked. As we progressed, everything we said began to seem indescribably funny and we were in continual stitches, giggling and laughing with each other.

Finally Julie sat down on a log. I sat down on it too. We looked into each other's eyes. She started to hum. Listening I became aware it was a familiar air. No, it couldn't be, but it was: *I Can't Give You Anything But Love, Baby!* Hearing this in Gorky Park in Moscow struck me as unbelievably incongruous. But I realized she was singing the words as well:

"Diamond bracelets Woolworth's doesn't sell, Baby!" I heard her chant with a lovely lilt. I could hardly wait till she finished. "I didn't know you knew English," I exclaimed.

"I don't," said Julie and explained. She had heard the song on a record. She liked it so much she had a Russian who knew English write out the English words in a transliteration into the Russian alphabet. Then she had learned the English words by heart, not understanding a one. She had managed to get even the accent and intonations almost exactly right.

"I love Western music," she said with feeling.

A couple of hours later we lay in the grass on a hill in the park still chatting.

"Only one thing in the world is important," said Julie. "And that's love. All the rest is nonsense."

I looked at her. Her face was serious. We discussed that for a while there in the sun in a state of luxurious relaxation. And I came to realize Julie meant it. This was her religion. By the time I dropped her off near her home that evening she had made a long start on converting me to it.

\*     \*     \*     \*     \*

It was an evening in early August. It was eight-thirty but it was still light. I stood in front of the gloomy statue of Nikolai Gogol, at the south end of Arbat Square where a narrow park stretched between the two avenues of the boulevard. I had been waiting fifteen minutes. Julie was returning from a concert outside of town and had warned she might be late.

I thought about the way things were. I was seeing Julie almost every evening. We never did much of anything, just walked, night after night, in the long twilight, looked into each other's eyes, and talked. We talked of anything and everything. And it was always interesting. I looked up. There stood Julie in front of me. "Are you sad, Tomochka?" and there was tenderness in her voice.

"I was just waiting—and thinking," I said.

"Never be sad, Tomochka," she said. "I wouldn't want you to be sad."

We walked off down the parkway. We walked and walked, sat on park benches, strolled to the Moscow River embankment, looked into the water, walked back. We talked and talked and looked at each other and held hands. I wouldn't be able to remember what we talked about. But I can remember the evening and the lovely feeling of being with Julie.

\*     \*     \*     \*     \*

The mid-August night had fallen outside the little window in Vera's tiny room. Julie and I sat across from one another with elbows on the table and our hands beneath our chins holding up our heads as we looked at each other. Between us on the table was the only light—a candle. It had been tall when we lit it, but it had burned and burned and little remained. And we had just sat there looking at each other for, I couldn't say, how many hours. We had said only a word or so now and then. Each of us was concentrating on the other.

It had been another chilly, sunny Sunday, much like that first one. We had met at the Stanislavsky Theater and seen *Eugene Onegin*— the light, gay and tender opera by Tchaikovsky, based on the poem by Pushkin. The cast consisted of fresh, skilful young people. It was unforgettable, particularly with Julie beside me, holding my hand and looking at me now and then. We came out of the theater together, in mid-afternoon.

"Where shall we go?" I asked.

She looked at me, hesitated a moment, then spoke out:

"You know, Tomochka, we've had luck. Vera's out of town today. She has, unlike me, a room of her own. She told me I could use it. Would you like to come for supper?"

"Of course! Can I bring anything?"

"If you have something you want to bring, you can. Why don't you go to your hotel now while I buy one or two things. I'll meet you in forty-five minutes on the Sretenka, just beyond the boulevard. You'll be walking away from the center and I'll be walking toward it—on the east side. Agreed?"

"All right," I hastened to reply.

So forty-five minutes later I was walking up the Sretenka in my bright blue suit again. In my left hand I held three roses which I had purchased from a street vendor. They were wrapped in a piece of a sheet of *Pravda*. In my right hand I held a package consisting of a can of peanuts, and a can of chicken. From out of my jacket pocket appeared the neck of a bottle of Iranian vodka.

Julie met me as she had promised and giggled. "Maybe I should be afraid of Americans bearing gifts," she commented. But she squeezed my hand.

We walked up the four flights of dismal worn-out stairs of an ancient tenement to Vera's room. The door to the apartment was opened by one of Vera's neighbors and Julie shoved me out of sight till the neighbor had turned.

"Vera doesn't want her neighbors to know a foreigner has come to her room," she said.

It was the first door on the right as I got inside and I ducked into it. Julie followed. Vera's room was small but cosy. An oriental rug, and a bright coverlet on the studio couch gave a feeling of warmth.

Julie took my vodka bottle and got a pair of thimble-sized glasses, called "ryumochki," out of Vera's cupboard and poured them full. She made a pair of caviar sandwiches and gave me one of the little glasses, took the other herself, raised hers to eye level, looked at me over it, and downed it in one quick little gulp. I followed suit. Then, hungry as wolves, we downed the caviar sandwiches.

We talked and Julie took my can of chicken and some things she had brought and made a little dinner on Vera's electric hot plate. It was simple, but it seemed as delicious as anything I might have got in the most costly restaurant in New York.

We talked some more after we finished the dinner and then—I don't know how it happened—we just found ourselves looking into each other's eyes, saying nothing. The intensity of emotion grew and grew, but neither of us made a move. Julie picked up one of the roses I had brought and started eating its petals one by one. I watched intently. The candle burned and burned till almost nothing was left. Still we sat and looked at each other.

Suddenly Julie shook her head as if to bring herself out of a trance. She looked at her watch.

"Bozhe Moi!" she exclaimed in Russian, "My Heavens— It's nearly midnight and you must be home before curfew."

I stood up and she did likewise. We stood within a few inches of each other. Our lips almost touched. We were like this for ten or fifteen minutes and I started to put my arm around her. Julie stepped back just a bit.

"Not now, Tomochka, not tonight . . . Not yet." And then her voice dropped a little. "Thank you for a beautiful day!"

She turned about as I slipped out of the door.

*     *     *     *     *

Our luck in having an evening to ourselves within the four walls of a room was not repeated. So we returned to our custom of long walks every evening she was in town—in parks and on the streets. One evening toward the end of August Julie said to me rather breathlessly when we met, "There is a new American motion picture. Will you take me? It is very good."

And so we went. In Russian it was titled "Uragan"—in other words "Hurricane." I no longer remember who played, but I shall not forget the picture. It was a South Sea drama—blue ocean, hot sun, white sand, palm trees, brown Polynesians, pure escapism. I watched it holding Julie's hand throughout. Somehow the impact of the "exotique" of this warm film seen in chilly, drab, wartime Moscow was so intense as to be unbearable. I wanted to break down and cry at the thought there were such places on earth as those—and that Julie and I were so hopelessly far away from them. We left the film in silence and went home, hand in hand as usual.

"What are you thinking about, Tomochka?" she asked.

"I'm thinking of that island—and wishing you and I were there right now," I replied.

"Let's make an agreement right here," exclaimed Julie. "We can't be on that island now. But let's agree, you and I, no matter what, we will meet on that island in the Pacific a thousand years from now."

"I agree—we'll meet on that island in a thousand years, no matter what," I exclaimed. I took her by the shoulders and pulled her close. Her lips were no more than an inch away from mine. "And we're going to seal our agreement with a kiss," I said, and put my lips over hers and kissed her with a long, passionate kiss which she returned.

\*    \*    \*    \*    \*

August wore to September and still we were walking the sidestreets of Moscow. There was now a chill in the air. We could smell the smoke of burning leaves. And darkness came a little earlier each nightfall—a fact we welcomed since the dark meant concealment in which we could steal long kisses. Our nocturnal wanderings were generally confined to one well-defined area located near the big apartment house on the Arbat in which Julie and her mother occupied one room. It was one of the most ancient and complex districts of the capital— one which before the revolution and also after was regarded as the best residential section. "Best" is an adjective which did not mean much in the Moscow of 1944. The homes, new and old, on these little cobblestone, often crooked, side streets off the main thorough-fares were mostly in a run-down, decrepit condition. If built before the revolution they had not been kept in repair. If built after they had often been jerry-built. Old mansions, built before the Soviet regime for single families of millionaire members of the merchantry, now become rabbit warrens for the dozens of people packed into them, stood side by side with four, six and eight-story apartment houses, old or new and equally overcrowded.

The buildings were constructed with interior courtyards, often muddy and filthy during wartime. One who knew these courtyards could navigate through them as short-cuts from block to block, emerging onto the little side streets only occasionally. Julie had lived here all her life and knew the "through" courtyards. She could find her way in them like an Indian picking his way through his forest trails in the middle of the night. Many an evening she and I delayed nearly till midnight curfew, and then she led me through pitch-dark courtyard after courtyard a half mile or more until she reached home. There at the back entrance to a whole series of "through" courtyards leading to an exit beside her own apartment building entrance she would kiss me goodnight. Then I would begin threading my devious way to the hotel a couple of miles away. I got to know the courtyards almost as well as Julie and could make my clandestine way back through court-yards most of the way.

There was this conspiratorial ring to our affair—for reason. The Soviet government has never approved of romances between its citizens and foreign representatives in the Soviet Union. There has always been the danger of police intervention, immediate or potential. In 1944, with the wartime alliance at its warmest, there was no direct crude interference, but arrests had taken place in the past and were a future possibility. There was surveillance. Files were accumulated on individuals. These might later mean tragedy. We were aware of this. Julie had accepted the risks because she was a daredevil, because she refused to be told by anyone what she couldn't do, and because she had a deep liking for me. We never supposed our connection, once we started meeting nearly every evening, would escape observation. The network of surveillance was too effective for that. But we hoped we could reduce the dangers by not drawing unnecessary attention. So we followed rules. We avoided putting ourselves under the police microscope unnecessarily.

Despite precautions, we would find now and then that we were in the net. The sensation of being followed is exciting but not pleasant. One evening we had gone to the theater. We walked home late. Not more than a quarter mile from Julie's home she stopped dead and whispered to me to stand still. We heard the soft footfall in the dark a hundred feet behind. Julie whispered to me, "Follow me—hold my hand." A few steps later we ducked into a dark doorway and hid, listening. A footfall, then silence, then running, then a whistle from behind and an answering whistle from ahead.

"Behind and ahead of us!" said Julie.

We waited—a welcome chance to kiss in a dark stairwell—and then slipped out and went on our way.

The conspiratorial atmosphere only heightened the feeling of romance. If we had tremors of fear, we had other tremors which affected us more vitally. The fact was that we were in love.

But as September wore on we became aware of the problem lovers have always faced in overcrowded Moscow, where even nooks and crannies are occupied by whole families, where there are no generally available hotels or motels, nor even many private cars. Out-of-door romances flourish in Moscow only in warm weather. Things get cold very fast in the fall. Even the most passionate Moscow love cannot outlast the summer without a warm indoor haven.

"What are we going to do, Tomochka?" said Julie one late September night, shivering in my arms. "Can't you find a room?" There wasn't a thing I could say. I was trying. Finding a room in Moscow— for a foreigner—was, as Julie knew, as easy as finding the proverbial cool spot in hell.

*     *     *     *     *

When I returned to Moscow in mid-October from my trip with General Fleming, Moscow was cold. I shivered from the frost as I stood on a small side street where Julie, whom I hadn't seen for three weeks, had told me to wait. I paced back and forth to keep the circulation going and watched my breath hover like a little miniature cloud in the frigid air.

"Just what are we going to do now?" I asked myself. Romantic nightly strolls on the streets were no longer practical except for Eskimos.

My heart skipped a beat as out of the dark a familiar figure loomed. I seized her and embraced her. She held me tight. It was so wonderful to be together again! There is something so final about partings in Russia! One never really believes in the reality of reunion. When reunion does take place it always seems a miracle. This is how we felt.

Julie shifted her feet and they came in contact with a small bag. "What is that?" she asked.

"Those are tomatoes, onions and honey I brought you from the Ukraine," I laughed. "There's a bigger sack at my hotel room which I'll bring in installments."

She jumped up and gave me a big kiss. "Tomochka! Now I know you're crazy!" she exclaimed with delight. "You did think of me!"

And then she paused. "I have a surprise for you too. Pick up your sack and follow me." I did as I was told. We went to the rear of the

block where her apartment building was located—where we had always said goodnight. She went through a gate in an old brick wall
and I followed. There was a passageway.

"Watch out!" Julie whispered. "There's a big puddle." I tiptoed
after her through a courtyard, a gap between two buildings and another
courtyard, and into a tunnel through another building.

Julie stopped me. "Now listen!" she said. "Outside this tunnel is an
entrance to a Cinema Theater on the Arbat. There is always a crowd
of people there. The first doorway to the left out of this tunnel is mine.
I am going ahead. You go out and mingle with the people at the
cinema entrance. After five minutes come into my doorway. Walk
straight ahead up the stairway. It's dark. Count nine landings. Be
careful not to trip for the stairs are worn. The ninth landing is mine.
Knock on the door on the right. I'll let you in."

I did as I was told and seven or eight minutes later a door opened
in the dark and a warm hand emerged to take mine and lead me
twenty or thirty feet down a completely dark hall to another door
which was quietly opened before me. Julie pulled me into a well-lit,
warm room and shut the door.

"This is the surprise," she said simply. "This is my room where I
live with mother. While you were away I told her about you. She's not
happy about my being in love with an American, and I don't blame
her. But we agreed you can come here to see me from now on. It's
not luxurious, but it's ours—and now it's yours too."

I gasped. I could write pages to explain the significance of my being
given the right of entry to the apartment of a Russian family. I still
could not make it clear to non-Russians. But I knew that for Julie
and her mother this act was irrevocable. By admitting an American
into their home they were setting themselves apart from the society in
which they lived, a society hostile to incursion by outsiders. It was a
gift too big to be comprehended.

I looked around. In the center there was a small round table. From
the ceiling over it there hung an enormous pink silk lampshade, or-
nately tasseled, which cast a warm light over everything. There was
a familiar sort of feel. As I glanced around I understood why. The
spirit of the room and its furnishings was similar to that of homes of
relatives in my own Ohio. It was that universal middle class style of
before World War I. It was characterized by a little picture on the wall
—of a fisherman rowing his boat with a small girl seated beside him,

a picture which also hung on the wall of the home of my maiden aunts in Toledo. The furniture was decidedly dark and massive. There was a broad divan with an oriental rug over it. In one corner stood an enormous buffet. Two items stood out—one, a tremendous rubber tree which looked as though it had been growing there for forty years, and a small iron stove in the front of the room—a temporary wartime emergency device—with a stovepipe leading out of a pane in the window.

Then there was a handsome upright piano against the wall.

"Sit down on the divan and be quiet," Julie said.

She went to the piano and began to play. For a time she played idly with the keys and improvised. But then she began to play songs and sing. I listened—breathless. One after another they came. This concert went on for an hour and a half. Russian songs, Western songs with Russian words, the old familiar *I Can't Give You Anything But Love, Baby!*, songs I knew and others I had never heard.

I stopped her after one and asked her, "What is that?"

"That's called *Sevastopol*—and I wrote it myself," she answered.

"You wrote it?"

"Of course," she replied. "Didn't I tell you that I am a composer? That's my real profession."

"I thought you were a singer."

"Oh, that! Well I do sing, but I thought you knew that on the stage I sing only my own songs."

"How could I know?" I started to break in. She knew very well I had not the slightest idea that she was a composer.

"Listen to this!" she said, continuing. She sang with tenderness a Russian ballad: "We met strangely and we will part strangely. With a smile of tenderness we will end our romance—like that. We will never return to one another—and we'll say it was all only a mirage."

Then came the haunting chorus: "Thus sometimes in the weary desert there hovers the image of far-distant, wonderful countries. But it's only an image. Again the heaven is blue—and in the distance there trudges along the tired caravan . . ."

"Is that yours?" I asked.

"I wish it were," she said.

I looked at her singing. She was inspired. She was in another world a long way away. It was her world. I could only look on from outside. I had heard Russian songs and Russian singers—but none like Julie.

There was a haunting intimacy to her singing that I have never glimpsed in any other artist.

Suddenly she got up from the piano. She went to the electric hot plate in the corner and put on the tea kettle. Soon we sat at the little table in the center of the room, sipping tea from glasses. She looked at her watch.

"Tomochka, you'll have to go. Mother is coming back in five minutes. You'll meet her soon, but not tonight. Go the way you came and tomorrow night you can come back. Remember your way and be here at eight o'clock. I'll be waiting at the door just as tonight."

We kissed lingeringly at the door in the dark and I left silently. I lay awake for a long time that night in my bed at the hotel before I went to sleep.

\*     \*     \*     \*     \*

My admission to Julie's home was the beginning of a new stage in our relationship. One aspect of this was that Julie began to talk to me much more freely about herself and her family. I met Julie's mother. She was a quiet, warm person—intelligent, perceptive, sensitive, fanatically loyal and affectionate to those she loved. Our acquaintance was at first superficial but gradually we came to know each other better. Every evening when Julie was not away I would come, slip in quietly, admitted by Julie or her mother. Then her mother would get up and leave us. She went downstairs to visit friends so we could be by ourselves. Then we sat and talked on the divan, or we sat at the table and drank tea. Or maybe we ate something which Julie's mother had prepared on the hot plate. Then maybe Julie would sit down at the piano and play and I would listen. The time went so quickly, and soon Julie's mother was opening the door with a slightly apologetic air. It was time to go back to my hotel, but sometimes Julie would ask me to stay longer and the three of us would chat or else Julie's mother would sit in one of the overstuffed armchairs and read a book in French or Russian while we whispered.

But then came the time when going home could no longer be put off. I got up, said my goodbys and left to make my lonely way through dark, cold Moscow to my hotel, where I would go to bed tired and lie there an hour or so before sleep thinking about Julie.

Fate left this talented girl with the responsibility of looking after herself and her mother. A few years before, this had been a happy family, close-knit and affectionate. There were vacations in the Crimea, summers at country homes outside of Moscow, good times at the apartment in Moscow, enough of everything, two vigorous parents in the prime of their lives, and two brilliant and gifted children with all the promise talent, plus background, plus opportunity could give. But perhaps I should let Julie herself tell about her father and mother as she told me during the long autumn evenings in her room.

Julie's mother came from a well-to-do family which lived in a small Russian provincial city. Julie's mother's mother died when she was seven. Her grandfather ran the house in a severe, old-fashioned way. Julie's mother's brothers both got whipped when they misbehaved and the little girl, from the time she was seven, had to learn to be a good housekeeper. Fortunately, Julie's grandfather, an intelligent, well-educated man for his time, and a bank official, got fed up with this way of raising children and one day sent both of his sons away to school and hired tutors for his daughter.

Then, a little later Julie's mother herself was sent away to a girls' boarding school in a nearby larger city. She became very friendly with one of her classmates and it was through this girl she met Julie's father.

It was a romantic story, but first a bit about Julie's father. He came from a family of the provincial intelligentsia which was quite poor, and in which there were many children. He was the youngest and from a very early age he had to support himself and help his family. He was a gifted, even brilliant person. He was quick of mind, had imagination, and was stubborn in getting things he wanted. When he was twenty-one or twenty-two he decided to go abroad to finish his education. This was not an easy thing for a poor young man. He managed, however, to get enough money to make a start, and chose a university in Western Europe. He was an acquaintance of Julie's mother's classmate and girl friend, and the train taking him abroad stopped just half an hour in the city where their young ladies' school was located. Julie's mother went down to the train with her girl friend to greet him as he passed through. This was the first time she saw Julie's father. It was enough.

She had nearly forgotten about him when one day she received a letter from him. The letter was so interesting that, after hesitating, she decided to answer it. He apparently liked her letter just as much, for he continued to write. In a short time, from being merely formal and descriptive, the letters became more and more personal. And after a year of correspondence he proposed—at a time when they had seen each other only half an hour. Julie's mother went home from her school and informed her father she was to be married. He refused flatly. This was what it took more than anything else to make her want to marry her sweetheart-by-correspondence. She tried to persuade her father to send her to get an education in Western Europe. He refused flatly again.

By this time Julie's father was writing Julie's mother frantic letters in which he said he would leave school and come to marry her in Russia if she did not join him. She, knowing he had money for only a one-way ticket, decided to go on her own to him, regardless of the family opposition. At this point her father gave in, forcing her to give a promise that there would be no marriage until the fiancé had met her family.

The two young people in love met in Western Europe, overcame all obstacles, and got married while both were studying at the university. Both graduated. They returned to Russia in 1913. Julie's father got a job, and her mother gave lessons in French, German and mathematics.

In 1918, after the revolution, they moved into the apartment on the Arbat—with all six rooms to themselves. By the time I met Julie's mother and Julie there was only one room left to them. They had been forced to give up one room after another as the Moscow housing shortage became worse and worse year after year.

"I was born in this building myself," Julie told me, "in a private maternity home one floor below us. I was not the first child. There was another daughter before me but she died in an epidemic during the period of the civil war. And after me there came my younger brother."

Julie's father was non-political. But, as a technically educated and able man, he made a good career under the new Soviet regime. With a separate income from technical writing added to his regular salaries in various positions in government offices concerned with economy management he provided well for his family.

Julie showed a marked musical talent. While still a small child, she picked out tunes by ear on her mother's piano, and was sent to the finest music school in Russia, that run by the Gneissen sisters, a few blocks from her home, as soon as she could be enrolled. The music school course she took simultaneously with a full course in regular school. Her music teachers urged Julie to undertake a career as a concert pianist, but her primary interest was in composition. And despite opposition at home and in school, she gave vent to a preference for popular music, particularly with a modern, Western flavor. When she sold her first popular ballad to the leading "Jazz" orchestra of the Soviet Union while still in her teens, it was a day of despair at home and a day of indescribable triumph for her. With this, she abandoned classical music and went over entirely to the popular field. She started to work with the Moscow Studio of Stage Arts—an organization producing variety or vaudeville programs—as a composer and soon they enlisted her as a performer as well but by this time the war had come. Julie had appeared in shows on Moscow's leading stages—the Hermitage, the Hall of Columns, and the like—and when I met her her troupe was presenting variety programs at factory and military units outside Moscow. Her act consisted of Julie singing her own compositions, written for herself, accompanying herself on the accordion.

It was the war that had destroyed this happy Russian family. It had taken and killed, first her younger brother, and then her father. Julie's mother was ill and grief-stricken and looked to her daughter for help. Julie was overwhelmed herself with grief for her brother and father, and for the family happiness which had been so quickly and utterly demolished, but this was something those who saw her outside her home never knew. She buried it deep inside herself and concealed it, but it was there all right. I had seen it myself. Beneath her external vivaciousness and sparkle there was a deep sadness. It left its imprint on her art and her personality. To both it gave great depth.

\*      \*      \*      \*      \*

As October turned to November and November wore on toward December I took to staying later and later with Julie. I used to take big chances of getting caught away from my hotel long after curfew time but I never did.

One very cold November night at about one A.M. I had wearily made it nearly to Arbat Square, half a mile along my way, when I saw a late trolleybus, empty, come down the line headed toward the center. It came to a sudden stop and I looked at it longingly. I had jumped trolleybuses before. Russians did it regularly. One got a footing on a narrow ledge at the back entrance to the trolleybus and a grip on handrails at the side of the doors and held on for dear life. It was precarious but exciting. I decided to try it. It was a wild thing to do— but it was a wild night. The wind was howling and snow was in the air flying in little gusts through the city.

I dashed out to the trolleybus and as I neared it it started moving. But I succeeded in boarding it. To my horror I discovered that, whereas most trolleybuses had hand rails alongside the rear door on each side, this had none. There was only a window ledge to cling to. I was about to jump off it but I saw a militiaman on the sidewalk. I decided to stick it. The trolleybus picked up speed. It headed down Comintern Street toward the Kremlin. I held on for dear life and the wind went through my thin overcoat as if it were cheesecloth. The driver went faster and faster. There was no question of jumping now. I would have to wait till he stopped. But then I felt my fingers slipping on the window ledge. And the driver went faster and faster.

We had gotten almost to the Kremlin when I fell. I went down backwards. As I went down I remember fearing a broken back. And then I hit. I hit hard and there were stars. But I hit flat on my back and went right over in a backward somersault. I landed on my feet. I was shaken but not bruised. I brushed myself off and went on my way.

The next evening I told Julie what had happened. Her reaction came as a surprise. She was first violently angry at me and upbraided me mercilessly for stupidity. And then she became tender and said to me with tears in her eyes, "Tomochka, please don't ever do things like that again. I couldn't bear to have anything happen to you!"

She kissed me.

"This whole business of your going afoot from here to your hotel has got to end. Heaven knows what will happen! There are bandits about. You'll get arrested or hurt. I think maybe I know the answer."

When her mother came in at eleven Julie took her out in the corridor. I heard the two speaking in Russian. They came in a little later and Julie's mother gave me a look which spelled out affection and despair. Julie came up to me and said, "You can go into the corridor, please."

"How is that?" I stammered.

"Mother is tired and is going to undress and go to bed in her little bed over there." I started to reach for my overcoat.

"No, no, you don't understand," she said and took my coat away. "You and I are going to sleep here on the divan. I just want you to wait in the corridor until Mother has gone to bed."

"You mean I am going to stay here?" I asked.

"Not unless you want to," said Julie with a twinkle in her eye. "But there aren't going to be any more midnight trolleybus rides, I can tell you that. Besides, as I've gathered, one of the reasons you came to Moscow was to find out how we Russians live under our overcrowded conditions. Well, this, Tomochka, is your chance."

She looked at me fondly. I looked at her and said,

"I love you, Yulochka, and I hope you understand how much."

I turned, went out into the corridor, and sat down on an old trunk stored there to wait for Julie's mother to go to bed.

*      *      *      *      *

Julie and I sat late before a fire in the apartment of a foreign journalist friend who had told me I could use his apartment while he was on vacation. The flames flickered through the open door of the big Dutch oven, and gave enough light to read by. All the other lights were out. Julie had been scribbling on scraps of paper and had repulsed my attempts to find out what she was doing.

She said each time I asked a question, "Be quiet, Tomochka!"

Then she looked up at me with bright eyes reflecting the blaze.

"Listen!" she said. And she started to read. It was a beautiful lyrical love poem to me. She finished reading it. We sat silently. Then she quietly got up, came over, and sat down in my lap and put her arms around my neck.

We looked into the fire. We looked and looked to see in the flickering flames what the future might hold.

*      *      *      *      *

"I'm going to run away from you—forever!" Julie exclaimed to me on a cold cold evening in December.

We were in the midst of a violent lovers' quarrel and something I had said—I don't remember any more what the quarrel was about— had angered her exceedingly. And she had really run away from me. She disappeared. I looked everywhere for her and couldn't find her. I phoned. I searched. Even her mother didn't know where she had gone. I was desperate!

Finally I remembered one more possible place. In the hotel Evropa one of Julie's friends, an actress from the Leningrad Comedy Theater, was staying with the rest of the theater's troupe. Maybe she could be there!

And so I invaded the Hotel Evropa at two A.M. in the morning. I got past the militiaman at the door by simply walking past him nonchalantly with a maximum of self-assurance. The doorman was dozing in the corridor and didn't see me as I mounted the stairs. But how could I find Galya, Julie's friend? How could I possibly find out her floor and what room she was staying in? I finally caught my breath on the fourth floor. I stood out there in the corridor wondering what to do next. At just that moment a young man whom I recognized as a Leningrad Comedy Theater actor stepped out of one room in the corridor and started walking down towards another a few doors away. I took a big chance. I stopped him and asked him whether he might possibly know which room was that of Galya R. of the Leningrad Comedy Theater. He looked at me very strangely indeed—and I don't blame him for I was pretty wild looking at that point.

"I think it's that one there," he said at last, and pointed.

I took my heart in my hands and went over and knocked. From within the alto voice of Galya finally answered.

"Who is it?"

"Is Yulya there?" I asked tremblingly.

A second later the door was thrown open and from a bed over against the wall a familiar face smiled out at me. I rushed in to embrace my runaway Julie.

"Don't you ever dare to run away from me again!" I exclaimed to her, covering her with kisses.

*      *      *      *      *

Out of the darkness there loomed the enormous cubic shape of a onetime Orthodox cathedral with its dome decapitated and neon lights on its roof spelling out the ungodly word "Avangarde." I made my way through the swirling, whirling snowflakes to the side door of this church turned cinema. I pushed my way past the squat female ticket taker, dressed in quilted cotton jacket, at the side door. In the anteroom outside the projection room Russian cinema-goers stood and listened in attention to the musical program presented for them before the motion picture. A svelte, attractive girl, in evening gown, was singing. The song was a Russian version of *Good Night Sweetheart*. The singer finished and the crowd applauded. She came out and bowed and the crowd applauded even more violently. "Bis!" I heard all around me, "Bis!"—the Russian phrase demanding an encore. But it was not to be. The musical program was over. The doors of the projection room opened and the crowd rushed to seats. I swelled with pride. It had been Julie, of course, singing on a limited engagement at this cinema.

Fifteen minutes later Julie and I trudged through the snow together on our way home. I carried her accordion. Julie looked at me. "It's nice, Tomochka, to have you here to meet me!"

*    *    *    *    *

It was well after midnight. I was in Julie's room, lying on the divan. From the other side of the room I could hear the quiet breathing of Julie's sleeping mother where she slumbered on her small bed behind a screen. I put my arm around Julie's shoulder. I felt her shaking. I turned her around to me. She tried to shield her face, but I found she was sobbing, silently, but violently.

"What is it?" I whispered. "Why are you crying?"

She said to me through tears, "I don't want you to leave me."

I put both arms around her. "I won't!" I said.

*    *    *    *    *

"They got married and lived happily ever after."

By all the rules of story book romance this is the way the story must end. In real life it hasn't always worked out in this way—least of all, perhaps, in the Soviet Union in the time of Stalin, when the matter concerned a marriage between a Soviet citizen and a foreigner. Such a marriage could mean a lot of trouble.

The Soviet government at that time did not usually give permission for a Soviet woman who married a foreigner to leave the country with her husband. This put the loving couple in a difficult position. The husband, a diplomat or journalist, might not be allowed to remain indefinitely with his Russian wife until she might be granted an exit visa. If the husband were forced to leave without his wife she would be left behind unhappy and defenseless. As a foreigner's wife she could become a pariah in her own society—with tragic consequences.

Some foreigners may have married Russian girls in ignorance of the risks, but not I.

I knew all about this—I knew the dangers. But I also knew there was a chance things could work out. I knew of several Russian wives who had been exchanged for tankers of American aviation gasoline at the beginning of the war. And there were others permitted to leave the Soviet Union in less sensational fashion. But one could never know. One was dependent on the political situation. One had to hope —and fear. And this was the most terrible thing, this uncertainty. So marriage to a Russian was not something to be undertaken lightly. At the same time the thought of leaving Julie became steadily more unthinkable. I found myself face to face with a horrible dilemma.

"You've been in a bad mood for days," Julie said one evening over a cup of tea which her mother had made for us. "I haven't said a thing. I've thought all along you would tell me what it's about but now I see you won't. So I have to ask you."

Finally I unburdened my soul. I told her what was bothering me.

"So you want to marry me!" she laughed. "Well, I don't suppose this is a surprise. I'm not against it. I'll go, if you wish, to the registration office and marry you tomorrow. We'll come back with a stamp on my passport saying that you and I are married. What good this is going to do isn't clear. Isn't it going to make things more difficult for us? What is your Embassy going to say? There is a lot to think about —and I have the feeling that whereas now nobody is bothering us, as soon as we marry a whole hornet's nest will descend. But that's not the main thing," Julie went on. "How have you liked your life since we met?"

"Wonderful!" I answered.

She retorted quickly, "That's what I thought, and that's the way it's been for me. I've never known such months before. But what are you doing now? You are letting fear for our future poison your mood. Remember, Tomochka, you and I probably don't have a future. But we have a present. I want you to live for now and forget about the future. I don't mean you and I shouldn't get married or that we shouldn't think ahead, but I do mean we shouldn't let any fears and uncertainties spoil what we have now!"

Julie had her way. I stopped my worrying—most of it, anyway, and buried myself in the awareness of what we possessed—the most precious thing that could be. But I had my way too, though that was later. Julie and I did finally get married.

\*　　\*　　\*　　\*　　\*

The long Moscow winter settled in upon the city. Outside, the winds howled through the streets. The snow got deeper. Janitors and their families kept up their never-ending battle to keep the sidewalks and the streets passable, wielding their brooms unceasingly. Inside, for Julie and me, things were warm and light. Our life had settled into a pattern of glorious evenings and nights apart from everybody.

And to me the deep darkness of the long, long Moscow winter nights seemed a friendly and affectionate darkness, meant for lovers, meant for Julie and me, so that we could enwrap ourselves in it like a warm blanket and find in it protection against the coldness, cruelty and brutality of the outside world.

Yet there were practical problems—one above all, the eternal problem of Moscow lovers and newlyweds, the question of housing.

Where to live?

The room on the Arbat where Julie and her mother lived had provided us with a warm haven—but it was only temporary. What Julie and I needed was a room to ourselves.

I looked. I was a resourceful person and I explored a number of leads. It was all in vain. I had not turned up anything in the smallest degree satisfactory. I was left with just one more lead and that a remote one, as I had been given to understand, for I had already made one call there.

On a cold, snowy February day I paid my visit. On a cobblestone side street called Malovlasevsky Pereulok, not over three blocks from Julie's own apartment, I entered a gate in a tall wooden fence and walked through a garden to an old and angular two-story gray stucco house. I knocked at the glass door and as I did an enormous police dog sprang to life inside and began barking at me at the top of his lungs. I stepped back with hesitancy. In a few minutes a tall, distinguished-looking white-haired old lady put in an appearance and looked at me through the door. Suddenly there came a light of recognition.

"Be quiet, Gero!" she said to the dog in a stentorian voice, trained at the Moscow Art Theater. He subsided instantly, looking at her in adoration.

"How do you do, Mr. Whitney," she said to me in over-exact English.

This was Perepetuya Alexandrovna Luzhskaya, widow of one of the actor-founders of the Moscow Art Theater, Vasily Luzhsky.

Piretra Alexandrovna—as she was known, had been herself closely associated with the Art Theater. She had acted and been a close friend of both Konstantin Stanislavsky and of Vladimir Nemirovich-Danchenko, the guiding geniuses of that theatrical group. I had come to Moscow with an introduction and had called on her the previous summer. We had had a delightful chat. Piretra Alexandrovna had been in the United States in the 1920's with her husband and with Stanislavsky. She treasured her memories of America. She had even had Americans living in her home there in the center of Moscow. And it was this that had led me to pay this winter visit.

But we did not get to that right away. We chatted over glasses of tea, which she served in her chilly little living room, about all sorts of things for at least an hour or so before I mentioned the housing problem of Julie and myself. Did she know of any place?

Piretra Alexandrovna thought. "Come with me, Mr. Whitney!" she said. She led me down the hall.

She threw open the door of a room. We went in. There was nothing in it except icicles. Big Dutch ovens lined the wall along two corners. There was an enormous frigid sun parlor with a vast expanse of glass in the front of the room. The ceiling was about thirteen or fourteen feet high. The wallpaper was in tatters.

"I haven't been able to heat this room since the war began," said Piretra Alexandrovna.

And then she looked at me speculatively:

"You know, Mr. Whitney, I could have rented this room a dozen times. But I never have because whoever lives in it would be a very close neighbor, using the same kitchen, bathroom and toilet and the same entrance. Maybe I'm making a mistake—but I don't think so. I like you very much. Would you like to have this room for yourself and your wife?"

I was overjoyed. Half an hour later Piretra Alexandrovna and I had completed the details of our bargain. There was much she needed from me in the way of assistance with fuel, repairs and food. These were all things with which I was glad to help her.

A short time later Julie and I moved in. The only furniture we had to start with was a bed.

# 8.     *Mokhovaya 13/15*

From the start of my Moscow stay I lived two lives—one during office hours in the Embassy in an American world, the other outside the Embassy after office hours, in a Russian world. With the advent of Julie my office hours' American life became even more sharply distinct from my after hours' Russian life. At nine in the morning I bade good-morning to the Soviet militiamen at the entrance to the Embassy at Mokhovaya Street 13/15, across from the Kremlin. I crossed the threshold, and was in the United States, a small piece of it, the more American for being so minuscule. At six in the evening I left the Embassy and made my way to the stucco home at 9a Malovlasevsky—and there reentered my personal corner of Russia.

At the Embassy the coming of George Kennan had opened up promising vistas in my work. Kennan himself was more interested in the political and cultural aspects of Russian life but he was aware of the need for good economic reporting. He let me take my initiative in work, advising me and checking my reports before affixing his initials. He suggested subjects for reports and made himself available to me for consultation.

For the last half of 1944 Kennan left me to work by myself. This is what I wanted. Gone was frustration, and the information and material I had accumulated in my first months in Moscow burst out in a flood of reports. I worked like a dog and I kept my faithful secretary, Louis Hirschfield, working like a dog too. I managed to help out Ed Ames, the clerk in the Economic Section, although he was not working under me. I helped push through the Embassy's machinery the pile of reports Ed had accumulated. They finally got to Washington.

Kennan's presence had had an electrifying effect on the Embassy. Able officers who previously felt frustrated found their work appreciated. They blossomed out. The Embassy began to acquire an esprit de corps.

The position of the Embassy in the conduct of Soviet-American affairs was also improved. Things worked out much as Ambassador Harriman had planned with Kennan in charge under him. Harriman maintained at his residence, Spaso House, a self-contained office staffed with a personal assistant, a diplomatic aide, and a pair of secretaries. Harriman rarely came to the Embassy on Mokhovaya Street. He worked in his residence and left Embassy operation mostly to Kennan. There was in Moscow a large American Military Mission concerned with all aspects of the war. Harriman had authority over its activities and it was under the immediate supervision of Major General John Russell Deane. Before Kennan arrived the Embassy did not play much of a role in Soviet-American relations. The Ambassador did—but he was working mostly through the Military Mission. This changed with Kennan's presence. Kennan and the Ambassador worked well together, and the Ambassador came to rely on him and through him on the Embassy. The boost this gave Embassy morale was great.

One day in late 1944 Kennan called me in. "You'll be taking over the Economic Section soon," he told me.

During the next weeks we had some talks on the section, what it should try to do and, as important, what it should not try to do. It would be, as Kennan outlined it, a small section to do only selective, vital work. It would consist of myself as head, Ed as my assistant, and a pair of American secretaries. There would be several aspects of its work:

1. Ed and I would scan the press and publications for new economic information. When major economic news breaks took place these would be reported in drafts of telegrams submitted to Kennan for possible signature by the Ambassador.

2. In other reporting we would emphasize collection, for dispatch to Washington, of economic information of types unavailable outside Russia. Thus we would carry out systematic observation on changes in the price and availability of goods. This could not be collected

except in Moscow. We would endeavor to get first-hand information and observations from persons who traveled in the Soviet provinces or who had some special access to economic information. This could be done in Moscow more effectively than elsewhere.

3. We would scan reports coming from Washington agencies, and when we found serious misconceptions of the Soviet economy in them, we would consider doing reports to pull together all available information and thereby attempt to get Washington agencies to reassess their views.

4. But we would *not* attempt to duplicate the major research projects on the Soviet economy being carried on by government agencies in Washington.

On a day in early 1945 I took over the Economic Section. I walked over to Ed's desk. He gave me a triumphant look—and put out his hand. I grabbed it.

*       *       *       *       *

It was early spring. The snow had more or less melted but warm weather had not come. It was that bleak, chilly time when in Moscow one must keep one's eye turned upward in wariness against the janitors throwing cakes of ice off the rooftops. It was that leafless, yet snowless, in-between time when the soul longs for the caress of the sun, when the Russian winter nears its end.

I had a problem in my work. I sought advice. I phoned the Chancery and asked for Mr. Kennan. The answer came, "Mr. Kennan is in his apartment. He is not feeling well. If you wish you can see him there."

I went upstairs. Attractive Anne Lise Kennan showed me into the Kennan apartment.

"Would you mind waiting for a while?" she asked.

"Of course not." And so I waited a bit.

Finally, I was admitted to Kennan's bedroom. He sat in his bed, pillows propped behind him. In front of him were sheets of paper with notes. His secretary, Dorothy Hessman, sat beside the bed with notebook open. She looked at me as if I had interrupted something important. But George looked at me tolerantly. I posed my question and I got my answer. After a few minutes I left his bedroom. On the way to my office I asked myself, "Why was George Kennan, sick in his apartment, working as hard as he worked in his office?"

I put the same question to one of the first secretaries of the Embassy. "George Kennan," he said, "is much too good an administrator."

"What do you mean?" I asked. For this was an enigmatic answer.

"The fact of the matter is," he said, "that there are few in the foreign service who deal with administrative problems so adroitly as Kennan. In the morning there is a pile of papers in his in-basket a foot high, and an hour later all have been handled—effectively. Kennan knows how to deal with organization problems but sooner or later he gets tired of them. His creative side demands out, and at that point Kennan may become indisposed. He is sick. He goes to bed. He launches there his most interesting work. Among his other talents he is a master of the language. He can write—and that is a rare talent in the Foreign Service—or anywhere else."

A week later I read a series of several telegrams from Kennan to the Department. They were brilliant essays, summing up conclusions to be deduced from the developing political situation. They had their effect in Washington.

*     *     *     *     *

Spring came to Moscow in 1945, a spring bringing with it an end to the war with Germany.

May 8, 1945 Julie and I awoke to knocking at our door. Our landlady, Piretra Alexandrovna, declaimed through the door, "Meester Wheetnee, Yulya Alexandrovna—there's been an announcement. The end of the war. It came early this morning. Everyone is walking around the city. It's a holiday."

"So they've finally announced it!" I said to Julie. Everyone in the world except the Russians had known at least a full day and only the Soviet government had withheld the good news. Precious few knew about it ahead of the official announcement, too. Julie and I got up and went out to see what was going on. And, truth to tell, it was a once-in-a-lifetime day. A holiday had been declared but the government had failed to "organize" it. This is the only time it has ever happened in the last three decades or more. No parades, no workers' demonstrations, no entertainment, no nothing. People did what they wanted! They milled around. They walked to Red Square. They basked in the sun. They shouted. They were full of that gladness that comes to weary souls after the end of a long period of unbearable hardship.

And a strange thing happened. The crowds began to gather in front of the American Embassy to salute the allies. Cheers went up when any American appeared. Americans were carried on the shoulders of Russians through Red Square, or kissed and hugged by enthusiastic Soviet soldiers. The day turned into a feast of Soviet-American friendship. This had never happened in the Soviet Union before, and it probably will never happen again. The very idea that Soviet citizens can express "unorganized" feelings of warmth for another country goes so much against the grain of all that the regime represents in terms of controlled opinion!

But that happened. Julie and I went to the center of town and watched. It was wondrous. I was in the crowd in front of the Embassy. George Kennan stood on the balcony of the Embassy and was cheered. The American flag hung there and it was cheered. I myself went up to the balcony. Kennan called me over and made a request. I went to carry it out—next door to the National Hotel. There I asked for a Soviet flag—a red banner. I carried it through the crowd, as all watched, and into the Embassy and up to the fourth floor. It was hung, next to the American flag, symbol of an alliance that won a war. A tremendous shout went up from the Russian crowd. And so the two flags fluttered there.

So often I have wondered whether that could ever happen again.

VE Day in Moscow—a glorious thing. Unfortunately its spirit was not to last for long.

\*        \*        \*        \*        \*

An evening in August, 1945 I stood in the enormous living room at Spaso House underneath the vast crystal chandelier and surveyed the situation. I was dazzled by the gleam of golden epaulettes all about me with bright red stars shining from them. Assembled was more Soviet brass than has ever before or since been brought beneath any American roof. The place was full of generals and marshals, so thick they were stepping on each others' feet. It was a special occasion. General Eisenhower had come to Moscow as guest of Marshal Zhukov. He had been given a royal treatment—and this was Ambassador Harriman's official reception for the visit. Zhukov was guest of honor, and he had brought with him nearly everyone of importance in the Russian high command. There were even present two top-ranking police generals.

Among this mob of brass there were a few Americans. I was one. Harriman in drawing up the list of Americans invited had ignored protocol and selected those of Embassy staff, regardless of rank, who spoke Russian. Those of us there were to make ourselves useful translating and conversing with Russians. We did.

The door to the terrace opened. There was silence. All eyes turned to the terrace doors. In came, arm in arm, Zhukov and Eisenhower. They had been chatting more than an hour. And now they had come back to rejoin the party. But Ambassador Harriman was not around, I noticed. I asked someone where he was.

"There's important news coming," I heard him say. "The Ambassador went to Mokhovaya Street for a teletype conversation with the White House. Wait."

A few minutes later Harriman came in. He held up his hand for silence. Everyone listened.

"The Japanese Government has surrendered unconditionally," he proclaimed proudly.

I looked around to see how the news was received. There was jubilation among the Americans. Next to me General Eisenhower was dancing a jig. "Now I can go fishing," he shouted.

I have often thought of that remark. One might say that he did, indeed, go fishing and caught a very big fish.

I looked at the Russians. I was astonished to note gloomy expressions on long faces. Hardly had Harriman finished his announcement than groups of the Russian brass began gathering at the exit, saying their abrupt farewells.

"To Frunze Street." I heard orders given to one Russian chauffeur. They were going to the War Ministry—though it was midnight. And then suddenly the thing became clear. Russia had entered the war in the Far East a few days before. Now had come the end. The Russian armies had not had time to advance to positions the Soviet government wished to have at surrender—in control of Manchuria, Korea and more. The Soviet generals had gone to the War Ministry to push forward Soviet forces as far and fast as possible. So it was that for days Soviet armies kept assaulting and advancing in Manchuria as if they'd not heard of the surrender.

A few Embassy officers remained as Harriman's last guests. One of our career diplomats laughed and said, "Well, our allies did not seem to receive with enthusiasm the news of our victory!"

"After all," laughed another of my colleagues, "it has been a short war there for them. What is it now—three days? They won one of the quickest victories of history!"

*       *       *       *       *

In 1945 I began to interest myself in the Soviet oil situation. In Washington all intelligence agencies were estimating that Soviet petroleum production was higher than before the war. This made me somewhat suspicious. In Moscow there were rumors indicating something different. The Commercial Attaché of the X Embassy, a well-informed person, had heard that oil production in Baku in Azerbaijan —from where seventy per cent of Soviet output had come in 1940— had fallen disastrously since the beginning of the war.

What was the real situation? I began to study. Preliminary results were indicative. I took the problem to Kennan. He directed me to follow this through. He understood the significance of oil. So I went to work. I read and searched. I picked up every item I could find on oil.

I started to go into the output of every single trust in the Baku area. One by one I managed to line up estimates of their production. How? *Pravda* reported the Kaganovich Trust in Baku had fulfilled its plan on December 20 and produced so many hundred thousand tons over plan. A quick calculation could give a rough rate of output. That for that trust. But how many trusts were there? Had there been important mergers since the beginning of the war? What were the other trusts? What cross checks could there be on this method? What had the production of the various trusts amounted to before the war? All these— and other—questions had to be answered. And the equation had to be worked out for every single production trust. And the same had to be done for every other oil field.

This was finally done but there had to be other evidence. Only two important Soviet oil fields had been touched by the Germans. The assumption in Washington had been that the rest—including the single biggest at Baku—had been functioning at or above prewar. What about this assumption? I began to question it. I found there was good evidence of a shortage of steel pipe for Baku, for the whole industry. I found there was evidence of serious trouble in Baku outside the pipe situation. I kept up my research. Soon everything began to add up: The war had brought a disaster to the Soviet oil industry. But it was one—and this was the real kicker—which would have come without the war.

The fact was that Baku, which had in 1940 furnished 70 per cent of Soviet petroleum output, was nearly exhausted. It had been over-exploited. The war had brought transportation problems and a pipe shortage, but the drop in output there was more than temporary. This was one conclusion. But there was another equally important. In the meanwhile, the industry had concentrated activities elsewhere in the so-called Volga-Urals area. There had been big oil strikes in the Kuibyshev Region and Bashkiria. This was evident from close reading. Production in this new area was still small but the future was bright. Possibilities, in fact, seemed unlimited.

Finally I came out with my field-by-field estimate. Production of Soviet petroleum, I estimated, was about 20 million metric tons in 1945. This compared with estimates current in Washington intelligence agencies of about 36 million metric tons for the same year.

I prepared a telegram summarizing the findings. I prepared it with trepidation. I was questioning serious work by able people. A few days before I completed the final draft of my report there appeared in the Baku Russian-language paper a news item. From this it was possible to deduce directly Soviet oil production for 1945—which worked out to be 19.4 million metric tons. This was so close to my figure as to be almost unbelievable. This filled in the final element in my equation. My telegram went in—and a storm descended on our heads from Washington, more ready to defend mistaken estimates than admit error. But eventually truth had its way.

This was just one way that my section and my work played an important role in the evaluation by the government of the Soviet economy.

*   *   *   *   *

It was a dreary, wet day. I made my way to Spaso House in a hurry because the Ambassador had asked me out to see him. I wondered what it was about.

Mike, the doorman, ushered me into the Ambassador's room and told me to make myself at home. The birch logs in the fireplace burned merrily away. I looked around at the room. Harriman had combined his personal bedroom and his office in this single long room. There he worked. And there he slept. What was he doing now, I wondered?

I heard someone calling, "Tom!"

The voice was coming from a door which, as I knew, led to a dressing room which led to a bathroom—the Ambassador's bath. I approached it gingerly. Was the Ambassador really asking me to come in there? I listened.

"Tom, come on in " I heard.

So I entered.

Belathered and in his trousers—shirtless with suspenders hanging down—the tall and handsome Mr. Harriman stood at the washstand shaving.

"I'm sorry to keep you waiting, Tom," the Ambassador said. "I'll be out in a second." So I went out and waited. I had thought for a moment that we were to conduct our business while the Ambassador shaved.

The Ambassador emerged completely dressed. He sat down opposite me and we talked. He outlined a situation. It was a question of giving some hundreds of millions of dollars to the Russians. How did I feel?

I outlined my reaction.

The Ambassador pulled out a telegram from his brief case, and said:

"You know, Tom, I agree—and this is the cable I have drafted. Read it and see if you have suggestions."

I quickly ran through it. One or two suggestions were accepted.

"Thank you, Tom," said the Ambassador. "I appreciate your help, but it's only fair to tell you I am fighting a lost cause. These grants have been decided on and I doubt that I can stop them. Still I'm going to try."

\*      \*      \*      \*      \*

One thing that troubled me as I studied my work as Chief of the Economic Section was the limited audience I was working for.

If I drafted a telegram and it was sent it might be seen by a few people in a few Washington agencies including the Department—and, if important enough, might be relayed to several of the most important American missions. The same was true of the reports I wrote. Yet, as I knew, there was the keenest interest throughout the foreign service in Soviet affairs. What the Russians did or planned always seemed to have implications all over the world. How could I satisfy this demand and have a bigger audience for the work of the Section?

I thought about this a while and hit upon an idea. I talked it over with Kennan. He told me to go ahead. It would be a lot of work but worth it. I proposed to produce a brief mimeographed monthly review of the Soviet economy with a number of short but pithy articles. It would be run off in as many as one-hundred copies and go to Washington in forty or fifty copies for distribution throughout the government and to every foreign service post of importance. This would broaden our readership.

The first issue went to press. I was very pleased with it. It covered, as it seemed to me, various aspects of Soviet economic policy, each in an effective way, and summarized succinctly major economic news and developments. But I was anxious. We might get some bitter attacks on our information and conclusions. We did not take the position—accepted on faith by some—that the Soviet economy was ready to collapse. So I waited for reactions. They began to come in and they were favorable. The Embassy monthly economic review was well received in and outside Washington. So it became a new regular enterprise of the section—one which made, I believe, a contribution to keeping the American foreign service and some other government agencies better informed on Soviet economic policy and development.

\*    \*    \*    \*    \*

In late January 1946, a few days after my twenty-ninth birthday, I was sent to Paris to represent the Moscow Embassy at a conference of American officials in the field of European economic affairs. It lasted two weeks, and took place at the Hotel Crillon.

It was a snowy day when I took off from Vnukovo Airport, south of Moscow. The DC-3 rose into the gray, cold sky overhead, and I watched lonesomely as Julie far in the distance waved her handkerchief forlornly. She had come to see me off. I hated to leave her behind. In any kind of a fair and decent world she could have gone with me. She had always dreamed about seeing Paris. But instead she had to stay behind. The situation hurt, but I knew the assignment was an opportunity to represent our Embassy at an important meeting and to make some important points about Soviet economic policy which had a direct relationship to American economic policies.

The conference was an active, vital gathering. Officials from various embassies and agencies presented summaries of the important problems in reconstruction and rehabilitation of Europe's economy. More than anything else I found the officials there deeply concerned with Soviet policies and their impact on European economics and American policy. What were the Russians up to? What were the chances of Soviet cooperation in the reconstruction of Europe? What was the Soviet economic program aimed at? How seriously should it be taken? I was showered with such questions at meetings, at luncheons, in chats in the Crillon corridors.

Among my colleagues I detected some delusions about Soviet policy. One was that one could hope for Soviet cooperation in the rehabilitation of Western Europe. Another was that the USSR had suffered such devastation that it could not recover for a decade or so. A third was the associated idea that Russia would be prepared to do anything to get American economic aid.

I was asked to speak at a general meeting. I stressed that the Soviet government would go to any lengths of ruthlessness to speed up reconstruction and develop rapidly the nation's economic might. Things would go fast. I commented that it was my view that the American government could not count on cooperation from the Russians in the rehabilitation of Western Europe—and could, in fact, count on the most bitter opposition. Things were looking very tough indeed.

My talk was followed by a heated question period. The Russian question was, it seemed clear, considered to be a key question. I had expressed for some of the officials present feelings and views they had reached in their own areas and work but which they had been hesitant to voice because of far-reaching implications.

The two weeks flew by in hard work. I sat finally in the airdrome outside Paris waiting for the plane to take me to Berlin on my way to Moscow. I felt I had done my job well, that George Kennan himself, now Chargé d'Affaires, would have approved. And then I suddenly remembered. Here I had come to Paris for the first time in my life. And I had not been in the Louvre nor ascended the Eiffel Tower.

\*     \*     \*     \*     \*

A day in early February 1946. I sat at dawn in a Soviet airdrome in East Berlin awaiting the departure of the Soviet plane returning me to Moscow.

A wife of a Soviet officer talked with another Russian woman sitting there. "What an awful place Lithuania is! My husband was stationed there for a year. The Lithuanians hated us. I was afraid to go out on the streets by myself. What spiteful people!"

She was talking about one of the "family" of Soviet peoples, united by Soviet socialism. I listened casually. I was thinking about Moscow —about the room on Malovlasevsky—about Julie. I hardly cared what Russians thought about Lithuanians or vice versa.

It was a long wait. I paced up and down in the airport building, a barren building with a barren exterior and a barren interior.

A Russian officer got up and left his newspaper behind. I went over and looked at it. It was *Pravda* of a day before. Stalin's picture was on the front page. There was bold-faced type. I picked it up and started to read. This was the first speech the Soviet dictator had made for a long time. It was a pre-election address in the Stalin election district in Moscow in anticipation of the Supreme Soviet election to follow. I sat down to study this speech which had to be an important policy statement—the first declaration in the postwar period of Soviet plans.

Stalin outlined economic programs for coming years—goals for steel, iron, coal and petroleum—"for three or more five year plans"— in other words for 1960 or 1965, as one might understand: 60 million metric tons of steel, 50 million tons of pig iron, 500 million tons of coal, sixty million tons of petroleum. They were big figures. In 1945, for comparison, steel production was about 12 million tons, as I knew from my own work; iron about 9 million; coal about 150 million and oil 19.4 million.

Considering possibilities these goals were not beyond reason. But they meant that again, as before the war, the government was going to put heavy industry first. This was a phrase Stalin himself used— "priority development for heavy industry." It meant that consumer goods were to have a poor second place, that war-weary people longing for the better things were to be refused, and that this would be imposed by ruthless force. Russians would not even be asked to tighten their belts. Their belts would be tightened for them by the government: economic, therefore political.

I had an empty feeling in the pit of my stomach as I headed back to Moscow. Stalin said the Soviet Union must attain these goals to be prepared against any "chance happenings." What sense did it make to be talking about "chance happenings"—in other words a new war just as peace had been attained? I thought about that. It did not make sense in terms of the given international situation unless the Soviet Union itself planned aggression—which the Soviet Union obviously was not planning then. But it did make sense in a perverse way in terms of Soviet internal politics!

The regime of ruthless dictatorship, of rule by police terror, imposed and maintained by Stalin from the early thirties on, required the presence of an external enemy in order that there should be a justification for repression and terror. In the thirties with the rise of Hitlerism this external enemy was self-evident and real enough. With the end of World War II, however, there remained no external enemy. But the regime had to have one. Therefore a new enemy must be created. Obviously the only possible enemy was "American imperialism." The Soviet press had already begun to sound the alarm.

We Americans in Moscow had long seen the storm signals. Soviet-American relations had never—even at wartime best—looked very cordial from the vantage point of the Soviet capital. And during the year of victory—1945—there had been marked deterioration, step by step, from VE Day on.

Stalin's speech of February 1946, however, proclaimed a new stage in the program of Soviet preparation for—and creation of—troubled times. It was the formal declaration of the cold war.

*       *       *       *       *

I sat in the office of the Soviet Minister of Foreign Trade, A. I. Mikoyan, and listened as the swarthy little Armenian Communist addressed a group of American Congressmen visiting Moscow. He had been asked by one of the Americans about Soviet plans for exports.

"At any rate," declared Mikoyan, "we do not plan to export revolution."

There was a rewarding chuckle from the Congressmen. This was a time-honored wisecrack of Mikoyan when he addressed distinguished Westerners—and it never failed to elicit a laugh from his listeners.

"How much gold does the Soviet Union have?" asked one of the Americans.

I translated the question into Russian. He replied quickly:

"I do not know the answer—and even if I did it is a secret."

That was that. I listened to the give and take. The American group represented a House Committee on Foreign Economic Relations. It consisted of high-ranking legislators who had come to Moscow to meet high-ranking Soviet officials and arrive at a few conclusions on Soviet economic intentions. They had spent a busy week. I had been with them constantly as an aide and translator. I had taken them to meet important officials. I had escorted them through factories. I had given them briefings. They had been appreciative and friendly.

This was not the first time I had been assigned to this sort of work. Generally when American officials had come to Moscow to interest themselves in economic questions I had been assigned to help. There were varied groups—from American banking officials of the Federal Reserve headed by Emmanuel Goldenweiser, who spoke Russian better than I, to James Carey of the C.I.O. who was concerned with the relations of the C.I.O. with the World Federation of Trade Unions. Many Americans whom I was assigned to help became fast friends as a result of our working together.

The interview continued. Mikoyan was engaged in an exposition of why it was in the interest of the United States to give big postwar commercial credits to the Soviet government. Mikoyan presented the case ably—but as I looked at the faces of the American Congressmen I noted skepticism. And this emerged quickly enough in the sharp questions which followed. If this American group was any index then Mikoyan did not stand much chance of getting the big American credit he was after. The climate was distinctly unfavorable to such things and the Russians had themselves to blame.

I listened to the Congressmen later at the Embassy giving their comments on Mikoyan.

"A pretty smart customer," said one. "I wish he were working on our side. If he were in the United States he would be a multi-millionaire."

"He didn't tell us anything," said another. "He's good at dodging questions."

Both the comments were on the nose. I saw Mikoyan many times before and after that interview. He is very bright, very sharp, and an old hand at not giving away something for nothing.

\*     \*     \*     \*     \*

By 1945 the Embassy under Harriman's overall supervision and Kennan's personal guidance had become an alive and creative organization. It continued to develop in this spirit through 1946 and 1947—even after Kennan left.

All of us there had the feeling of being privileged to be at the very *center* of things, the "decisive point." This was not a geographical point but the fact that we in the Embassy were in the heart of Soviet-American relations which were "of the essence."

We there felt ourselves to be the only Americans with a window into Russia and the Russian question. True, sometimes we couldn't see much through our window. That made it the more intriguing and our position the more crucial.

There was a sense of adventure, exploration, of investigation into the unknown—all the time. And in this kind of an atmosphere individuals blossomed out. Playboy third secretaries came, some in a state of dejection because Moscow was notoriously not a center for "play," and they stayed to acquire a sense of purpose, a sense of the importance of their profession. Serious career diplomats, senior and junior, who had been in a chronic state of frustration and dejection with their careers, came to the Embassy and there, for the first time, found that their work was needed by their country. The Embassy became literally a "school for Ambassadors." Service in the Embassy soon became a qualification in itself for rapid advancement in the service. And all over the world today there are American heads of mission who found themselves and were found in that yellow pillared building at Mokhovaya Street 13/15.

This was a place in which to work! And work I did as never before.

*    *    *    *    *

In March 1946 the Supreme Soviet—the Soviet Union's rubber-stamp parliament—met to approve the new first postwar five-year plan for economic development. The plan ran from 1946 to 1950. Its aim was to provide for reconstruction from war devastation and for expansion of production beyond prewar levels.

The five-year plans had been inaugurated by Stalin in 1928 as programs of "construction of socialism." They were launched with fanfare. They had both practical and propaganda significance. They were actual economic plans. True, in prewar plans there was a notable tendency for the political leadership to override the economists and set propaganda goals which were fantastic and unattainable. But when reality caught up—as it soon did—targets had been lowered to more reasonable levels. Even at their worst the plans did provide a blue-print. As important was their usefulness in dramatizing Soviet economic accomplishments. Soviet citizens could be urged to sacrifice for the future as symbolized in five year plan goals. To foreigners Soviet propaganda could point out that the plans exemplified the fact there was no economic crisis in Russia, that the Soviet Union, in contrast to the capitalist world, was making continual economic progress. The tremendous hullabaloo about the "great" five-year plans also served to conceal in some degree—or to make a little less obvious—more seamy sides of Soviet life such as the famine of 1932, the economic hardship and suffering of everyone, and the great purge of the thirties. Before World War II came to Russia the Soviet Union had completed two full five-year plans and several years out of the third.

The return to the five-year plan scheme in 1946 was an important development and the plan a vital document. It was my task to study and analyze it. As new figures and facts on it kept coming out for a period of over half a year, this work took up most of my time and energy in the first six months of 1946.

It was a delight, at last, to have some figures, officially released, to work with. Up to this most of my work had been devoted to the ferreting out through the perusal of vast masses of published materials and the putting together of one figure and another of some, just a few, of the basic production figures for the USSR, such as those for steel, oil and coal. Precious little time and energy remained after this for real study or analysis of trends, directions and bottlenecks.

With the new plan this aspect began to improve. The Kremlin, it's true, retained a psychosis, not overcome till long after Stalin's death in 1953, against release of current economic data in other form than percentages of some other year, such as 1940 or 1950. There was still a lot of "detective" work to be done even after the new plan came out. But, nevertheless, in connection with the plan masses of figures were revealed. These constituted real hard material with which to work.

The new plan was most ambitious. Overall industrial production was scheduled to rise nearly 50 per cent. Steel production was to go up more than 100 per cent, coal by 60 per cent, oil by 75 per cent, electric power by just a little less than 100 per cent. Total production of agriculture was to exceed by 27 per cent in 1950 that of 1940. The standard of living was to rise by 30 per cent in 1950 compared with 1940. These were the way all the goals ran. If one believed in them then there was in store a rapid advance all along the whole front of economic effort.

How did this jibe with previous experience? I asked myself this. How did it jibe also with Point No. 1 in the official preamble to the plan which provided for *priority* reconstruction and development of heavy industry and railway transport?

To analyze the plan I broke it down into three sectors—heavy industry, agriculture and standard of living. To estimate how it would work for each of these sectors I looked at previous experience. I found that in the prewar period actual experience had shown remarkable progress in building up heavy industry—steel, coal, electric power, oil, basic chemicals, and particularly machinery, a category embracing both armaments and capital equipment. The level of annual increases in this area had been so consistent as to make it possible to predict what the same system could do from any given starting level.

At the same time prewar experience showed something quite different about the course of things in agriculture and standard of living. Here the Stalinist system had shown not progress but regression. This regression, it could be shown, was the result of two principal factors: first, collectivization of agriculture and the way collectivized agriculture was then being made to operate; and second, the fact that whenever bottlenecks were encountered in heavy industry they were invariably solved by pulling up the belt another notch on the population; in other words, by reducing the already atrociously low standard of living.

I looked then at this new plan in the light of this previous experience. My conclusions, in reports, were that the goals set for heavy industry for 1950 were not unrealistic, though ambitious. It was even possible that in some key lines, such as steel and oil, they might be exceeded. In particular, I felt, the war had broadened the human base of the Soviet machinery industry. Tens of thousands of young people had been graduated as engineers specializing in machinery production. Scores of thousands of citizens had been trained to operate lathes, to carry out all the complex operations of the metal-working industries. One could expect that after reconversion there would be rapid rises in the output of all machinery. I was certain Soviet capabilities in this key area were being seriously underestimated in the West.

I concluded that the plan goals for agriculture and standard of living were unrealistic and would not be attained. They were not so much unrealistic in themselves as in terms of Stalinist policies. The agricultural plans could possibly be attained by relaxing the rigor of the collective farm system to allow scope for individual enterprise and give greater incentives to peasants to produce. The whole line of policy was, however, in the opposite direction. The goals in standard of living might be reached if either the slogan "priority for heavy industry" were relaxed or if the determination of the government to re-equip immediately all its armed forces with the most modern weapons were abandoned. Neither of these things were going to happen. Stalin's February speech had told the story on this. Of course, some quite significant increases in both agriculture and living standards could be scored, even in this situation, merely as the result of the return of millions of men from the front to peacetime economic pursuits, but not enough. Life in Russia would still be hard—and foodstuffs insufficient.

And, I felt, here was a dangerous political situation. Weary people . . . More sacrifices . . . Lack of enthusiasm . . . Passive resistance . . . A campaign of terror on the part of a ruthless government . . . More passive resistance . . . A vicious circle.

But I was still certain that the increases in production of the main materials of basic industry programmed in the plan would be realized. And in this, as in the rest of my analysis, I was, as things turned out, right: In 1950 the Soviet Union produced actually 27.3 million metric tons of steel compared with an output planned of 25.4; 261 million tons of coal compared with a plan of 250 million; 37.8 million tons of oil compared with a plan of 35.4; and 91.2 billion kilowatt hours of electricity compared with a plan of 82 billion. Total industrial output rose in the period, according to the official government index, to a level of 73 per cent over 1940 compared with a plan, in terms of the same index, of 48 per cent. Machinery production, scheduled to double in terms of the official output index, actually increased, according to the same index by 115 per cent.

(Careful analyses by American and other Western economists, supported in some degree by some studies by Soviet economists, suggest that the official Soviet output indices for industry as a whole and the machinery industry tend to distort in an upward direction by an appreciable percentage increase in the physical volume of output. However, short-term comparisons of relative magnitude of increases within the same index still retain a fair validity.)

On the other hand the picture in consumer goods was the opposite:

The USSR produced in 1950 3.9 billion meters of cotton cloth compared with a plan of 4.7 billion; of woolens 155 million meters compared with a plan of 159 million; 203 million pairs of shoes instead of 240 million pairs planned etc. (In all these items the increases over the war-end year of 1945, which was a very meagre year, were nevertheless very considerable.)

And so far as agriculture was concerned things turned out miserably indeed, so miserably that no meaningful statistics were released on the subject by the Soviet government for many years after the plan period was over.

But to me, surveying the economy in 1946, the decisive element was not the coming failure in agriculture and the standard of living sector, which could be foreseen—but the success in development of heavy industry. Given continued success in heavy industry, failures in other areas could be regarded as temporary. A heavy industry increasing its production could pour capital resources into whatever sector of the economy required them—whenever the need was realized by the leadership and the decision made to direct them there.

The prewar period and the war itself had demonstrated what the Soviet regime could do in development of heavy industry. Given the difficulties encountered—those imposed by the natural and cultural environment, those created by external foes, and those created by the system itself—the accomplishments had been spectacular. (The cost in human life and happiness had been horrifying.) A powerful foundation of basic industry, including particularly a highly developed machinery industry, had been created. By 1940 the Soviet Union had lifted itself into the first rank of the world's industrial nations. During the war Soviet industry had proven itself in the difficult conditions of occupation by the enemy of important industrial regions. With most of metal and fuel supplies cut off, Soviet industry nevertheless had turned out a steady stream of first-class equipment for the front in big quantities—some of the best tanks in the world, fine artillery, plenty of ammunition, good fighter and assault planes, even some revolutionary new rocket weapons such as the famous "Katyusha." I knew about this aspect of the Soviet economy because I had studied it in Washington and in Moscow.

And, it seemed to me, that given continued success in development of heavy industry the USSR government could do much. In postwar peacetime it could create a powerful construction industry to build new factories, mills and plants on the broadest scale and even spectacular projects such as giant hydroelectric dams. It could equip them with modern equipment. It could assure increases year after year in output of all the basic materials: fuel, metals, power, chemicals. It could, assuming it was willing to devote the resources to it, turn out also ever-increasing quantities of consumer goods. It could re-equip Soviet agriculture with modern tractors and farm machinery and lay the foundation for eventual increases in food production. It could re-equip its armed forces with the latest weapons. It could even, I was certain, begin the manufacture of nuclear weapons in a short time. I never felt, given Soviet energy, resources and resourcefulness, given the Soviet technological and scientific base in existence, given the fact it was known through American experience and information, publicly released, that atom bombs could be made and in general outlines how to make them, that it would take the USSR more than a few years to explode its own first atom bomb.

So far as I could see, the Soviet Union could, given peace, in the longer run of two or three decades challenge the United States in economic growth. The Russians could by adding steadily to their production year after year after year eventually hope to outproduce the United States in everything that makes the sinews of economic-military might: steel, fuel, power, armaments and capital goods, all types of machinery and equipment, and everything else that constitutes national wealth.

The Soviet Union, in short, as I foresaw could hope to become a *richer,* more powerful nation than the United States. All it would take for this, as it seemed to me then right after the war at a time when the Soviet economy in its volume of output looked puny alongside that of America, was time, a continuation with a good many incidental adjustments as things went along of the already mature Soviet policy and practice of forced rapid industrial development, and in particular the unwillingness of the American system and the American leadership to do anything to prevent this happening—to meet the Soviet challenge.

# 9.   *Malovlasevsky 9a*

My "other life"—the after-hours Russian part which centered on the Luzhsky home on Malovlasevsky and was so distinct from the American part of my life centering on the Embassy—was always fascinating. But it was not luxurious, and in some respects not even comfortable.

Let me begin with the Luzhsky house itself. It had been built for Piretra Alexandrovna Luzhskaya and her actor husband, Vasily Vasilich Luzhsky, by her wealthy father around the turn of the century. It was an historic house because on many occasions there had been held in its ample chambers first-night celebrations, attended by all the Art Theater company, following the new Art Theater productions.

It was a posh "modern" home for the Moscow of its time with big expanses of glass windows in large tall-ceilinged studio rooms in a spirit of revolt against the traditional styles of town mansions of the Muscovite merchantry. This was what one would expect from the Luzhskys who were in the forefront of the Moscow theatrical intelligentsia. The Luzhsky home however, was not a particularly successful experiment. It was neither beautiful nor practical. It had, for instance, been constructed to be heated with firewood, using gorgeous large green-tiled dutch ovens from floor to ceiling throughout the home. There were at least half a dozen of these. And it was an enormous job to fuel them! It had been built, calculated for maintenance on eight or ten full-time servants. Both firewood and servants were cheap in the Moscow of 1900 and the idea there might ever be a shortage of either would have seemed outlandish then, I guess.

110

This was the establishment—with some nine living rooms—which the Soviet government in a fit of generosity on the death of the great actor, Vasily Vasilich, had given back to Piretra Alexandrovna and her two sons for their lifetime as their personal property. (The same Soviet government had confiscated it during the revolution but allowed the Luzhskys to continue to occupy it as tenants.) And this was the monstrosity with which poor Piretra Alexandrovna had to cope in a socialist country which provided no facilities for fuel, repairs or maintenance for privately owned mansions in the middle of the capital. No wonder her broad shoulders were slightly bowed. From office to office she went, trying to get fuel, trying to get roofing iron, trying to get labor to fix the house, trying to get this, trying to get that.

"I am the widow of the actor, Vasily Vasilich Luzhsky," she would introduce herself. And she commanded attention—and did get assistance with her problems. But there were a lot of problems. And she was old and during most of the war all alone, left to do everything herself. It wasn't easy. But she was always cheerful. And she had always a good word for everyone.

The house was on a plot of somewhat less than an acre. It was in the center of a block and surrounded by buildings on every side but the front where there was a partly vacant lot. Around the courtyard was a board fence six feet tall.

The garden, once carefully kept, by 1945 had become a shambles. In the early part of the war much of it had been put under potatoes but by 1944 this part had been allowed to grow up to weeds. There were fruit trees none of which produced fruit except one apple tree whose apples were just sufficiently large to lead small boys to scale the fence. Clumps of bushes had grown wilder and wilder year by year. There was an immense dented metal vase, a dull rose-maroon in color, about four feet tall which stood on a stone pedestal for décor. A cast iron fence was still left along one portion near the house and there was one large bench on which Piretra Alexandrovna used to sit by the hour—where in clement weather in the summer she received visitors.

The inside divided up into three separate "apartments" and one separate single room. One of these "apartments" was on the second floor, had its own entrance from the rear outside, and was occupied by two families. Another consisted of a spacious ground-floor studio apartment rented to a foreign diplomat. The separate single room, divided from the main house by the woodsheds, was occupied by a Russian grass-widow.

The Luzhsky family occupied two of the three rooms of the remaining "apartment" which they and we jointly used. Julie and I had the other room in it. We shared with the Luzhskys toilet, bathroom and kitchen. All three of these jointly-held facilities were something. The toilet was unheated. It never did freeze, not quite. It was down a dark corridor, and it was always very cold. One never stayed there long because one feared catching pneumonia. It was just as well since there were quite a few people using it, always at least five during our stay there, sometimes twice as many.

The bathroom had a sunken bathtub which was tiled in white and had a border around it. It looked like a miniature swimming pool. It was a Hellenistic luxury in the midst of barbarian Moscow—except for one thing—there was almost no hot water. The hot water came only after the janitress had worked for half a day or the like at building up a fire in the wood-burning hot water heater—the "kollonka"—in the bathroom corner. We had one bath day a week and we all took our turns beginning with Piretra Alexandrovna. And woe to the one—and those nearby—who missed the bath. For him or her it was eau de cologne and sponge baths for the next seven days.

The kitchen, however, was the biggest white elephant in the establishment. There was a stove. It was literally twelve feet long, designed for firewood which it consumed cheerfully by the carload. The best we could do, pooling our resources, was to heat it up once a week for washday. Then the tubs of water could be put out on the cast iron hot plates stretching out like a great table and baking could be undertaken at the same time. The fire would roar and everything would get hot.

The rest of the time cooking was done on two hot plates and a pair of primus stoves. This naturally limited the repertoire. Most of what we had was fried or boiled. The kitchen was impossible to heat without lighting up the stove. Therefore the cooking was conducted—at cold times of the year—in semi-frigid temperatures. In the winter whoever cooked wore an overcoat—a pot-holder in the hand to keep from burning one's fingers on the frying pan and earmuffs over one's ears to keep them from frostbite.

There wasn't any question of our doing our own housekeeping. We were both working full time. So we employed a cook whom I found through one of the cooks in the Embassy. She fed us for six months on buckwheat grits and farina porridge. And during this period, as we later discovered, she provided a set of new clothes for her married daughter, including half a dozen silk dresses, a fur coat, and lots of other things. She also apparently provided all kinds of goodies to her associates and other relatives and herself steadily gained weight, despite all her running up and down the stairs from our room to the kitchen and back, and all that work she had carting our provisions out of the house. Julie and I were so absorbed in our romance and our work that we hardly noticed. But finally Piretra Alexandrovna took pity on us and called it to our attention.

There followed a whole succession of other cooks—all good hard-working Russian women, much more typical of their kind than our first. But none of them could stand the kitchen and the stairway. Sooner or later they fled, leaving us to our own resources. "Our own resources" consisted of Julie's mother, who fed us in her own room during periods between cooks, giving us delicious meals off her hot plate. I suppose without her we would have soon come down with malnutrition illnesses.

Our never-ending problem was keeping warm. Our room—because of the front sun porch with three sides glassed—was almost impossible to heat. Our two big Dutch ovens were fired up early. When the fire had roared away for a time dampers were closed. The heat was kept inside and the tiles warmed up till they got almost too hot to touch. Warmth radiated out from them into the room. And we were warm. But then, usually early in the evening, the stoves began to cool and the room also. Cold air flooded in from the sun porch. We would begin to shiver. We resorted to electric heaters and this caused poor Piretra Alexandrovna untold anguish.

"Meester Wheetnee!" she would expostulate. "Please, the leemeet!"

The "limit" was the amount of electricity allowed the house without payment of penalty rates which were several times higher than the normal rate. I always paid the penalty rates without complaint and begged for the installation of a separate meter. But there was never a separate meter and the penalty rates did cause problems, so there was always poor Piretra Alexandrovna standing at our door, wringing her hands and begging:

"Meester Wheetnee! Please, the leemeet!"

But for all the problems, our room took on a warm, golden glow in contrast to everything around. We papered it with Russian wallpaper which I went myself to get from Moscow's only wallpaper factory. The first piece of furniture to appear after our bed was a concert grand piano which I rented. I bought some furniture from an Embassy officer who left his things behind him when he departed in a rush. Two rich Guatemalan rugs—one on the studio bed and the other on the floor—gave a touch of brightness.

It was delightful beyond description to come home and walk up that driveway through the wooden gates and through the bleak garden and into the house through the glass doors, being careful not to skin my knuckles on the very poorly placed handle, and take a few steps down that dark corridor with walls covered with pictures which represented the history of the Art Theater and the Luzhsky family, including one of Piretra Alexandrovna, her actor husband, and Konstantin Stanislavsky himself at the White House in Washington, and then open that enormously tall, white double door and enter our own room. Julie more often than not would be at the piano. She would come over and kiss me—and I would be home again, home in my Russian home. Cold toilet or not it was a happy, lovely place, the kind that one remembers forever with a warm and tingling sensation.

*     *     *     *     *

There is a great plenty of many things in the Soviet Union—snow, birch trees, open space and vodka—but one of the scarce things is privacy. In Russia one lives in close quarters with one's neighbors. God grant that they should be more or less pleasant and kindly people, as they often are, for if they are not life can become a hell. And pleasant or unpleasant they inevitably, even if they are not nosy, find out a good deal about one and one finds out a good deal about them. Nothing much one can do about that.

So, of course, I inevitably came to know well my neighbors in my Russian home on Malovlasevsky and they came to know me well. Perhaps even now, some fifteen years later, they reminisce about me once in a while. I certainly remember them and my memories of them are warm for they were friendly, generous, good people.

The Luzhsky family consisted of half a dozen people of whom five lived in the family residence and one outside. There was, of course, Piretra Alexandrovna, the matriarch, who governed the establishment with an autocratic but kindly hand. Her two sons were Alexander

Vasilich Luzhsky, who lived in the home, and Yevgeny Vasilich, who lived outside it but often visited his mother. The wife of Alexander Vasilich—Piretra Alexandrovna's daughter-in-law—was Ilena Alexeyevna and they had a small son, Vasya, aged about three. Another grandson lived in the home, Sasha, son of Yevgeny Vasilich by a previous marriage, whom Piretra Alexandrovna had taken into her home to bring up herself. Sasha was about fifteen.

Piretra Alexandrovna herself was nearly seventy. In the mornings about six-thirty we would awaken to the stomping of her old-fashioned ankle-high shoes down the corridor outside our room and to the penetrating tones of her Stanislavsky-trained voice as she greeted the janitor and janitress. And the picture will forever remain in my mind of tall and erect Piretra Alexandrovna, with kerchief about her head binding up her flowing mane of lovely white hair, marching through the front courtyard, behind her her dog, Gero, with his head high and behind Gero the Siberian cat, Lemon, with his tail always straight up in the air. What a procession! In her youth Piretra Alexandrovna had been a ravishing beauty. Over her iron bedstead in her simply-furnished bedroom hung an enormous photographic portrait taken of her when she was in her mid-thirties. It showed a woman who, despite her height, possessed a soft and gentle fullness of feature and limb. This had disappeared, of course, in the sharp angularity of old age, but she retained the beautiful liquid blue of her eyes. And even at seventy she was handsome.

The way Piretra Alexandrovna talked about Stanislavsky left in my mind a question. I never asked her, but the portrait over her bed showed an attractive woman who did not look like one who would reject the opportunities life might offer. And she used to sit and reread now and then the letters which Stanislavsky had written to her. Piretra Alexandrovna had enjoyed her life to the full and this was one of the things that gave her that breadth of spirit, that joy in life, so characteristic.

Piretra Alexandrovna's elder son, Alexander Vasilich, was a specialist in cancer. He was a large man with an expressive face and a courtly manner who went out of his way to be polite. When we first moved in he was absent in military service. He had been in the army since the beginning of the war. He returned home in late 1945 after being demobilized and then returned to work in a Moscow cancer clinic. Before the revolution he had traveled extensively in Western

Europe and had participated in the intense social life around the Art Theater. Alexander Vasilich inherited the histrionic ability of his great father and I considered it regrettable he had not taken up acting.

He and his wife, Ilena Alexeyevna, a short roly-poly nurse, lived happily for two decades in the Luzhsky home before World War II. They always wanted a child but none came. She was mobilized with him and they served in the same hospital in the North. At the worst possible time Ilena Alexeyevna became pregnant at over forty for the first time. She was sent home and gave birth to little Vasya. The two of them settled in with Piretra Alexandrovna who till then had been alone with her other grandson, Sasha.

Sasha had come to her as the result of a typical Russian tragedy. The offspring of a short-lived marriage between his father and an attractive member of the leading family of seamstress-stylists in Moscow, he had remained with his mother when his parents separated. His mother had remarried to a high-ranking Red Army officer. In the great purge of 1937–39 the stepfather had been arrested and executed and his mother arrested and sent into exile. Piretra Alexandrovna stepped into the breach and took little Sasha in. He was tall, gawky and handsome. He had an appealing personality and a quick mind. He was studying to be an actor at the Art Theater Studio, following in his grandfather's footsteps and those of his father. His father, Yevgeny Vasilich, was an actor and administrator in the Art Theater.

The Luzhskys were not the only people in their home, for they had several tenants. Upstairs were two families. The actor, Babanin, had been with the Art Theater from pre-revolutionary days but had never progressed beyond bit parts, which he always played beautifully. He was the eternal footman, playing nearly always the roles of waiters or butlers. The thing I remember best about him aside from his genteel, self-effacing, quiet way was the fact that he collected newspapers. He had been collecting them for some thirty years, I guess, and he had them stacked up in an enormous bookcase in his high-ceilinged room which had a big window overlooking the front yard. Perhaps he read them when he could not sleep at night. Who knows?

His daughter, Tanya, also played bit parts in the Art Theater. One could spot her now and then in a crowd scene in *Tsar Fyodor Ivanovich* or some similar well-populated production. Later, she left the Art Theater to go to another theater where she would have more opportunities for development. That was after she met the character we all called "the circus man." This chap, always jovial, was an actor in another Moscow theater where he had good roles. Piretra Alexandrovna christened him with this epithet because he actually had been a strong man in a circus. He was Mr. Five by Five himself, nearly as broad in the beam as from tip to toe, with an avoirdupois up near three hundred. When he came into our happy home one day, hand in hand with Tanya Babanina, there was a good deal of raucous speculation as to how the ceiling beams and Tanya herself were going to hold up.

I can remember a feast one night in the room of Alexander Vasilich with my whiskey furnishing part of the enlivenment and everyone in a good mood when suddenly from upstairs came an horrendous thud.

Piretra Alexandrovna raised her liquid blue eyes to the ceiling.

"Aha!" she declared. "Tanya must have kicked the circus man out of bed." We all roared till the tears came.

The other upstairs tenants did not provide amusement. They were two victims of TB—father and son—and both had it bad. The father was bedridden but his son, Julius, could get out and was a student of philosophy at Moscow University. He was a sensitive boy. He talked with Julie by the hour, sitting in the garden on the bench there. With me he was more shy. Father and son died within a year of each other. The hopelessness of their illness hung over them.

Out in the single room at the other end of the woodshed lived our grass widow, Lyuba. We didn't see much of her. Her husband deserted her just before the war and she was left to look after herself by being a clerk in an office. The most notable thing about Lyuba was her nocturnal visitor once or twice a week. A dark shadow would sneak in and out after dark and Lyuba the next day would look a bit happier. I guess he was a non-com from an AA unit in the suburbs and he probably sneaked off duty to see his sweetheart.

The most pitiful figures in the household were Tyotya Pasha—Aunt Pasha—the janitress and her husband, Dyadya Vasily—Uncle Vasily —the janitor. The two were loyal family servants and had worked there years. She was lean, spare and solemn and clothed in a dirty old apron and a dark gray woolen scarf around her head and showed in every inch her peasant background. He was rough, unkempt and poorly shaven and did his work cutting and splitting firewood and the like rapidly despite his withered hand. These two elderly people loved each other with a clinging, wonderful sort of faithfulness, and never gave up hopes of seeing their only son again. Actually, there was no hope. The last time they had seen him was when he had come to them for shelter—a deserter from his army unit during the siege of Moscow. They had persuaded him to try to return as the only hope of avoiding execution. But he had evidently failed and no doubt had been caught and shot. But they never stopped hoping. Their only son, their beloved son. Perhaps one day he would knock on their door and say:

"Mother, father, I've come home . . ."

But he never did.

\*    \*    \*    \*    \*

People did come home in the Soviet Union—sometimes. And it could be a strange thing, as if they had returned from the dead. They were gone. The emotions surrounding their missing dear ones had grown cold. Much had changed. Nothing, or next to nothing, was heard from them . . . And then suddenly, one day, like Rip Van Winkle, they appeared from out of nowhere, and lives cut and fitted to allow for their absence had to be readjusted. Sometimes this readjustment was painful.

Young fifteen-year-old Sasha had lost his stepfather and his mother in the purge in 1937. He was seven. The police came and took them away, and that was that. Little Sasha was too young to understand. And then he found himself with his grandmother, Piretra Alexandrovna, in her big house with its big garden and life went on. It was a happy life. Things were hard during the war and he was left alone with his grandmother during the siege of Moscow and the hungry winter that followed. But she was an imposing figure that could inspire both love and confidence. As time went on Sasha nearly forgot his mother. She became a shadowy figure in the recesses of his mind— and he pushed her back even further subconsciously, no doubt, for there was always a taint, felt even in the presence of a keen sense of injustice, to an arrest in the family. He grew, became tall like a beanpole, and approached adulthood. He was admitted to the Studio of the Art Theater, an important thing because of family tradition. He became accustomed to the fact that he was in a way alone—with a father with whom he did not live and a mother who had disappeared, almost non-existent.

And then one day . . .

It was late winter—a dreary time. Julie put on her fur coat to go outside, wrapped a scarf around her head, and stepped out of the door.

Coming up the garden path through the snow came a tall woman. She was poorly dressed even for Russia, partly in rags, her feet in well-worn "valenki" or felt boots, a dark gray dirty shawl covering her head not quite so completely as to conceal snow-white hair. Julie looked at her. One tended in Russia to eye all callers with circumspection. The woman's garb seemed to place her as a poor peasant but her face belied this. It was wrinkled and tanned but it was the face of a woman who had been beautiful, the face of an intellectual. How can one tell? One can.

The woman addressed Julie hesitantly. "Could you please tell me whether this is the home of the Luzhsky family?"

"Whom do you wish to see?" asked Julie, following the Russian custom of being noncommittal with strangers.

"Is Perepetuya Alexandrovna here. Is she still alive? Is she in?" the woman asked, still with hesitation.

"Piretra Alexandrovna has gone out," replied Julie. "Is there anything I could do?"

By this time Julie had sensed this was not an ordinary visitor. The woman spoke with a cultured Moscow accent. There was something very pitiful about her.

"Ah, you live here?" asked the woman and then went on quickly as if she had already made up her mind to trust Julie: "And what about the boy, Sasha? Is he here?"

"Yes, he is," answered Julie. "He is here right now—only he's not a boy. He's a young man."

"Oh, oh!" the woman exclaimed. She wrung her hands and tears came to her eyes: "I can hardly believe this is happening at last. Could you please, please call him and ask him to come out and see me?"

"Who shall I say wants him?" Julie asked.

The woman looked frightened but with great effort pulled herself together. "Tell him that his mother, Ksenia Vladimirovna, is here."

Julie finally grasped the situation. "Stay here, I'll get him," she said quickly. Then she caught herself: "Please come into the corridor."

Ksenia Vladimirovna came into the house and waited while Julie went to call Sasha. In a few seconds she returned with Sasha behind her. Sasha stood there and looked without recognition at the woman before him. Julie had, of course, not told him who it was waiting. It was for the mother herself . . .

Ksenia Vladimirovna looked at Sasha and gave a little scream.

"Sasha, don't you know me? It's I, your—your mother."

And then she approached him and embraced him and covered his face with kisses. Sasha stood there awkwardly, his hands at his sides at first, not knowing what to do, taking in the initial impact of the meeting, the meeting after eight years, eight long motherless years.

Ksenia Vladimirovna drew away in confusion.

"Sasha, it's your mother. She's come home." said Julie.

And suddenly a light came into Sasha's blue eyes. He looked at his mother with a gleam of recognition. And suddenly he blurted,

"Mother, oh, mother, it's good you're back. It's been so long . . ."

And then he turned and fled down the corridor to Piretra Alexandrovna's room and the two women could hear his sobs all the way where they stood as he threw himself on the bed and cried. With sheer shock, with joy, with fear or shame, with what emotions? Who can know?

*     *     *     *     *

Russian life flowed and rippled around us there in our home on Malovlasevsky Pereulok. There were happy events and sad. There were problems and hopes. There were holidays and week days. And, as it does into every home, sooner or later, death found its way into ours.

A bright sunny early summer day in June. At Malovlasevsky there was unwonted activity. People, dressed in their best, crowded into the house. Men took off their hats as they entered and held them uneasily.

They walked into Piretra Alexandrovna's room and stood there with bowed heads for a moment before her. Piretra Alexandrovna lay in her bier, nearly covered with flowers. She had given up the ghost, dignified and brave, after a long painful struggle with her final illness. And she was resting in her small room for the last time before leaving that house of hers that had given her so much joy—and so much trouble. No longer would she have to worry about the firewood and the leaky roof and the over-expenditure of electricity. No longer would she clomp down the corridor at six-thirty in the morning awakening us with her stentorian and happy voice.

A little while later the funeral procession led out of the courtyard to the waiting autobus, provided by the Art Theater. The bus started up and chugged away across town to the Moscow Crematorium—and there in a dank and dismal funeral room above the crematorium furnace she was laid out.

An actor and friend from the Art Theater spoke briefly about this woman who had watched that great dramatic organization grow from its earliest days into worldwide fame. And then we filed past, all of us, including among us some of the leading actors and actresses of the Soviet Union, and each of us kissed her on her cold forehead. We stood and watched as the crematorium machinery was put into motion and the bier sank lower and lower, and finally out of sight.

Julie and I looked at each other. There were tears in the corners of our eyes. We had lost a good friend.

After the funeral I took Julie back home and returned to my office. When I myself got home in the early evening from work I found a real wake in progress. Yevgeny Vasilich sat on the front steps of the house, swaying, trying to put his arms about old Gero's neck. The giant police dog kept lifting up his paws and shoving him away gently but firmly, and kept turning his head away from the actor-administrator. Gero could not stand the odor of alcohol but Yevgeny Vasilich nevertheless continued his vain efforts to kiss the great animal who only occasionally warned him with a low growl.

Alexander Vasilich stomped through the corridor when I entered and threw his arms around my neck.

"Meester Wheetnee!" he exclaimed. "You must have a drink!" I disentangled myself and went into our room to look for Julie. She sat on the couch holding her head in her hands.

"Oh, Tomochka," she exclaimed, when I entered. "I'm so glad you've finally come. Tomochka, you know I think I've had too much to drink! Oh, Tomochka!"

And she put her head back in her hands. The wake continued till the last of us had collapsed and sunk into alcoholic sleep. My only regret is that I got there so late. I never did catch up. As for the propriety of thus marking the exit from the world of a beloved individual—I know this is how Piretra Alexandrovna would have wanted it.

A month to the very day after Piretra Alexandrovna died, old Gero, the dog, passed away. From canine broken heart, from ever-thinner oatmeal, from some other cause? Who knows?

Once Piretra Alexandrovna died, we started looking for a new

place to live. Ilena Alexeyevna, our new landlady, obviously wished
to work things out according to her own plans. It seemed likely she
would sooner or later want us to move. That we would move as
abruptly as we did, however, we could not have foreseen.

\*     \*     \*     \*     \*

It was a damp night in November. There had been an early freeze
that autumn and then a sudden thaw. The atmosphere was raw. The
drip-drip of melting ice on tin roofs was omnipresent. Julie and I had
been out for the evening to see one of our favorite plays, *The Living
Corpse* by Lev Tolstoi, at the Lenin Komsomol Theater. It was in
the sad yet mellow mood that it induced that we returned to our little
glass-fronted room on Malovlasevsky. As we walked up the garden
path to the house, attempting to avoid the puddles, it seemed to me
that there was a strange light from our window, brighter than usual.
I thought nothing of it—till we entered the house. Our doors had
been broken down. We rushed into the room. There greeted us a
scene of devastation. In the ceiling there gaped an immense black hole
about five feet wide. Shreds of plaster and lathe hung down from it
dripping with mud. All about the room there was splattered this black
Russian mud. Across the room there lay atop a heap of broken plaster
an enormous wooden beam which had fallen out of the ceiling. It
became apparent with a glance why our light had seemed brighter from
outside—the lampshade had been knocked off the bedside lamp and
the bulb which had somehow survived the maelstrom shone there
naked.
Alexander Vasilich rushed in, waving his arms and explaining
hysterically. A picture of confusion, he apologized for breaking down
our door and recounted the events of the evening. I listened intently,
attempting to find out what had happened. Finally, out of muddled
fragments, I pieced together a fantastic but true-to-Russian-life story.
The roof of the Luzhsky house leaked whenever there was a thaw.
This was not new. On such occasions, to minimize the damage to
beams and ceilings, Ilena Alexeyevna went up to the garret and put
beneath all the major leaks washtubs, pails, basins and kitchen pots
and pans in order to catch as much water as possible. It was never
possible to catch it all and he water which got away ran in between
the big beams and formed a mud paste with the dirt there, which the
turn-of-the-century builders had used for ceiling insulation. Ilena

Alexeyevna had followed the same procedure with this particular thaw which was an especially heavy one. While we were at the theater she had gone up to empty the full pans and put them back. The beam broke beneath her and she came right through our ceiling, falling to the floor some twelve or fifteen feet below. The ceilings were very high.

Fortunately the piano broke the fall for her. She had come to, locked inside our room and unable to move. She had called for help and finally Alexander Vasilich, who had run all over the house in search of her, had discovered that her cries were coming from inside our room. So he broke down the door. He found she was in a state of shock but had not suffered serious injuries and he had managed to get her into her own bed.

As Julie and I grasped the import of Alexander Vasilich's story we rushed in to see Ilena Alexeyevna. She lay pale and woebegone. She moved with great difficulty but assured us she would be up and around in a few days time.

"It's just as well you weren't home," she said to us.

I began to think about that remark for a moment or so. The picture I got in my imagination was vivid enough. Julie, sitting at the piano in a typical pose. I standing beside her, listening to her latest song. Suddenly down comes the ceiling. The beam cracks me across the head and Ilena Alexeyevna lands with her one-hundred and fifty chubby pounds on Julie. Mud pours over all of us. What a vision! It had almost happened, after all. I came out of the nightmare to stare into Julie's eyes. She, with her creative sensitivity, obviously pictured the situation to herself with even more horrible embellishments. We soberly bade Ilena Alexeyevna goodnight with wishes for her speedy recovery and returned to our devastated chamber.

"Well, it was a lovely home for us," I said.

"Was!" declared Julie.

# 10. *Tin Samovar Alley*

I have gotten a bit ahead of myself again. It was long before the ceiling fell on our little room, while Julie and I were still living in the Luzhsky home, that I got a glimpse of the Moscow music and entertainment world. It was fascinating—and frustrating. But to tell the story I shall have to introduce Julie's two lyric writers, David and Sasha.

"Just what made you decide to be a writer?"

I put this question to a pleasant young man with dark curly hair in our cozy, well-lit room. He was David Mikhailov, talented Moscow journalist, who had come to work with my wife on a song. Julie had been called out of the room to answer the phone.

"I never wanted to be anything but a writer," David said. "My father was a writer, and he encouraged me. So I just naturally took it up at an early age."

"What was your first published work?" I inquired.

David laughed. "That's an amusing story," he said, "I completed my first book—a novel—in 1928. I was exactly twenty and full of enthusiasm. I got on the train and took it to Moscow. I showed it to a publisher. He accused me of having got my father to write it for me."

"Well, you were young!" I commented.

"Oh, I proved that it was mine all right, and he accepted it. I was on top of the world. I was certain my career was made."

"Wasn't it?"

"Hardly! The book had come out and been distributed before

critics discovered serious 'ideological errors' in it. The entire edition
was recalled and destroyed."

"Did you rewrite it?"

"If I had the patience then that I have now, I would have. But I
made a decision. I was through writing novels. It was too uncertain."

"Where did you go from there?"

"After that it was journalism. I've never regretted it. I'm good at it
and I've never been unemployed."

David was not one to underestimate his ability. It was true he was
a skilled journalist. He had a sharp mind and a good sense of humor.
He was outstandingly articulate.

"During the war I was a war correspondent," he said. "We war
reporters shared the dangers of the front with the soldiers. But it was
a big opportunity. I went into magazine work after the war."

"Is your song writing a sideline?"

"Sometimes I earn more from it than from my magazine work. I
want to write an operetta next. Maybe Julie will do the music. She
has a wonderful talent for writing catchy tunes."

The door opened and Julie entered.

"So, you're talking about me when I'm out of the room. You might
have waited till I got back. I like such phrases!"

"No, we've been talking mostly about me," said David.

"How disappointing! In that case let's get to work," she said.

I resumed my role as observer. Julie would knock out a theme on
the piano. David would listen and come up with a phrase. Back and
forth it would go, like a tennis ball. Soon order began to take shape.
A song was coming to life. When it was finished Julie sang it over
several times. She was in a good mood. Afterward she and David
discussed future plans. David glanced at his watch and jumped up.

"I'm late!" he declared. "I promised to meet my wife at six."

"I'll bet it isn't your wife!" laughed Julie.

"Of course it is!"

His denial was so vehement it made me wonder whether Julie's
joke had not hit home. David had a way with women. He was short—
about five foot four. He was self-conscious about his shortness and
because of it slightly belligerent toward bigger men. He wasn't handsome in the classic sense. He had a gold tooth in his mouth which
gleamed now and then. It was a result, he later told me, of a fight in
his youth. His hands were small and his face large for his body. He
had a short neck which made it appear as if his head grew directly

from his torso. His light brown eyes carried an eternal sadness. To-gether with high, thin eyebrows, high forehead, curly hair, thin mouth, and a lively personality, they endowed him with appreciable sex appeal. David was well-dressed. It was his only extravagance. His suits were of good cloth and all hand tailored.

"Tomorrow I'm bringing Sasha Borisov," David said in parting.

This was the origin of a trio which worked smoothly for many months.

Sasha came with David the next day.

"You're the first American I've met!" Sasha said. He looked at me with curiosity and friendliness. I had come upon the three when they were laughing hilariously at a joke which David started and Sasha continued.

"If you can make the audience laugh as loudly at your humor as you are laughing yourselves, you'll have a hit!" I commented.

"You should hear what we've been writing," said Sasha who was smoking a pipe. Sasha was a handsome chap of average height and erect bearing. Curly dark hair combed back straight from his forehead and a thick mustache combined with the rest of him to give the im-pression of a pleasant, easy-going fellow—which he was.

The contrast between David, raised in Tiflis in Georgia, and Sasha, raised in that musical city, Odessa, was great. David was super-quick, Sasha was slow and deliberate. David was aggressive. Sasha was gentle, almost shy. David's creative work was often slick and glossy. Sasha's was quietly humorous—sometimes truly poetic. They com-plemented each other. Their different personalities were symbolized in clothes. David wore hard worsteds. Sasha wore tweeds.

"Are you going to listen to us working?" Sasha asked. It was a friendly question.

"After all," I replied, "this is the only room we have. Besides I enjoy watching geniuses at work."

"Don't blame us if you get bored," David cracked back. "Think how hard it is going to be on the audiences." We all laughed and then the three went back to work on their newest song.

\*       \*       \*       \*       \*

The series of events leading to the song-writing team of Julie, David and Sasha had started months before when Julie decided she wanted to go back to work full time as a composer.

"Why haven't you done it before?" I asked when she told me her feelings. I knew that, very young as she was, she had written wonderful songs, that several had become popular through performance in wartime by well-known singers. I always felt keenly that her future was as a composer.

Julie did quit the stage and began spending all her time writing songs. Since she was a poet she could write her own lyrics as well as the music. She was fast. She could turn out songs, lyrical and varied— sad sad Russian ballads and rolling Western blue blue blues—at the rate of one every day or so when her mood was right.

So Julie wrote songs. They were lovely. I sang and whistled them all day long. I couldn't get the tunes out of my head. And she kept writing more. She ran out of her own lyrics and called on her close friend, the talented poetess, Galina Romanova. They would loll about all day in our room on Malovlasevsky smoking packs and packs of cigarettes. Songs would be produced and cigarette smoke. There would be intermissions for gossip about friends from the art world. Galya would compose a satire on the foibles of so-and-so whom both knew. They would toss that one back and forth. Then someone would find a vodka bottle or a bottle of my whiskey—which Galya adored. More often, quite without alcoholic euphoria, the creative activity in that little room would move faster and faster till all was in a whirl of music, poetry and exhilaration. I would come home from my prosaic work counting Soviet oil wells into this heady atmosphere. The pieces they were writing were lovely. Things, I thought, were going well. But I returned one evening to find Julie in a state of dejection.

"What's the matter?" I asked sympathetically.

"Oh, I've had more trouble with *Glavrepertkom*. Today they refused visas for two songs."

She named the songs. They were among her best. They were love songs—completely non-political.

"What did they find wrong?" I asked.

"Too much Western influence," Julie replied. "There wasn't much I could answer. There *is* Western influence there. Anyway, it's not just *Glavrepertkom*. It's the whole thing of having to do my own business—sell my songs, get them documented and everything else. I'm a composer, not a businesswoman. I need help with this. It takes all my time and all my energy and kills my desire to work."

*Glavrepertkom* was the abbreviation for the full name, in Russian, of the Chief Repertoire Commission, organ of government censorship over the performing arts including music. It was charged with keeping "harmful" works from being performed. The definition of what might be "harmful" depended on the party line. An anti-Soviet ditty was "harmful" by definition at any time. But, at times, it was enough for a song to be a non-political love song, without a touch of propaganda, to be "harmful." The party wanted propaganda songs at such times and none others would be allowed. Julie had run into this sort of a block. However, there was rarely total rigidity in the policies of *Glavrepertkom* which could give its "visa"—permission for public performance—with any qualification desired. It could limit it to one artist, to one type of performance, to a specific time period, or anything else. And, as things were in actual practice, a leading performer could often secure a "visa" for a song which otherwise would have been refused. Here the question of the organization of the Soviet popular music business as a whole was closely related to that of artistic censorship. Popular songs could and did become popular in the USSR through mass communications outlets.

But there was another important outlet for popular songs in the USSR which made it possible for a song that had never been recorded, published or sung over the radio to become well-known. This was "the stage" or the "estrada"—what we would call "vaudeville"— except that the Soviet "estrada" is not the same as American "vaudeville," since it includes a broader range of materials, some of them classical, in its scope. And the vaudeville stage in Russia is still a very much alive and exceedingly popular medium, employing thousands of artists and attracting big audiences. It plays a key role in the popular music business.

This was Julie's native milieu in which she herself had worked. Via "the stage" her songs went everywhere. The key to success here was to sell to a popular performing artist a particular piece—or write one for him or her to order. The performer would secure the "visa" from *Glavrepertkom,* pay the composer a substantial fee for exclusive or semi-exclusive performing rights, and popularize the song all over the country so that later other artists would perform it, too.

"What you really need is an agent," I said to Julie, joking.

"What's an agent?" Julie asked. And then I had to explain.

"That's not a bad idea," she said thoughtfully. "But we don't have them here. I have an idea of my own, however. I'm thinking of getting a new lyricist."

"What's wrong with your own lyrics, or those of Galya?"

"Nothing—but through Galya I've heard of another lyricist. He's good and he's successful. He's clever and hard-working and not only at writing but also at selling. If he should write lyrics to my music he couldn't sell his lyrics without selling my music, could he? I'm inviting him over tomorrow. His name is David. Why don't you come from work early to meet him?"

So this was how David came into the picture. And David brought in Sasha.

*      *      *      *      *

As soon as Julie began to work with David and Sasha things started to move. Money began to roll in from the sale of performance rights and for royalties. Julie got numerous calls from artists who wanted her music. Much of this success was due to David's acumen and energy. He had a golden touch. He had techniques and ways of selling the performance rights to a song not once but several times. He had contacts with important artists and knew how to sell material to them. He had ways of getting at the *Glavrepertkom* to get "visas" for his songs.

Julie made a big contribution to the business side too. Once someone showed her how to do things she could do them. And she had some top contacts of her own. Julie, for instance, knew Leonid Utyosov, top band leader and star of several famous Soviet cinema musicals. Long before she had sold him her first song. David knew Utyosov also. And it was this contact that led to the biggest project of the trio.

"Guess what!" Julie exclaimed one day early in 1946. She could hardly wait. . . . David and Sasha had been engaged to do the next for Utyosov's new musical program scheduled in August for the Hermitage, Moscow's largest summer vaudeville stage. Julie was to write a group of songs for the program. In effect the trio was to do most of a musical.

This task could be appreciated only by one who felt the mood of Russian people. It was 1946. The war was over. People had just begun to recover from the numbness of wartime hardship and grief. People wanted to laugh, dance and sing. For this they looked to their entertainment idol, Utyosov, who more than any other artist had a feel for the popular mood. The new 1946 Utyosov show was, in the maestro's concept, to reach out to the hearts of Russians with gaiety and light-heartedness.

So the trio set to work with delight. This was the sort of thing they wanted to do. They slaved away every day in our room. As they worked I saw the program taking shape. It was gay, funny and light. I liked it. But there was one thing that bothered me.

"It's going to be a success!" declared David one day. "Rehearsals start in three weeks."

"It sounds wonderful," I told him. "But there's a question I'd like to ask. This program is non-political. It has, in text and music both, hardly any of what you call "political content." It's just entertainment. I'm sure that will go over well with the public but how about the critics? There's more and more talk nowadays in the press about the importance of ideology. And Stalin's February speech didn't sound as if the government is ready to give people a chance to relax and be gay—which is what you want. Have you thought about that?"

"What about Churchill's speech?" David retorted. Like many Russians he was terribly sensitive to any idea that it might be the USSR that was against peace and relaxation. I saw David was not to be drawn into a discussion and I shut up. The work went on as before.

Utyosov's show went into rehearsal in July. The trio transferred their work to the rehearsal hall. They awaited the opening August 25. Julie had three new songs in the show. It was a big thing.

\*     \*     \*     \*     \*

On August 11 David and his wife, Natasha, Sasha and his wife, Valya, and Julie and I, gathered in our room for an evening together. It was a warm summer night and we opened the window to let in the air from the garden. Julie had laid out a small banquet of hors d'oeuvres—*zakuski* as they were called in Russian—anchovies, shrimps, crab meat, red and black caviar, and a lot else. And of course there was vodka.

"Here's to Julie and Tom!" David proposed a toast. Every Russian party has to have a lot of toasts. They were always drunk—in respectable company—from minuscule glasses not much bigger than a thimble. And one did not have to drink every one to the bottom. Still, the effect of a series of toasts on the spirits of the company was always marked.

"Here's to Utyosov's program—and to us!" declared Sasha. That was drunk down gleefully.

"How is it you've forgotten the most important toast?" asked Julie.

"What's that?" David, Sasha and I chorused. The three girls looked at each other and laughed.

"To the women, of course!" exclaimed Valya. "What kind of gentlemen are you?" David was never to be caught at a loss and declared, "Of course I was saving that for the last and most important place."

Like so many of the evenings I spent with friends in Russia this one had about it an old-fashioned and courtly air. There was something turn-of-the-century in this spirit which is typical of gatherings of friends in the Russian intelligentsia. It can be a bit stuffy but it can also be very friendly.

After we had had coffee and brandy Julie sat down to play and sing some of the trio's latest songs. From there she went on to some old favorite Russian songs. I noticed David seemed to be anxious to say something and that Sasha kept looking at him.

"What are you up to?" I asked. David pulled a sheet of paper out of his pocket on which there were verses. He read them aloud to us. They were a parody on one of Julie's songs, cleverly written in a warm spirit of friendliness. Julie and I were overwhelmed. I raised my glass once again.

"Here's the last toast of the evening," I declaimed. "This time it's a toast to the trio of David, Sasha and Julie. May it—and this friendship of ours—last forever."

All of us were enveloped in that little moment in the aura of cordiality which flooded through the room and crossed the borders of nationality.

*        *        *        *        *

The day of the opening came at last. Everyone was on edge. At the last minute difficulties developed with *Glavrepertkom* which was not certain about the political acceptability of some of the material. Last minute changes were made. Utyosov brought his own prestige to bear and at last there was the "visa" for the program. But when the curtain went up in the big Hermitage Concert Hall on August 25, these difficulties were forgotten. The auditorium was packed. In a dark corner of one of the boxes sat Stalin's daughter, Svetlana, with her officer husband. Outside the hall hundreds of Utyosov fans clamored in vain efforts to get inside and ticket scalpers reaped rich profits. The audience included dozens of leading figures of Soviet society.

On stage was Utyosov's famous orchestra called "The State Jazz Orchestra of the Russian Republic," the word "jazz"—or as it came out in Russian "dzhaz"—meaning any kind of popular music in modern Western dance or jazz rhythm and style. The old maestro himself came out to the center amid applause.

He waved his hands and a familiar syncopated melody rolled out, one of his old favorite songs. It was his custom to begin this way and it got his audience in a receptive mood. Utyosov was not a young man. In comparison to his peak, fifteen years before, little was left of his voice. But he had that rare quality of being able to project his infectious personality beyond the footlights. He was a magical artist.

The audience concentrated on him, watching and listening intently. The men in his orchestra took delight in their performance, and their enthusiasm was infectious. There was a hush—and then a new song. Rich, ripe blue notes came from the orchestra. A trumpet climbed and quavered. Blue, blue music! He started to sing.

"Shtorm i vayter!"

It took me a moment—but, of course, the old American favorite, *Stormy Weather* now in a Russian version! I looked around me to watch the audience reaction. I saw interested, absorbed faces. It was new, but it was getting across. It came to an end. There was applause.

Utyosov stood for a minute, waiting. And then he gave the signal again. And again there came blue notes, but a different piece. Then I looked proudly at Julie next to me. This was her blues—a Russian blues—*The Moon and I*. A hot solo on the cornet ripped through the auditorium. The sax and the clarinet took their turns on the theme. The musicians were old hands at modern rhythms and blues. They loved them. People in the audience sat on the edge of their seats. Utyosov finally came through with the lyrics—a clever little verse about what the moon saw down below on a romantic evening, a love song without a touch of political content. The song ended. There was laughter and amusement in the audience and a strong wave of applause. "Bis!" shouted some loud voices, "Bis!"—in other words, "Again!"

The program went on. Another of Julie's songs came up, this one about a Soviet mail delivery girl in the Cossack country who kept observing the sufferings of a young man who was waiting continually for letters from his sweetheart—but never got any. His heart was broken until, of course, he fell in love with the mail girl herself. This was very Russian and high-spirited. It struck home. The applause for it was long-continued.

Her third number was received equally well. Julie was aglow. The whole program was received with enthusiasm. Utyosov came out repeatedly to give encores from his favorite old songs. He was finally forced to cut it off in the midst of an ovation. And his last number was that old Ray Noble piece *Good Night Sweetheart* in a Russian-language version.

That was all. It was over, that first night for which Julie and Sasha and David had waited so long. The three went backstage to congratulate Utyosov. I stayed outside listening to comments from the audience.

Everywhere I heard enthusiastic remarks: "Gay!" "How wonderful!" "The old man has still got it in him!"

But I heard another comment.

"No political content!"

"But who wants political content?"

"The Party."

But it was obvious the public approved. Everyone associated with the show went home happy that night. Utyosov was delighted. The next day I saw David. "Everyone's talking about it!" he exclaimed joyfully. "It could play to a full house for months." He looked at me with a warm and friendly expression.

"And you can be proud of Julie. She's a great success."

I didn't really need David to tell me this. But it was nice to hear it.

\*     \*     \*     \*     \*

A few days later Julie and I went off in high spirits for a month's vacation. And while we were away the cruel blow fell. A letter came from Julie's mother enclosing a review of the Utyosov program in one of the leading Moscow papers. Julie and I read it together:

"Can a talented artist count on the attention and gratitude of the audience if he appeals to . . . low tastes? Can a high degree of professional skill in performance make up for an emptiness in ideological and artistic content?" Julie and I looked at each other with sinking hearts. We read further:

"The new program of the Utyosov Jazz Orchestra . . . bears witness to the unprincipled and a-political attitude of its authors to the tasks of Soviet musical art."

By this time neither of us wanted to read further. The review then became a welter of clichés and hack phrases such as "decadent," "vulgar," "awkward," "stupid," "nonsense," and worse. The critic sadistically attacked the program. It was a vicious job. He wrote pompously: "What does the song *The Moon and I* say to the listener?"

The fact the audience had obviously enjoyed Julie's song was irrelevant. The only important thing was its lack of propaganda content. I put the clipping down—for I had had enough of it—but Julie finished it to the bitter end. She looked at me. She laughed sadly.

"Well, I guess the only career I have now is my career as your wife."

"But this is only one review."

"Oh, this reviewer is nothing. No one ever heard of him. The thing is that he wrote this on instructions by his editors who got their instructions from higher. He was told to try to kill the show. It won't work that way for people in Moscow wait till they hear of a review condemning something as 'unprincipled' and 'a-political' and rush off to buy more tickets as soon as they can. It's what they want."

I interjected: "Then why does it bother you?"

"It's the spirit behind the review that bothers me," she continued, "and I'm afraid it's the spirit of the times. There's an anti-Western, anti-American twist to it which I'm sure you noticed. That's not the reviewer's personal taste—that's the line. There's also the demand for 'political content' that he makes so much of. No, Tomochka, I conclude—not just on the basis of this review but on the basis of other things I've read and know about—that the powers that be don't want people merely to be entertained. They don't want people just to relax and enjoy life, to laugh and dance and sing, as people long so much to do. People instead must be driven to 'storm the heights'—there are to be more heroics and more sacrifice. I guess when David and Sasha and I were so absorbed in the new show we let ourselves forget in what times we are living."

"You mean you think this means an end to your work as a song writer?"

"Who knows?" Julie said. "Maybe not. I'll keep on trying. But I have the feeling it may. After all I write songs about love and I'm certainly not going to write songs about happy collective farms. If people aren't to be given the chance to relax and have a good time, then my work isn't needed."

"I hope it isn't that bad," I said. In my own heart I feared it was. I knew that in the Soviet Union politics rule art no matter what people want and the political future looked bleak.

"You don't mind my making a career of just being your wife, do you?" Julie asked. "I think I have worked enough for a while and that it's time I was just a parasite for a change."

She joked—but I knew she was an unhappy girl. And her presentiments were unfortunately all too true. This was the end of her career as a composer in the Soviet Union but this was a question of far more than bad reviews of one show.

One day, after we were back in Moscow many weeks later, I came home. Julie lay on the divan sobbing. I rushed to her and put my arms around her shoulder.

"What's happened?"

Gradually as she came to herself after a time I got the story.

"I went to see David today—I wanted to work on some more songs with him. But he acted terribly ill at ease—and then he told me. He said that things are very difficult. He's afraid to see you any more. He's also afraid to see me, because I'm your wife. What am I going to do? Everyone is going to be afraid to see me. How can I work if no one will have anything to do with me?"

And then she broke out sobbing again. And the worst of it was that there wasn't a thing I could say to comfort her. I knew that things were getting difficult—difficult indeed. And it looked as if they were going to get a lot worse before they got any better.

# 11.    *The Cut-Off*

As I look back now I can't think of that period in late 1946 and 1947, when Julie got cut off from her work as a composer, without a shudder. It was as if an icy hand had suddenly emerged from nowhere and begun touching things all around—turning everything it touched also to ice. The cold war was well named. We in Moscow felt its coming directly in our own personal lives.

At the same time the descent into the deep freeze did not take place all at once. At first one didn't realize what was happening.

On an evening in early September 1946 Julie and I sat with some interesting and attractive new friends from a Leningrad theater on the terrace of the Gorka Restaurant in Sochi, located on the peak of a knoll right in the center of this famous Caucasus resort. Earlier we had watched a dazzling sun sink behind the blue waters of the Black Sea, flooding us with a torrent of light as it descended. Below us the main street of the city was already in semi-darkness. In the restaurant's main room the dance orchestra tuned up, ready to start its nightly session lasting to early morning, playing dance tunes in rhythms more typical of Chicago than of the Soviet Union. I caught the eye of our ancient waiter who was scurrying around like mad, attempting to satisfy the voracious needs of Russian vacationers. He approached. "More vodka!" I commanded.

For a month Julie and I basked in the sun in Sochi. I was often thankful for that vacation spent lolling on the fine pebbles in front of the Riviera Hotel. It was a long time before we were to have another holiday in the sun. And evil times were creeping up.

In late 1946 we had heard rumors of a harvest failure. In Sochi the rumors were specific. There had been a disastrous drought, travelers reported. The harvest in many places had been completely lost. The nation was ill-prepared. In September came the government's move to meet the desperate situation. Two sets of prices existed—very low prewar prices charged for all foodstuffs and a few other items purchased on ration cards—and the very high prices charged in the unrationed market: in unrationed "commercial stores" operated by the state, and on the open collective farm markets for foodstuffs sold by the peasants themselves.

The Kremlin, in September 1946, moved to meet the food shortage by raising the official prices charged for rationed foodstuffs by nearly 300 per cent. Simultaneously prices charged in unrationed commercial stores were significantly cut. At the same time an order went out tightening up all rations and reducing sharply the rations of most citizens. The idea was to force consumers to tighten their belts, reduce their food consumption and get more of their food at commercial stores on an unrationed high price basis, thereby turning in tremendous tax-and-profit revenues to the state. Thus foodstuffs were to be conserved, state revenues to be greatly increased, and a foundation laid for a subsequent derationing. Thus the standard of living in all urban areas of the Soviet Union was sharply reduced in one fell stroke. It had already been very low. Things were tough.

In early October Julie and I flew back to a Moscow already covered under a blanket of snow. The faces of Russians on Moscow streets were somber and their lips tight. The war was over but the hoped-for easier life seemed further away than ever.

* * * * *

Most of October 1946 I spent in a sick bed. During my last days in Sochi I had come down with hepatitis. Julie and her mother put me to bed and nursed me under the direction of a Russian woman doctor. The three did a wonderful job. Gradually I began to feel more energy. In a little over three weeks' time they had me up and around. By the first of November I was back at work in the Embassy. It was just as well, for there was plenty to be done.

My first assignment was to write a comprehensive report on the effect of the price and ration changes of September on living standards. Only in small part had these measures been reported in published decrees. Their full scope could only be grasped by firsthand research among Russians—finding out directly how rations had been cut and supplies of rationed foodstuffs reduced through "unavailability" in ration stores. This was a report which could only be written in the USSR. It involved much work and the bringing together of a mass of varied information, much of it gleaned by going to stores and markets to collect prices, and onto the streets to talk to people.

Out of this work I came to understand how bad things were that winter of 1946–47. The relationship of the political clamp down steadily taking place, to the economic tightening of the belt became clear. The government showed some signs of nervousness. The salaries and allowances of all police personnel were greatly increased—in an obvious effort to insure their loyalty. In the cultural world, Communist Party Secretary Andrei Zhdanov set in motion purges, first among the writers, then among other creative artists, to keep these elements in line. Meanwhile relations of the Soviet Union and the United States grew worse.

My standard of living report went to the Embassy counselor who had replaced George Kennan earlier in the year. This was Elbridge Durbrow, active, energetic career diplomat who himself had conceived the report. From him it went to the new Ambassador, Walter Bedell Smith, for final approval before going to the Department.

*     *     *     *     *

Smith ran a very different Embassy from Harriman. He evicted the offices from his residence and kept it as an official residence. He came to the Embassy building on Mokhovaya Street every day and worked regular working hours there. He kept familiar with Embassy personnel and administrative problems which Harriman had left to Kennan. They absorbed a fair amount of his considerable energy. He held regular weekly staff meetings at which key Embassy officers reported on developments in their areas. Smith was hard-working and hard-bitten.

Ambassador Smith was a forceful representative. He had a good staff in his Embassy and he showed perception in promoting some able career officers. However, nothing—not intelligence, hard work or strength of character—can ever make up in the post of American

Ambassador to the Soviet Union for lack of previous first-hand experience in dealing with Russia, and knowledge of Soviet affairs like that possessed by such career diplomat ambassadors as Charles Bohlen, George Kennan and Llewelyn Thompson.

Under Smith, my own Economic Section in the Embassy was expanded. I had lost Ed Ames, however. He went home to America to get his Ph.D. at Harvard. I don't blame him for wanting to go—but I missed his adroit mind and his thorough work.

Time moved swiftly.

\*     \*     \*     \*     \*

January 26, 1947. My thirtieth birthday. I celebrated it a long way from home. Outside in the courtyard a cold wind howled, but inside our room there was a warm glow. In front of us was a festive table organized by Julie. There were even a few presents. With us were several Russian friends, wonderful people who, unlike most, refused to be frightened away from seeing us now and then in a quiet way. I have always deeply valued their friendship. We banished the gathering clouds on the political horizon that one night and enjoyed each other's company. It was good.

I am not a person who gets homesick yet there were thoughts of mother and father and of other dear ones far away. Would I ever see them again? I knew one thing—I was going to stick it out with Julie however long it might take and that might be very long. We could not know what might lie ahead.

\*     \*     \*     \*     \*

In early 1947 things stood still for several months in Soviet-American relations. A Council of Foreign Ministers session was to be held in Moscow in April. The Russians were anxious to put on a good show. They perhaps hoped for concessions from the West. They did not wish, at any rate for the time, to make things worse. The effect was a period of relative relaxation in the small but important things influencing the life of foreigners in Moscow.

In April 1947 the Council of Foreign Ministers assembled. Several hundred Western officials and journalists flooded into the Soviet capital. It was the greatest foreign invasion since long before World War II. They occupied all the hotel space—in the Hotel Moskva, the Metropole, the National, and elsewhere. They swarmed to the Bolshoi

Theater to watch Galina Ulanova and Olga Lepeshinskaya star in such ballets as *Swan Lake* and *Sleeping Beauty*. They wandered into stores looking for souvenirs. They poured out to see such famous places as the Tchaikovsky Museum in Klin and the Monastery at Zagorsk, both within easy drives of Moscow. They walked in Moscow and stared at the Russians as if they were men from Mars while the Russians stared back in the same spirit.

Meanwhile negotiations went on at a building on Leningrad Chaussée, once the famous pre-revolutionary Yar Restaurant, shortly to become the deluxe Sovietskaya Hotel. I sat one day in the meeting room. Secretary of State Marshall, Soviet Foreign Minister Molotov, French Foreign Minister Bidault, and British Foreign Secretary Ernest Bevin talked in turn. They talked and talked—and got no closer to each other's position. Rock-ribbed old Molotov, expert in immobility, sat unsmiling and listened. Then he restated his own position. The others, likewise unsmiling, restated their positions. And so it went. No negotiations, no compromises, and no settlements. That was the Council of Foreign Ministers.

It was a failure diplomatically but a howling success socially for us foreigners in Moscow. It was a breath of fresh air to have so many compatriots in town. They descended on us like flies, asking questions, requesting all kinds of assistance, glad to have a good time when one was offered. I had friends among the American diplomats and journalists and I saw much of them.

Came the end of the session toward the end of April and they all packed their bags and left, leaving us behind, forlorn and lonesome, the more so for our having had a bit of a fling.

\*     \*     \*     \*     \*

As soon as the Council of Foreign Ministers closed down things got worse fast. All along the line, in everything, we began to encounter difficulties. Foreign diplomats who wished to travel in the Soviet Union found they were refused tickets. It became more difficult to get servants from the Soviet agency handling this kind of request. Foreigners often waited months before an applicant was sent and often the applicant was completely unsuitable. Sometimes foreigners would be picked up by the Soviet militia and held for an hour or so. Often this was the result of carrying cameras or taking photographs. It was an annoyance. Matters which previously had been rather simple, such as getting passes to use the Lenin Library, became difficult problems. Foreigners were generally refused drivers' licenses. Soon, the only foreigners who held them were a handful like myself who had passed the examinations at a time when it was still possible for a foreigner to pass them. And so many other things happened, not all at once, of course, but gradually, steadily.

The real heart of the cut-off that took place over a year or two from mid-1947 on lay in the ban on fraternization between Soviet citizens and foreigners. This was enforced by arrests of Soviet citizens who maintained contacts with foreigners. There were even frequent arrests of individual citizens authorized or assigned to work for foreigners. Every large foreign embassy in Moscow lost one or more Soviet employees as a result of the clamp down. The atmosphere created was one of fear of foreigners.

\*    \*    \*    \*    \*

I suppose the series of events which brought home to me more than anything else the impact of the cold war cut-off was the "KR Case." I was personally involved in it—unwittingly.

In early 1946 in looking through the Soviet press I ran into several articles claiming that two Soviet scientists, a husband and wife, the man named Roskin and his spouse named Kluyeva, were working on a cancer cure which was said to have given promising results. I read the articles carefully. Allegedly there was a tropical disease which attacked cancer cells more ferociously than ordinary cells. The disease was generally fatal but the theory of Kluyeva and Roskin was that a vaccine made from the bacteria causing the disease might cure cancer. They supposedly had on this basis produced a substance called "KR" —from their own initials—which had brought about miraculous results in experiments with animals and even on humans.

I wrote up a report on "KR" for the Department. An American newsman in Moscow heard about my report and was allowed to peruse it. He sent home dispatches on "KR" and one or two others followed suit. Articles were published in the American press.

I sat in Ambassador Smith's office several weeks later. He had called me in for consultation.

"What are we going to do about these?" he asked.

He passed over a sheaf of letters. I looked them over. They were pitiful requests from cancer victims for information on "KR." Smith didn't wait for my answer. He told me, "I've reread your report—and it's good as far as it goes. But I feel in all fairness to these poor people that I ought to get as much information on this as I can. There may be nothing in it, but we ought to follow it up. Work out a plan and report back."

I did. I reported that the best approach was direct action. We should seek appointments directly with people who knew—Academician Abrikosov, President of the Academy of Medical Sciences, the Minister of Health, G. A. Miterev, and the scientists Kluyeva and Roskin. If we could get these interviews we could make a comprehensive report. Smith approved. I got on the phone.

A day later the Ambassador and I sat in the office of Academician Abrikosov. He received us cordially, as well he might, considering how much American medicine was sent the Soviet Union during the war. He talked frankly about "KR." We gathered he had many reservations. Finally the interview was over. I had translated and taken notes. I had a full notebook.

Minister of Health Miterev, an amiable and courteous gentleman, always appreciative of American medical assistance to the Soviet Union in wartime and afterwards, chatted with us the next day for half an hour. He too had reservations about "KR." He did not consider that it had been tried in conditions capable of giving conclusive results . . . Yes, the work was interesting, but . . . Would he make an appointment for us with the two scientists, the Ambassador asked? He picked up the phone and called. Yes, they would receive us the next day at three P.M. at their laboratory. He gave us the address. I left with another notebook full of information.

The next day the Ambassador and I entered an old building and looked at each other speculatively. The "KR" laboratory was next door to Soviet police headquarters at the Lyubanka. The two scientists received us. Silently there sat with them a grim-faced man who watched us like a hawk. He had been introduced as an assistant. To me he looked as if he had been sent over from that building next door. Nevertheless Kluyeva and Roskin, friendly types, were talkative about their work. They had not tried it on humans. That was an error. They could not consider they had standardized their product. There had been interesting results on experimental animals. Could they show us through their laboratory, we asked? They consulted each other with glances and then looked at the character with the grim face. They read the answer there. No, they were sorry they could not take us through. I went home with another full notebook.

I drafted a report. The findings were precise enough. There was not any such product as "KR" for use on human beings. The experiments had been inconclusive. There was no disposition on the part of the leading Soviet medical authorities to think they had a cancer cure. But they did feel there was an interesting line of investigation in the Kluyeva-Roskin work which deserved encouragement. The Ambassador could answer the letters from cancer victims and he would have to disappoint them. So, thought I, that was that. The matter was finished. And so, indeed, it was so far as I was concerned. But on the Soviet side the story hadn't even begun, and before it had run its course lots of heads fell.

I sensed something was in the wind when I read long afterward on February 26, 1947, that Minister of Health Miterev had been fired. The brief notice of his dismissal in *Pravda* carried an ominous notation. It said he had been dismissed for dereliction of duties. This boded ill for his future. Only later did I establish a connection between Miterev's dismissal and "KR." I was told by an acquaintance familiar with the medical world, that Miterev's "dereliction" of duties was his interview with Ambassador Smith and myself.

A short time after I heard this I picked up a rumor. There was a great scandal involving Kluyeva and Roskin. They had been dismissed from their posts. There were grave accusations. These accusations, I was told, centered on the fact they had received Ambassador Smith and me and made available information on "KR."

Something most unusual was said to have taken place. Kluyeva and Roskin had not been arrested at night, held incommunicado, tried in secret trial or none at all and then shipped out to exile in Siberia or executed as in the usual case of a political crime. They had been put on trial but not before a criminal court. They had appeared, I was told, before a panel of scientific colleagues and an audience of the same in "a court of honor." They had confessed to a number of sins—publicity-seeking, dishonesty, "lack of vigilance" towards American "agents," and "sycophancy before things Western." The "court of honor" had allegedly held Kluyeva and Roskin up to public derision among scientists. Their further fate was in question.

Not so dubious was the fate of another individual involved in this, Dr. V. V. Parin, Secretary of the Academy of Medical Science. It was said he had been arrested and sentenced to exile. His sin? He was said to have given samples of "KR" to American researchers so they could make a trial of it. Thus he had been convicted of giving away a "state secret."

As I discovered one fact after another indicating the ramifications the "KR" case was having, I asked myself why so much was made of it. The question concerned not a hydrogen bomb but a cancer cure, something without military significance. And it was, of course, not a cure at all. So why had the Soviet government decided to make an issue of this? Soon I began to get my answer. Things began to fall into a pattern.

A law was shortly promulgated forbidding Soviet officials to deal with foreigners except through the Ministry of Foreign Affairs. The list of materials and information constituting "state secrets" of the USSR was broadened in a special decree to include almost all scientific and economic information of any importance. The penalties for inadvertent or careless divulgence of such "state secrets" were made severe.

A campaign was launched demanding "vigilance" of Soviet citizens against Western, particularly American, "agents."

Simultaneously, the propaganda machine of the Soviet state was put to work condemning what was termed "sycophancy before things bourgeois or Western."

It was at this time that the campaign was launched to prove that every invention or discovery of any importance had been first made by Russians or Soviet citizens, from penicillin to the airplane.

The close connection of all these things with the "KR" case was demonstrated by two separate plays put on in Moscow in the late forties. Each represented a dramatic version of the "KR" case. Each was awarded a Stalin prize and each was made into a motion picture shown with great fanfare. One was called *Court of Honor* and was written by Boris Shtein. The other was called *Alien Shadow* and was written by the famous journalist-novelist-poet, Konstantin Simonov. The plot of each was similar. Here is how one of them ran:

A leading Soviet scientist is engaged in perfecting a new drug to kill all pain. Working with him are two associates—a young woman Party member who admires the talent of her chief but despises his "cosmopolitan" faith that science is international and knows no boundaries, and a middle-aged man, a sneaky type, frank in his contempt for things Soviet.

The American "imperialists" decide they must have the secret of the pain-killer and send to Russia to get it a leading American scientist accompanied by a professional intelligence officer disguised as a scientist. Profiting from naiveté and lack of vigilance of the Soviet scientist and his male assistant, they are about to get the secret when the vigilant woman assistant breaks the lab apparatus at the crucial point of demonstration of the process. Thus the American agents are foiled.

There follows a court of honor which tries the culprits. The leading scientist comes to understand the error of his ways, confesses his "lack of vigilance" and his "sycophancy before things Western" and asks forgiveness of his colleagues. His male associate is exposed as an American spy. The patriotic woman associate receives her appropriate reward in praise and advancement.

The payoff in this plot was the motive ascribed to the "American imperialists" in desiring to have the secret of the new pain-killing drug. They were said to need it so that they could send their troops into battle against the Russians without fear because they had been given doses of the drug ahead of time to deprive them of pain.

Thus it was in part through the medium of the "KR" case—and its publicized dramatic versions in theaters and in films—that "cosmopolitanism" in science and culture was declared to be a crime in the USSR. Soviet science and culture were declared to be superior to those of non-Communist countries. It was an error to consider science and culture to be international and a crime to put one's scientific discoveries or one's cultural contributions at the service of all peoples. One must keep them for the Soviet Union which would guard with the most jealous care and vigilant eye every accomplishment of Soviet citizens, be it a cancer cure or a nuclear weapon.

Why was it that the "KR" case was chosen as the pilot case for the launching of this whole campaign? This in a way typifies it. Involving as it did something with no possible military or state significance, and being in fact a secret which by definition could not be a secret since it didn't work in the first place, it points up the artificial nature of the entire campaign waged over it. The "KR" case was obviously picked by Soviet authorities because it happened to come along at a time when they wished to drive home to the Soviet intelligentsia the points they wanted to make. And the fact that it had no practical significance was from this point of view irrelevant.

And so it was that things closed in about us and all the other foreigners in Moscow in that year of 1947. And they closed in about Russians just as tightly.

\*    \*    \*    \*    \*

June 30, 1947. A fateful day. I finished packing my books in the office in the Embassy building I had occupied for more than two years. A chauffeur came to take them downstairs to my car. I went to the Chancery on the third floor and waited outside the Counselor's office till I was shown in. We chatted briefly.

"So you're really going to stay here as a newspaperman for the Associated Press?" he asked.

"That's right, Derby," I said.

"You won't change your mind?"

"No," I said with a smile. He already knew.

"All right, Tom. I wish you success in it. Be a good journalist and a fair journalist."

"Of course," I said.

He had already thanked me for my work for the Embassy. He had already told me that there were good jobs waiting for me in Washington. There wasn't anything more to say. We shook hands and I left. I walked out of the Embassy with a twinge of regret. I had spent interesting, productive years there. But I had much to look ahead to in my new work. When it had become known that I intended to leave the Embassy in June I had received several feelers including three from leading American higher educational institutions. Would I be interested in an appointment? I answered all in the negative. I had other plans. I had already decided that I wanted to stay on in Moscow as a foreign correspondent. My three reasons were good ones. I had much left to learn in Moscow as a student of Soviet affairs. I wanted to become a journalist and a writer. And finally I was determined to remain with Julie. I knew that the only way I could protect her was with my own person. The Russians had never molested the wife of a foreigner whose husband stayed with her so long as he was there with her. There was no question of her leaving. The most categorical turndown had been given by Stalin himself to requests that Russian wives of foreigners be allowed to leave to go with their husbands. She was stuck in Russia, no question of that—and I was going to stay with her.

I had applied for a job and the Associated Press had hired me. The fact I had had no previous journalistic experience was not a barrier. My subject was to be Russia—inside Russia—and this was something I knew something about. And so by the grace of God and the AP I became a foreign correspondent.

# 12.     *Foreign Correspondent*

July 1, 1947. I sat at my new desk in Room 225 on the second floor of the Hotel Metropole and looked out the window at the sunlit summer scene below.

Stretched out there was the broad and barren emptiness, as it was then, of Revolution Square. At its far corner was the Metro station nearest Red Square with hundreds of serious-faced Russians scurrying in and out. Across the way one hundred and twenty-five yards or so was a block of ancient plaster fronted dirty yellow buildings including the decrepit and aged Grand Hotel. Behind them, rising in its ugly bepillared majesty was the new and tall Moscow Hotel, built shortly before the war. Nearly behind me was the well-proportioned classical grandeur of the Bolshoi Theater façade.

This scene I studied that day with the foreknowledge that I might be seeing it often from then on. And in fact I was destined to stare at it daily for a good many years. Room 225 in the Metropole was the Moscow headquarters of the Associated Press.

It was a little before noon. Across, behind his own desk with typewriter beside him, sipping from a glass of carrot-colored tea brought a few minutes before by a superannuated waiter, and puffing on his daily cigar, was Eddy Gilmore, veteran newsman, an AP correspondent in Russia from 1941 on. Eddy had invited me to join him in the AP bureau. He got the Foreign Office to accredit me. And he undertook to teach me journalism.

All morning long, as I assisted Eddy in getting out telegrams to New

148

Julie

The Luzhsky police dog, Gero, before the front steps in the courtyard of house on Malovlasevsky.

The glassed-in sunporch of our room in the Luzhsky home on
Malovlasevsky—as seen from outside.

The Luzhsky home on Malovlasevsky—a view from the courtyard.

A Norwegian boy and a Russian girl with their playhouse in the courtyard of the Luzhsky home on Malovlasevsky.

Julie seated at her piano in the apartment on Sadovo-Samotech-naya Boulevard.

A Halloween party at the American Embassy dacha in Tarasovka.

The dining room of our apartment on Sadovo-Samotechnaya Boulevard.

Julie, Tom and Candy, the cocker spaniel, in the apartment on Sadovo-Samotechnaya Boulevard.

The
Saltykovka
dacha.

Julie poses in front of our Chevrolet in the yard of the Saltykovka dacha.

Tom in the yard of
the Saltykovka dacha.

The vegetable garden at the dacha: Julie seated on the grass.

The brick house which Col. Borisov built for himself at Saltykovka.

Four Russian neighbor
children at Saltykovka.

The winter landscape at Saltykovka—looking toward **Dachnaya St.**
on which the dacha was located.

York, he had assiduously been giving me advice: pointers on AP style, formulae for dealing with stories, how to write a good lead, the accepted abbreviations, and much else. Eddy was a good teacher.

Once the work was out of the way he sat back, relaxed, and lapsed into reminiscences of his earlier days—in Atlanta as a police reporter, in Washington as a reporter and feature writer, in England as a war correspondent during the days of the blitz, and then in Russia—in Kuibyshev and later in Moscow. Eddy had a vast fund of anecdotes and gossip about the great, the near-great, the not-great-at-all, particularly about other newsmen. And he had a way with a story. One wasn't always certain of its literal accuracy but it was always amusing and usually had a bit of an edge. Eddy looked out on the world with his own individual melange of humor, sentimentality and cynicism, and he had a keen nose for the foibles of his fellow humans. Eddy's reminiscences were as fixed a feature of my new life work as the scenery outside the Metropole, though a good deal more varied and interesting. Between Eddy's advice, my own knowledge of things Russian, and my already extensive writing experience, I slipped into the news business quickly. I took up immediately the routine that was to become second nature for several of my remaining years in Moscow.

Every day I arrived at the Metropole at around nine A.M. Sundays I worked by myself. On the other days I went through the morning papers with Eddy. Major stories we did immediately with a pair of gray-scarfed Russian female couriers or the chauffeur running our copy to the telegraph office. Less urgent stories we laid aside and did later, dividing them between us. The duration of this morning stint depended on the amount of the material. When there was little we might finish by eleven or earlier; when there was a lot we might still be at it at one P.M.

If we got through the work quickly Eddy and I might set out to pay visits to acquaintances in the American, British or other Embassies. This was a matter of maintaining contacts, and more particularly of picking up news stories. An important portion of our news originated with foreign diplomats. We cultivated them. They cultivated us as assiduously for news trading was a two-way street.

After lunch at home I returned to the office by myself to go through the flood of Soviet publications in the afternoon mail. This was my private preserve because I read and translated Russian fluently and easily. I could and did comb through several dozen newspapers and magazines daily in the course of two hours or so. And I always got some news stories.

In the afternoons I could also write up less urgent feature stories out of observations of the Moscow scene or from my research. This sort of thing I liked best. Such stories could often be sent by mail.

Late in the afternoon I returned home to Julie who was waiting to see me and hear the news of the day. I was eager to see her too. Often then I could relax, but never completely. The news business never ends. Stories break any time. They can come from any direction. When you're a foreign correspondent in a one or two man bureau, responsible for covering the news of an important country for a news agency, you can never rest comfortably. There is always that haunting sense of urgency, that feeling something may be happening. Sometimes there is. There is always that fear you will wake in the morning and tune in the BBC, only to hear the biggest story of the year from right out of your own bailiwick—reported by someone else. What a feeling that is! It happens. In the news business you can read your successes in the headlines. On occasion, alas, you can also read there your failures or, worst of all, your errors. Combined with this immediacy of result there is also that feeling of being on the inside. You learn about things almost before anyone else. And even though you report them to the world a few seconds later, there is in this possession of momentary inside knowledge an indescribable thrill.

One has in news work, particularly as a foreign correspondent in a remote place, a sense of urgency and importance for one's function in life which is often lacking in other work. I suppose this is one reason so many good, even great, men remain newsmen all their lives when they could easily win an easier, more luxurious livelihood by applying their energy and talent in other more lucrative fields. The news is a fickle but demanding mistress whom some find so eternally fascinating and satisfying that they cannot break away. I don't suppose that I shall ever get from anything the thrill I used to get in Moscow so often—of hearing the BBC announcer in faraway London repeat back to me in his lead bulletin the very words that came off my typewriter a few hours before.

The work of a foreign correspondent in Moscow has always had peculiarities in comparison with other capitals. During 1947 to 1953, when I was with the AP in Moscow, these peculiarities were especially marked. Perhaps the best starting point is to give a glimpse of the actual physical conditions of our work.

It was six A.M. in Moscow (ten P.M. EST in New York City) in a small room with a tremendously high thirty-foot ceiling in the Central Telegraph office on broad Gorky Street just a few hundred yards from the Kremlin. We correspondents did most of our work on important stories here and sometimes almost lived there. Several telephone booths with double-paned glass doors lined one wall. A large round table covered with an orange plastic top graced the center of the room. There was a bureaucratic look to the furnishings—chairs covered with leather and plastic fabrics and a small table or so. From the walls there glared down several poorly-painted portraits of Soviet leaders, including one of an unsmiling Molotov.

In a small anteroom outside this particular room was a long wooden counter and on it a frosted glass barrier punctured by three small swinging windows behind which sat and dozed two Russian women telegraph clerks and a telephone operator with her head down on the desk in front of her switchboard. She was sound asleep.

Several correspondents including myself were in various states. I paced the floor nervously and kept looking out the tall many-paned window into the Moscow night on Ogaryov Street outside. A colleague sat at his typewriter and pounded out a letter home. A third had his head on the desk catching a nap. This was a typical scene in the life of correspondents in Moscow.

Fifteen minutes later and the whole somnolent picture had sprung into life. Two cars had stopped outside the entrance and a pair of Russian chauffeurs had sauntered in with packets of mimeographed sheets bearing the label "TASS"—referring to the official Soviet government news agency. Here was a new Soviet note on the German question. This was what we were waiting for.

The journalists began to read the mimeographed sheets, starting usually at the end after a quick glance at the beginning. Two—and then a third—began hurriedly to type out fast one-sentence leads on "books," consisting of four half-sheets with carbons in between, already set up in ready typewriters. There was a rush to shove telegrams over the counter—and to order telephone lines to London.

The correspondents made four copies of each telegram including the original. One copy they kept and the other three they turned over to the clerks who registered serial numbers and time of receipt, and carted them off to a hidden back room, the room where the censors worked. The censors were never seen. Their work was anonymous but omnipresent. The correspondents could transmit nothing by telegraph, telephone or mail without the censor's prior approval. In dispatches consisting largely of quotations from official Soviet government statements, as with this, the censor might process copy fairly quickly—in from five to forty-five minutes. When copy was ready for transmission the telegraph clerks received signals from the censor and went to get the material. The clerk was returned two of the three copies of each "take" or separate telegram in a series handed in— each with deletions of censor marked. The third was kept in the censor's own file. Of two copies given back one was returned to the correspondent who could see for himself the censor's depredations. The other was used for telegraphic transmission if the correspondent selected that mode of transmission. If the correspondent chose, as he often did, to use the telephone, which was faster, he had to transmit his own story, dictating it, as censored, to his office in London or elsewhere. This was hard work. And foreign correspondents' international telephone calls could be made *only from this room* where the censor had facilities for monitoring.

Imprisoned in the stuffy phone booth I sat and waited for my connection with London. I needed to get more copy written, yet I feared to leave the booth lest I lose my line. I knew there were only two lines to London—sometimes only one—and three or four correspondents competing for them. If I lost my line I would be out in the cold dependent on slower cable transmission to New York. Finally I was told that my office was on the line. I prepared to dictate. Alas, the line was fading and my AP colleague in London protested he could not hear. I shouted. He still had trouble. Then things improved and I could proceed.

Halfway through—an hour later—he told me abruptly,

"We've begun to receive the text from the Soviet monitor."

I knew what this meant. In London the BBC monitoring service had picked up from Radio Moscow the text I was reporting and was pumping it by teletype into the AP London office. My job was finished. London had it all and didn't need any more from me.

I hung up. Outside I gathered my things—typewriter, papers and copy—and wearily, my voice a bit hoarse from shouting, made my way home to get a wink of sleep before going to the office—this day at ten-thirty instead of nine. By the time I got back into bed it was close to nine. Even an hour's sleep was precious. I never sneered at it.

\*     \*     \*     \*     \*

Of such scenes and problems my life consisted from 1947 to 1953. We American correspondents in Moscow, a small and hardy band, smaller as time went by till in the end there remained but five, had a tough lot. In return we had a few unusual compensations.

We had to wage continual struggle with poor communications— slow telegraphic service, poor telephone connections and too few, and physically inadequate facilities at the Central Telegraph office. The little room used by foreign correspondents—a room called suggestively "International Call Office"—was used by other non-diplomatic foreigners resident in Moscow for international telephone calls. There were days when we journalists were fighting an unequal battle with hordes of Mongolians, Hungarians, Poles, Rumanians and Bulgarians, students and officials, for the three or four phone booths there. They wanted to talk to their families and we wanted to report the news. One could hardly blame them but it was not easy for us.

We were forced continually to compete on stories with the Soviet radio. This was strange. Such was the functioning of Soviet bureaucracy that it was simpler for it to broadcast important announcements direct to the outside in such fashion as to guarantee that they would appear everywhere with a "London" dateline rather than to make the simple arrangements involved in releasing stories to the foreign correspondents in Moscow so as to insure the Moscow news would appear with a Moscow dateline and the enhanced prestige for the story resulting.

The Soviet government treated foreign correspondents in Moscow at that time with a cold neglect. There was no effort to exploit the opportunity our presence offered. The Kremlin, which spent millions on propaganda abroad, nevertheless had no public relations program to make use of foreign news facilities available in Moscow. In a way we could be thankful since one would have good reason to fear Russians bearing gifts—even news. But it also meant we could not expect the most elementary official cooperation and minimum advantage, so far as official statements were concerned, from being on the spot in Moscow. During the half-dozen years I was an AP correspondent in Moscow the Russians held no more than a dozen news conferences altogether—all trite performances consisting of nothing more, in several cases, than the handing out by the Foreign Office Press Department of mimeographed documents without opportunity to ask serious questions. We got no news releases from the government except as we found them in the morning paper like everyone else. For news agency correspondents, to be sure, there was some assistance from the Soviet official news agency, TASS, under terms of its contracts with foreign news agencies for exchange of TASS news for their respective news. This took the form of occasional special delivery by TASS of the text of important statements to the correspondents—as in this scene at the telegraph office which I just described—a few hours before they appeared in the papers—sometimes even before they were broadcast. But this useful channel was also sporadic. TASS might call us and might not. One never knew what to expect. Even when TASS did deliver, the censor might refuse to pass the copy for hours.

Our work as correspondents had also to be carried on in the face of restrictions on access to news and our movements. The restriction on access to news was carried to an extreme. Thus, for example, the Soviet Sports Committee was sending a Soviet soccer team to Sweden to meet a Swedish team. All the details were big news in Sweden where the AP had many client newspapers. But I could not telephone the Soviet Sports Committee and get from it such information as the date and time of departure of the Soviet team, the list of team members, their biographies, etc. This was forbidden. In January 1948, a special law was promulgated which said all foreign officials must deal with Soviet officials *only through the Ministry of Foreign Affairs*. The fact that I was not an American "official" but a private person was irrelevant. This was too fine a distinction for Russians. I had to direct my inquiries not to the Sports Committee but to the Soviet Ministry of Foreign Affairs which often did not answer.

If I desired an interview with a Soviet citizen—for instance, composer Dmitry Shostakovich—I could not call him on the phone and arrange it. I had to write a letter to the Press Department which sometimes did not reply, sometimes said no, and never arranged such an interview. If I wished to visit a factory, a school, a collective farm, a hospital, a research laboratory, a university, or any of a thousand enterprises about which I might like to write a news feature I could not arrange my visit myself. I had to write to the Press Department asking them to arrange a visit. Occasionally they did—very rarely. One day in response to requests for a visit to a factory they took us to a "bread factory"—a bakery.

Another irritating restriction consisted in limitations in our movements about the USSR. Within Moscow we were free to move about as we pleased, so long as we stayed out of forbidden compounds and buildings, all government offices with security guards and pass systems. The situation varied from time to time in the environs of Moscow. For a time we were free to go anywhere up to 60 miles outside the city, but in 1947 this was changed. Some of Moscow's suburbs were put on a forbidden list for foreigners. As time went on the forbidden list was expanded and areas we could formerly visit were put off bounds. For travel outside the Moscow area we journalists were in a difficult position—worse off than the diplomats. To leave Moscow and visit another city, such as Leningrad, I had to have permission of the Ministry of Foreign Affairs—and have this confirmed by the Section of Visas and Registrations for Foreigners (OVIR) of the Ministry of Internal Affairs (MVD—the police) by a special stamp in my Soviet Residence Permit. Such permission was hard to get except for Leningrad. It was made difficult for resident correspondents to make any trips. Journalists coming on short visits for some special event, such as international game or sports competition, might be permitted to go where they pleased during their stay—but not us resident journalists.

*     *     *     *     *

The most burdensome restriction on foreign journalists in Moscow was the censorship. The name for it was *Glavlit*—an abbreviation for a name meaning "The Chief Literary Administration." *Glavlit* was an invisible, powerful organization which spread its tentacles over all the USSR, reaching into every publishing house, printing establishment and newspaper; having the function of passing on every word printed or spoken over mass communication facilities. *Glavlit* insured there were not published works or articles hostile to the regime. *Glavlit* tried to insure that nothing got into print that the government did not want known. *Glavlit* hovered over our typewriters as we tried to report the news. *Glavlit* haunted our dreams. Our copy went to *Glavlit* and sometimes never came back. No explanations, no reasons given, just eventually the single word "killed" as its obit. Sometimes it was kept there for days or weeks, and then suddenly when one had forgotten it, it was returned—passed, maybe without a word deleted. Run-of-the-mill news stories, referring to the daily diet of Soviet press and political commentary on international affairs, were returned usually with fair dispatch with only here and there a penciled line through a word or sentence and now and then a missing "take" or telegram in the series making up one story.

There was a wide variety of material, particularly in stories the least bit beyond the mere reporting of Soviet official commentary, which fell victim to *Glavlit*'s long pencils. I remember a story written by a colleague in which he described a gawky young Russian boy as a "gangling youth." *Glavlit* cut the word "gangling." He and I puzzled a long time till we realized the censor—possibly some young lady from the Institute of Foreign Languages—thought this adjective "gangling" was related to the word "gang." As everyone knew, there could not be any juvenile delinquency in the Soviet Union—not for *Glavlit*.

*Glavlit* refused to pass any stories estimating Soviet production of such items as steel, oil, coal, power and the like. I might even spell it out as if for a small child:

"*Pravda* said today steel output this year was higher than prewar. Steel production in 1940, according to official published figures, was 18 million metric tons. Therefore, steel production this year was over 18 million metric tons."

Of this story the first sentence would have been passed by *Glavlit* and the second two sentences deleted from the dispatch. One could not, in *Glavlit*'s book, make any deductions, not in economics, at least not during the years 1947 to 1951.

Severity of censorship of correspondents' dispatches varied a little from time to time. Now and then things were eased or tightened. Some subjects or categories of material which previously were deleted would suddenly be permitted. In early 1951 I noted a slight relaxation of several of the most irritating practices of *Glavlit*.

Before then *Glavlit* consistently deleted from my dispatches, even much material published in the press, in Soviet newspapers, maga-

zines, and the like. *Glavlit* had been killing many news stories from
the fifteen or so provincial newspapers we received from the capitals
of the various Soviet republics, the Ukraine, Georgia, etc. Even material taken from central papers like *Pravda* or *Komsomel Pravda*
might occasionally get the knife. This was happening even though
everything published in the USSR already had *Glavlit*'s approval once
since otherwise it could not have been published. All the Soviet
publications in question could be subscribed to abroad and read there
by anyone who knew Russian. And, in fact, in part because of this
senseless practice of *Glavlit* there had sprung up a corps of Russian
experts in the Western press who read Soviet publications—and wrote
articles based on the same Soviet press articles whose contents *Glavlit*
prevented us from reporting. Carrying censorship to this length was,
of course, cutting off one's nose to spite one's face. Finally even the
Soviet government came to realize this. From early 1951 we received
more latitude in reporting materials found in the press, including the
provincial press.

*Glavlit* generally pursued a steadfast policy of remaining invisible—
a sensible policy under the circumstances. But not always.

One day I received a call. A highly pitched female voice addressed
me nervously in careful English, "Mr. Whitney? Is this Mr. Whitney?"

"Yes," I replied.

"Mr. Whitney, this is *Glavlit* speaking."

I nearly fell over. This was the first time I had heard from that
agency. It was like getting a telephone call from God Almighty. Suddenly the humor of it hit me. I had all I could do to stifle my laughter.

"This is *Glavlit* speaking!" I tried to picture the female who was
pronouncing these so solemn words and so carefully preserving her
anonymity.

It was a trifling matter. There was a word to which *Glavlit* took
exception. Would another word do? In fact it didn't matter and the
whole telegram didn't matter. And this was the occasion for me to get
a phone call from God Almighty! The only time, too.

Then there was the occasion on which I met God Almighty in
person, and even had a conversation with him.

His name was Mr. Omelchenko and he was Chief Censor. Some of
my colleagues knew him from wartime when censorship had been
less inaccessible. One year he came to the reception on the Anni-

versary of the October Revolution at the official reception house of the Minister of Foreign Affairs on Spiridonovka Street.

When the correspondents saw Omelchenko they surrounded him. We had so many beefs we could have started a cattle ranch and here was a chance to express one or two to the main source of our troubles. By the time I caught up with the conversation Omelchenko was telling my colleagues that if they would only stick to the "truth" they would encounter no difficulties from *Glavlit*.

I interjected: "But Mr. Omelchenko, today your office killed a story of mine which was a complete and accurate translation, without a word added or subtracted, of a story published in one of your own newspapers, *Komsomol Pravda*. Do you wish to tell me that *Komsomol Pravda* was printing untruths?"

Mr. Omelchenko replied curtly: "Mr. Whitney, it's time you understood we have our own *considerations.*"

He turned on his heel and left. The situation could not have been put more aptly. *Glavlit* had its own considerations. Omelchenko knew what these considerations were. The truth was that censorship had been set up and given authority over communications of foreign correspondents from Moscow. From that point anything published abroad with a "Moscow" dateline was *Glavlit's* responsibility. Omelchenko's personal skin and the skin of *Glavlit* depended on preventing anything appearing under that dateline which might seem questionable to any higher authority, including Stalin himself, a man of impatience and brutal habits. Whether censorship resulting from the instinct of self-preservation of Omelchenko and *Glavlit* served the interests of the USSR became almost irrelevant.

The fact, of course, was that Soviet censorship of foreign correspondents' stories always did serious harm to the self-interest of the Soviet government. The fact there was censorship indicated to outsiders there was much to be concealed. There was—but not so much in the more obvious ways as most people outside thought. The censorship system always resulted in a premium throughout the non-communist press on news least favorable to the USSR. Apparently in the end, the Kremlin finally realized this itself. At any rate in early 1961 the formal *Glavlit* censorship system I describe here was replaced with a less formal "responsibility" censorship under which a foreign correspondent can report whatever he pleases—and is expelled if Soviet authorities do not like it. How this will work remains to be seen. It could be even worse than the formal *Glavlit* censorship if administered that way. But not necessarily. By 1961, in any event, the censorship had been greatly eased in comparison with my times in Moscow.

The essential thing about censorship is that it is degrading to work under. By attempting to express oneself through a censorship one inevitably participates in it to some extent. This happened to us correspondents in Russia. We were forced not only to submit to censorship but in a certain degree to participate in it. Every telegram we submitted had at the bottom of it, written according to the rules established for us, the phrase "my corrections" with our signature over it. By writing this we were saying ahead of time that whatever the censor chose to delete was our "own" correction. Thus, similarly, we were always forced, while I was in Moscow, to re-type every sheet of any mail story on which the censor had made deletions, thus making those deletions our own "corrections." We had the right to see any story we had written *after* it came back from the censor, *before* it was sent out. We didn't have to send it. Often I made use of this right. With competitive stories it was out of the question. It was standard *Glavlit* practice to hold important stories till two or three A.M. when they would finally get a clearance. Any agency correspondent who insisted on seeing his copy before it was sent would find in such a case he had to get out of bed to go and see, and as a result would have his story arriving an hour or so later than stories of competitors.

*Glavlit,* it needs to be said, was in my experience honest. I never encountered a case in which the censor replaced a word of my own with a different one of his. *Glavlit,* in my experience, was careful that the censored copy returned the correspondent was identical with that actually sent. It even happened that *Glavlit* saved one or another of us from embarrassing errors. Of course, one could not depend on this. *Glavlit,* naturally, became the pet hate of every foreign correspondent in Moscow. The fact was, it was the Soviet government that was responsible for censorship over the dispatches of foreign correspondents.

\*        \*        \*        \*        \*

And in my bitterest moments over *Glavlit* I had to remember that whatever censorship I was encountering was a mild shadow of that which Soviet journalists and creative artists endured. They got it both ways—in formal censorship of *Glavlit, Glavrepertkom* or other similar institutions which made deletions in their work or refused them "visas," and in the severer form of criticism by the Party. They got it both for what they said they were not supposed to say, and what they did not say which they were supposed to say. With me, the only thing the Soviet censor could do was to cut things out of my work he did not like. He could not force me to say anything I didn't want to say. Soviet journalists could not protest—and I could. They could not get out from under the system, and if I lived long enough I would.

The atmosphere surrounding my work as an AP correspondent in Moscow from 1947 to 1953 consisted not only in restrictions imposed by the Soviet side. There was another factor, more subtle yet perceptible enough to me as I acquired experience in my new profession. This consisted in the relative receptivity for various kinds of news about the USSR in the West—particularly America. I watched the American press closely—kept tabs on what stories involving the USSR got what kind of play and saw how my own articles fared; which of my articles fared better and what kind worse. The increasing impression I got was that American editors, and to a much lesser extent editors in Western Europe and Britain, in selection of the news they printed about the USSR rather consistently showed bias in favor of news indicating the Russians were doing poorly and against news indicating they were scoring impressive achievements. Faced with a choice between two stories, one reporting a farm crisis in the USSR and the other reporting that the USSR was graduating more engineers than the United States, it was my impression that from among a typical group of American editors a large majority would choose the first and bypass the second. Both stories were sides of the same coin. But wishful thinking and hostility to a hostile regime had created an atmosphere in which the adversary's strong points were often overlooked. This in the long run could only lead to complacency and over-confidence, and to sad surprises. And it did. Yet despite all these surprises there is still even now much wishful thinking about the news from the USSR. As a result there is still complacency and over-confidence in America, and more sad surprises impending. While I was in Moscow, this sort of thing strongly influenced the entire business of reporting on the USSR. No one told me to angle a story, to play up Soviet failures and run down Soviet successes. My bosses in the AP leaned over backwards in honesty and objectivity and were ready to defend me in my work, as I learned from experience. But the fact remained that I always knew I could get better play with a story telling how the Russians claimed to have invented the first airplane thirty years before the Wright brothers flew theirs (which made the Russians appear to be absurd) than I could with one telling how the Soviet government was raising steel output several million tons a year which might make Americans think twice before laughing off the Soviet economy. Well, I did the best I could. I wrote both stories. Both were part of the picture of the big and complicated Soviet Union with all its contrasts. Both were legitimate stories. It was too bad both would not get equal play but there was nothing I could do. Just keep writing, I said to myself. Report everything you can that seems news-worthy. So I did.

Now if one adds up the Soviet limitations on news coverage, then throws in this other factor of Western wishful thinking, one has made a case for "Frustration" with a capital "F" for every American correspondent in Moscow, for stomach ulcers and ultimate nervous breakdown. This outcome should have been as predictable as in the cases of Pavlov's dogs, conditioned for reflexes violating fundamental instincts, who went crazy. There was frustration. From 1945 on it drove out one after another correspondent. They couldn't take it any longer and departed. Finally there were just five of us left. We were the free world's press in Moscow and we stuck with it: None of us had a nervous breakdown either. Why? I can only tell for myself. I know why I didn't crack up despite plenty of reasons. The reason I was able to keep myself together, to deal with the continual frustrations of reporting from Russia, to face all the other frustrations of Moscow life in the coldest point of the cold war, was because I had with me continually the sense of the importance of my job. There I was, working for the world's most important news agency, sitting on the most important news story of the world—the Soviet Union. I was one of the few who could really cover it. There were limitations, restrictions, problems. There was censorship in Russia and wishful thinking outside, but these things made the story that much more difficult, and that much more vital—to the world, to me, to everyone. There was in the West the most intense interest in what was going on in the Soviet Union and in its import for peace.

Anyway, in my case, just as I had come to the Soviet Union originally with a good knowledge of what one could not do, and a determination to focus instead on the things one could do, and do them, so I had entered the work of a foreign correspondent in Moscow.

I had known much about censorship and other restrictions on journalists. What I also knew was that there was still much, despite restrictions, a foreign correspondent could do in Russia. There one was in Moscow. All around one was life. There were theaters, stores, museums, soccer games, zoos, markets, circuses, and a thousand other things anyone could go to. One could walk in the park and see how Russians spent their Sunday. One could go to church and see how Russians worshipped. One could go for a walk in the woods and watch Russians hunt mushrooms. One could go to the Hippodrome and watch Russians bet on the horses. And one could report much about these things. One could write—and so long as every single word one wrote was fair and truthful—one could communicate, no matter how many words were deleted by *Glavlit* along the way, with each one that remained a small, infinitesimal fraction of the infinite truth about Russia to the outside world. And in the outside world there was such a longing for the truth about the Soviet Union! I could not, at any rate, imagine any task in the world more vital.

# 13.   *Headlines from Moscow 1947-50*

I used to sit at my typewriter hammering out a news story and sometimes I would pause a few seconds and recollect what a long way away I was from the academic career I had planned for myself when I set out in 1937 to study Russian history. And yet, was I really so far away from Russian history? Was not the news I was reporting for the next day's newspapers in the West also Russian history? Is not a foreign correspondent an historian of current events? Would I not in the end be able to write the Russian history of those years out of my own AP dispatches? So I fancied now and then. How right I was and how wrong!

Much of what I reported was history—but how much there was of the history under my nose that escaped my typewriter! During the last half-dozen years of Stalin's rule many important things were kept secret. Some have since become known but others remain hidden. Yet when I list the most important news stories which I helped cover from Moscow, the significant thing to me is not what is left out but what is included—the breadth of the spectrum they embrace of Soviet development and directions of that era.

\*   \*   \*   \*   \*

October 10, 1947. I picked up the papers in the AP office in the Metropole and looked them over. Spread across *Pravda* was the headline: "Meeting of Representatives of Several Communist Parties." I read with interest. Nine parties had been represented at a conference "somewhere in Poland"—seven parties of Communist bloc governments of Eastern Europe and also those of France and Italy. A long declaration followed. It consisted of a bitter assault on the Marshall Plan—the European Recovery Program. The nine parties formed a new international Communist organization called the Communist Information Bureau (Cominform) which would maintain a center and issue a regular newspaper. Here was a partial revival of the old Comintern, dissolved during the war. This was certainly a big story! I wrote till my fingers were stiff and got it off to New York as fast as possible. From New York I got my first congratulatory telegram from the AP back the next day. Everywhere my story had received banner play.

What did Cominform mean, I asked myself? Ever since early July, 1947, I had seen the Soviet campaign against the Marshall Plan rapidly building up. The Russians evidently were not going to spare any effort to campaign as vociferously as possible against European economic recovery. They would raise as much hell as they could with the Western European economy and the slogan of the era was to be "Down With American Imperialism!"

\*     \*     \*     \*     \*

In the first half of December, 1947, most Muscovites spent long hours worrying how to hedge against the coming Soviet currency reform. Everyone knew new money had been printed and was ready for distribution. How could one avoid the loss of value of one's old currency? That was the puzzle. One foreign ambassador invested in vodka—a wise investment. Some Russians took their savings out of the savings banks and bought whatever they could buy—and this usually proved to be a mistake. They would have fared better by leaving their money in the bank.

Finally on the evening of December 14th came the announcement. The reform was drastic: one new ruble for every ten old rubles. But savings held on bank books would be converted at much more favorable ratios. Total derationing was simultaneously declared. The next day I went around to the stores in Moscow watching Russians eagerly buying everything they could get with ten old rubles for each ruble of unrationed price value. I went to my office and wrote my articles. A few days later the whole thing was completed. The Soviet government had financed a large part of the cost of World War II by printing in war years vast quantities of currency and now, by this reform, the values of this money had been almost completely destroyed. In this single ruthless blow the Soviet government wiped out what amounted in effect to a large part of its war debt—and most of the savings of its citizens.

*     *     *     *     *

Early in February, 1948, there appeared in *Pravda* one of the most extraordinary documents of Russian political and artistic history. This was the decree of the Central Committee of the Party on music. Among those condemned were the three greatest modern Russian composers: Serge Prokofiev, Dmitry Shostakovich and Aram Khachaturian.

As I wrote this startling news story, I wondered. Why would the Soviet government go so far out of its way to scold, to degrade, its own best cultural advertisements? Was this not, indeed, folly? By what right had Andrei Zhdanov, a Communist politician, become an arbiter of music? Then I began to contemplate the action in the light of what had gone on before. Here was a decree on music. Before, there had been decrees on literature and other creative arts. The slogan under which all these decrees had paraded was *"socialist realism."* And what was "socialist realism"? It meant that art must be "socialist" —in other words Soviet propaganda—in subject matter, and "realist"—in other words, readily comprehensible and unambiguous in its mode of expression.

Under this definition a poster-like painting of a cheerful red-cheeked Soviet milkmaid, milking a contented cow on a Soviet collective farm, was healthy art while modern French impressionist painting was unhealthy, and the magnificent Soviet collection of such masters as Cézanne, Renoir, Manet, Degas, and even Communist Pablo Picasso himself, was at the time stored in cellars where it could not pollute Soviet taste. Under the dictum of "socialist realism" all abstract graphic art was forbidden.

But how did music fit into this? All instrumental music is, of course, an abstract form of artistic expression. There were Communist experts, indeed, who claimed they could determine whether a given symphony was "fascist" or "progressive"—but this was obviously a subjective judgment. So what could the Party do about music? The

Party found a way—and this was the most important aspect of the music decree. The stress must be put on music with words, on works with tangible political content such as oratorios and operas. These the Party could grasp. Soviet composers could still write instrumental works, at the price of putting a large portion of their creative genius at the service of the Party propaganda machine composing works glorifying the Soviet Union and Stalin.

*     *     *     *     *

The end of June, 1948, I opened *Pravda* and read that the Cominform had met again. I scanned quickly, expecting a new flood of invective about "American imperialism" and the Marshall Plan. But the target this time was instead one of the leading figures of the Communist world, the other Joseph—Iosip Broz Tito of Yugoslavia. What a blast!

That day I went to the Yugoslav Embassy in Moscow to talk to their officers. The Ambassador was not there. The Yugoslav diplomats were puzzled young men. Yes, they said, they had been informed of the dispute but had not expected it would be brought into the open. No, they said, the Soviet-Yugoslav alliance was still in effect. There would be no change in government-to-government relations, they felt, or so they said. The dispute was solely a Party dispute. I did not believe this, nor do I think they did. It was apparent from the start that the Soviet assault on Tito and the Yugoslav Communist Party and government would be extremely prolonged and bitter.

*     *     *     *     *

From July 31 to August 17, 1948, there was held in Moscow one of the strangest scientific meetings ever to take place. I covered the story day after day and had to try to make sense of it, first for myself, and then for my possible readers. I had no doubt it was one of the most important news stories I had reported. But to make this significance clear, particularly through censorship, was almost impossible.

It was a special session of the Soviet Academy of Agricultural Sciences. Presiding and dominating was Trofim D. Lysenko, regarded by some as a genius of plant breeding and of practical farming techniques; by others as a dangerous charlatan. Spare and fanatical, he wielded the whip over assembled Soviet biologists, agronomists and geneticists. In his hand was the approval of Stalin for his pet theory—

called by the name of Michurinism after a Soviet plant breeder named Ivan Michurin—of the possibility of inheritance of acquired characteristics. Discredited in the West, this theory held that organisms could pass on to their offspring directly, traits acquired during their lifetime.

Lysenko and his cohorts went so far as to ridicule the established scientific fact that chromosomes and genes are a mechanism of heredity. This very idea was denounced as capitalist and imperialist. Those who believed in it were called "lackeys of American imperialism." As dictator of biology Lysenko extorted abject confessions of error from some of the proudest and most famous Soviet scientists, it was indeed a dismal spectacle! And after the session was over "Michurinism" had become an integral part of the Soviet Communist Party line. Anyone failing to believe in it was treated somewhat like a heretic in the Middle Ages.

\*     \*     \*     \*     \*

It was a warm evening in late August, 1948. I sat in my little blue Ford, parked in front of the American Ambassador's residence, Spaso House, and watched the Soviet police guards in their car parked in front of his driveway, ready to follow the Ambassador whenever he drove out. I was parked there—and had been parked there already three hours—waiting to see whether the Ambassador was going anywhere that evening.

In that August, West Berlin was under Soviet blockade. Only the airlift got supplies through. In Moscow, meanwhile, high-level talks were taking place, quietly, but with the whole world watching. Ambassador Smith was the American representative. Since these were "secret" talks he had steadfastly refused to tell us correspondents ahead of time when he was going to the Kremlin for meetings with Stalin. This made for a serious reporting problem. The only way to meet it was to park in front of the Ambassador's door till he left and then tail him—behind his Soviet security escort.

I saw a figure come out on the Spaso House porch and eye me for a time. Then I heard a call, "Tom!"

It was the Ambassador. I got out of my car and went up to him where he stood, by now out on the lawn.

"Do you have to stay there all evening?" he asked, with irritation in his voice.

"It's my job, Mr. Ambassador," I replied. "I'd look pretty sad if you went to the Kremlin and I didn't know about it."

"All right, all right," he said. "But you'd better come in and get some dinner. Mrs. Smith and I are ready to eat—won't you join us?"

And so I did. The three of us hardly filled the tall and murky dining room. After the meal the Ambassador said to me, "Now go on home, Tom. I give you my word nothing will happen tonight."

I went home. Later the Ambassador agreed to let us know ahead of time whenever he went to the Kremlin. The Four-Power Kremlin talks of August and September, 1948, did not solve the Berlin problem. At one time Smith was hopeful there was understanding with Stalin on conditions for resumption of land traffic to West Berlin. But at the last minute this agreement fell through. In fact it took many months longer to lift the blockade—in early 1949.

\*       \*       \*       \*       \*

I stood one day in early August 1948 on Red Square. It was early afternoon and the sun shone out of a blue sky. Silence hung for a few moments over this center of Communist power. A funeral dirge wailed and into the square rolled an artillery carriage carrying the bier of Andrei Zhdanov, leading Secretary of the Party's Central Committee, second only to Stalin himself. Behind the coffin marched the members of the Politburo of which Zhdanov had been a member. When it came to a halt in the center of the square the Soviet leaders mounted Lenin's mausoleum for the funeral speech.

I looked around with interest. I wanted to observe what kind of people were attending this funeral. Zhdanov's career had been exclusively within the Party's own apparatus and he had been one of its leading personalities for years. During the immediate postwar years from 1945 to 1948 it was apparently Zhdanov who administered for Stalin the Party Secretariat and its machinery—the apparatus of the Central Committee. Zhdanov's funeral obviously had brought out in force the shadowy but powerful men who staffed these institutions.

Though it was midsummer it was chill. The several thousand mourners standing on Red Square listening to the drone of the funeral oration wore dark overcoats and suits, mostly navy blue or black. Almost all were men—hardly a woman in the crowd. They all had dark felt hats, doffed for the ceremony. I recognized hardly an individual whom I knew but I knew well the highly standardized physical type represented. Most were a little on the short side, running from about five feet three up to five feet eight or nine, rarely much more. They were squat and had large heads and grim faces. Their grimness was accentuated by the funeral atmosphere but they seemed to take to it naturally as if it were their habitual mien. They were typical Slavic faces, Russian, Ukrainian, Byelorussian, and there were among them seemingly few from among the other nationalities of the USSR. They looked a hard, tough, stolid, determined and uninspired lot.

This was the Party elite, out en masse to bury a man who had been one of them, one of their leaders— A formidable crew!

*     *     *     *     *

In late October 1948, "the Great Stalinist Plan for Remaking Nature" was proclaimed amidst fanfare. This plan, which would extend over a fifteen-year period would, it was claimed, abolish that ancient curse of Russia—drought. Through forestation of the Southern plains, and the planting of vast shelter belts of trees, it was said that the dread dry winds of Central Asia would be stopped from periodically invading Russia and drying out grain crops of the Volga region, the Ukraine, and even those of Central Russia. The forestation program would represent a vast effort, mostly based on free labor exacted from collective farms and school children. It was to be on a tremendous scale. The propaganda built around this program was intense. Painters were set to painting pictures of farmers planting trees. Dmitry Shostakovich was told he could redeem his past errors by writing an oratorio glorifying the great Stalinist tree-planting plan.

The forestation work went on year after year in the glare of constant press publicity until Stalin died in 1953. Then, as suddenly as it had been begun, the plan was dropped. Nothing was said. It was just dropped and that was all that was heard of it. Evidently a little realistic examination by the new post-Stalin government of what the plan was costing led to the conclusion that it was uneconomic. Forestation efforts did not cease but they were kept within reason.

Out of "The Great Stalinist Plan for Remaking Nature" came this phrase so characteristic of this time in the USSR, "remaking nature." Stalin was evidently possessed of what one can call a "King Canute psychosis." This was the time when, on Stalin's initiative, broad efforts were made to acclimate tropical and subtropical plants to Northern areas of the USSR: tea bushes to the frosts of the Karelian Isthmus, watermelons to the cool Moscow Region with its short summers, lemons to the Southern Ukraine, and the like. All this fitted in with Michurinist biology preached by Lysenko. Even the hot drought wind from Central Asia—the feared "suhkovei"—would submit to the will of Stalin! And all the vast power of the Soviet state would be used in order to prove it—no matter what the cost.

*    *    *    *    *

It was a Sunday morning in early January, 1949. Alone in the AP office I started going through the papers. There was little of interest until I got to *Komsomol Pravda,* organ of the Young Communist League. A headline hit me in the eye: "The airplane—a Russian invention." A full page spread was devoted to proving the first airplane was flown by a Russian inventor named Mozhaisky two decades before the Wright Brothers flew theirs at Kitty Hawk.

Here was a good article for the day. This would cause some belly laughs in the West. It was worth thorough coverage and that's what I gave it. The next day I got a warmly-phrased congratulatory telegram from the AP in New York. The story got excellent play. It was an AP exclusive.

This Soviet claim was only the latest and most absurd of a whole series made for Russian priority in important inventions and discoveries. From 1947 on these claims began to come in a flood. The list of "Russian inventions" grew and grew—the radio, the free balloon, penicillin, the steam engine, the railroad, the discovery of the Antarctic continent and so many other things. Some of the claims were fair enough. Russia had had a distinguished scientific history and nurtured many famous scientists and inventors who had made important discoveries. But in the late forties justified claims were not enough to satisfy the Soviet regime. Claim must be laid to the discovery of everything, even if the world was set to laughing and the data had to be forged, as with Mozhaisky's "airplane" which, as the Russians themselves confessed years later, had never in reality got off the ground.

This indeed was an era of xenophobia.

*    *    *    *    *

In March 1949 important changes in government positions were announced. A. I. Mikoyan resigned his post as Minister of Foreign

Trade and V. M. Molotov his as Minister of Foreign Affairs. At about the same time another important shift was announced: Nikolai A. Voznesensky, leading figure in the formulation of economic policy, was removed from his position as Chief of the State Planning Commission. In reporting these changes I tried to analyze what they meant. It immediately became apparent that neither Molotov nor Mikoyan was in serious trouble. They appeared in public with the rest of the leaders. Indications were that both retained important supervision authority within their respective fields. They remained members of the Politburo.

But I wondered about Voznesensky. Did he still retain authority? This seemed to be different. In the press there had been no indication of reasons for his removal from his post. There was no way of knowing whether he was still a member of the Politburo. So long as he was in the Politburo he was not in serious trouble. But if he had been booted out of this body he had clearly had it.

I waited for some further indications. Not until a month later, in early April, did I find the definitive answer I sought. It came in a dramatic but quiet way. At a meeting of the Young Communist League all the leaders of the Communist Party and Soviet government, present and absent, described and listed as such in the Soviet press, were given an ovation. I went through the list. Molotov's name was there. Mikoyan's also. But no Voznesensky. He was no longer a member of the Soviet leadership, clearly no longer in the Politburo.

This was an important story. But I knew from experience that if I reported that Voznesensky had been purged the censor would kill it.

I finally figured out how to attack the problem. I wrote a deadpan article about the Komsomol meeting and reported in exactly the same words as *Pravda* the ovation for the leaders and inserted, as *Pravda* had, the names of the leaders given in *Pravda* in quotation marks. This, I hoped, would get through the censor. It did. But would my editors in New York understand? I didn't think they necessarily would. They had too much else to think about. How could I put it across? Any telegram calling special attention to the list of names would be killed by censor. But I could simply ask the telegraph office to repeat the telegram containing the list of names—once, twice, three times, even more. By that time in the AP in New York someone would wonder why Whitney was sending the list of names over and over and start checking. I hoped so.

That is exactly the way it worked out. I repeated the list of names three times, and the AP foreign desk in New York realized I was trying to tell them something. That is how the AP—and I—got a scoop on the definitive news of Voznesensky's ouster from the Soviet leadership. The story was carried under a New York dateline, saying my dispatches indicated Voznesensky had been ousted from the leadership. The story got top play.

The Voznesensky case illustrates the "silent" purge technique of Stalin in the postwar period. Here was one of the half-dozen most important men in the Soviet Union. One day there was an announcement that he was dismissed from his main job. Then *nothing* more, not *one* word said about him in any Soviet publication for nearly five years. He disappeared. His portrait was no longer hung among those of the other leaders on holidays. His recent book, originally awarded a Stalin prize, was removed from public sale. So everyone knew he had been purged. But no one knew why.

What actually had happened to Voznesensky? Even now only part of the story is known. According to Nikita Khrushchev, who told that part of the story in his secret speech of February 25, 1956, attacking "the personality cult" of Stalin, Voznesensky was arrested on Stalin's orders, tried in the so-called "Leningrad Case," and shot for treason in 1950 or thereabouts along with a group of his prominent associates arrested around the same time. The "Leningrad Case" was one of the most important political happenings in the postwar Soviet Union yet not a word about it was published at the time in Russia nor for half a dozen years after. Very little of the matter is known still though more than a decade has passed. And this illustrates the fact that one could live in Moscow and know nothing of some of the most important happenings in the country.

\*       \*       \*       \*       \*

On January 28, 1949, *Pravda* carried an editorial entitled "Concerning an Anti-Patriotic Group of Theatrical Critics." It declared there had been discovered "an anti-patriotic group" of theatrical critics consisting of "followers of bourgeois estheticism" which had "penetrated" into the Soviet press. These, said the editorial, were critics infected with "homeless cosmopolitanism." They had set themselves the task of discrediting Soviet literature and art, attacking patriotic works, including particularly the works of Soviet dramatists who depicted the heroism of the "new Soviet man" on the stage. The editorial went on to name names of the critics.

Declared *Pravda:* "The top priority task of Party criticism is the ideological crushing of this anti-patriotic group of theatrical critics . . ."

The call to action, using words like "smash" and "crush" and stressing the existence of a "plot," was foreboding.

Clearly a purge of the arts was signaled. I asked myself, as I studied this news story and wrote my articles, what this was all about. Who were the "homeless cosmopolitans"? Soon the answer began to come. There were reports of meetings of writers and creative artists of all kinds. A chorus of condemnation of the "homeless cosmopolitans" arose. Everywhere—in music, social sciences, philosophy, graphic arts, literature, cinematography—"nests" were discovered of "homeless cosmopolitans" or "passportless beggars." With monotonous regularity in these attacks there appeared names of Jewish origin. In the Soviet humor magazine *Krokodil,* and elsewhere, cartoons appeared, some even by artists of Jewish origin, attacking "homeless cosmopolitans," depicting them with hooked noses. The attacks often gave not only the pseudonym or adopted name, often russified, of the person attacked, but also an original family name, often Jewish, in parenthesis, to make clear what was meant.

The censorship, of course, killed any attempt on the part of Moscow correspondents to report the anti-Semitic storm. But the story got out fast enough and enabled my editors in New York to point up the significance of the daily reports from Moscow. As the campaign continued rumors spread, reporting the arrest of prominent members of the Moscow Jewish community. The Yiddish language newspaper published in Moscow was closed. The Jewish (Yiddish) Theater in Moscow was shut down. The Jewish Anti-Fascist Committee, rumors said, was dissolved and most of its members arrested. Jewish writers were said to be disappearing—arrested. The Moscow Jewish population was said to be in terror.

Then suddenly, after several months, the public manifestations in the press of the drive against "homeless cosmopolitans" subsided. The attacks eased. "Cosmopolitanism" was still a curse word in the Soviet vocabulary but the drive had seemingly been called off.

But why, I pondered, had this campaign happened? The answer that suggested itself was frightening. The last of the Tsars, as I knew, had used anti-semitism as a deliberate device to distract acute popular discontent and unrest away from their government. Was this sordid aspect of Russian history now repeating itself?

*     *     *     *     *

On September 23, 1949, President Truman announced that an atomic blast had been detected in the USSR. On September 25 a Soviet statement followed which hemmed and hawed about "large blasts" in connection with construction work and went on to claim the USSR had had atomic weapons since 1947.

Though this big story originated in Washington and not in Moscow, it was not entirely due to lack of effort on my part. I did not have secret information about Soviet nuclear explosions. But I had found a clear indication in a Soviet publication before September 23 that a nuclear blast had taken place or was planned. It came in the unusual form of a poem in the literary magazine *Novy Mir,* which told at length in emotional verses about a big blast in the remote regions of the USSR and how now Russian children and their parents could sleep more easily because this new power was at Soviet disposal. I filed the story but the censor killed it.

The Soviet atom bomb came long ahead of the schedule predicted by American "experts" on this subject. Few Americans in or outside the government had any realization of the intensity and scale of the Soviet scientific-technological effort or of Soviet ability to concentrate material and human resources at decisive sectors—of which the nuclear weapons field was certainly one. Americans—the populace at large and even the most highly placed government officials as well—had been lulled by over-confidence in American technological superiority into the feeling that the American monopoly on nuclear weapons might continue for a long, long time. It was highly popular at this period to depict Russians as technological oafs who couldn't even make elevators work.

Not even the Soviet A-bombs nor later the H-bombs shocked Americans out of this dangerous state of mind. The beautiful dream that America would always be on top of the technological-scientific world went on and on—and even continues today despite the Sputniks, despite Yuri Gagarin, and everything else.

*     *     *     *     *

December 21, 1949. Stalin's seventieth birthday. A big day . . . A special celebration in the Bolshoi Theatre . . . Decorations up all over town, stressing the genius of J. V. Stalin . . . Encomiums, praise, fawning adoration, sycophancy and flattery . . . Thousands of birthday messages received, and lists of them reported in *Pravda* for months.

Perhaps the height of the adulation came in the statements of the Politburo members printed for the occasion in the press. And perhaps the most sycophantic of them was the article by Police Chief Lavrenty Beria:

"Comrade Stalin's name stands among the names of the greatest geniuses of mankind—Marx, Engels, Lenin. For the creation of scientific communism, mankind is indebted to Marx and Engels. For the victory of the proletarian revolution and the formation of the Soviet social and state system mankind is indebted to Lenin and his faithful pupil, Comrade Stalin. For the victory of socialism in the USSR and the rescue of its civilization from fascist barbarism, mankind is indebted to Comrade Stalin." And he also declared, "Comrade Stalin firmly holds the rudder of leadership in the struggle for the triumph of communism. Our leader's genius is combined with his simplicity and modesty, with an extraordinary personal charm, with implacability towards the enemies of communism, with sensitivity and paternal concern for individuals. He possesses extreme clarity of thought, calm greatness of character, scorn and intolerance of all boastfulness and outward effect."

\*     \*     \*     \*     \*

February 15, 1950. The Soviet-Chinese Pact of Alliance—a strange treaty after strange negotiations.

Mao Tze-Tung had come to Moscow weeks before. His visit was a contrast to the usual routine when foreign Communist leaders came to Moscow. They came, were feted, signed agreements, were given a reception and sent home all in a few days time. But not with Mao. He came in early December. And though he was badly needed in Peking where his regime had only just acquired control over all mainland China he stayed on and on. There could be only one explanation. There was no agreement on a treaty. And why not? That was a question on which the censorship would not let me speculate in print. But I could speculate to myself.

The agreements finally signed gave a part of the answer. Mao got little out of Stalin for his wait. There was a niggardly Soviet loan of three hundred million dollars in gold. The Russians kept special rights —for the time being—in Port Arthur. And there was a weasel-worded alliance. The whole course of Mao's visit showed that though Stalin and Mao might smile at each other in public neither was giving the other anything for nothing. There had been long and drawn-out haggling in the ancient tradition of the oriental bazaar between these two hard-bitten oriental bargainers. Stalin now had to deal with an *independent* Communist regime not under his control.

It seemed to me that as things developed there was going to be a new center of the world communist movement in Peking to match that in Moscow. Perhaps the Peking center might wait for years before vigorously expressing its independence but the independence was already a fact in 1950.

*    *    *    *    *

It was a Sunday afternoon late in June 1950. Summer had come at last to Moscow after a late, wet spring. The sun was out and there was a soft, gentle breeze.

Julie and I spent the day outside of town on a picnic with three young men from the American Embassy staff who had asked us to show them a bit of Russia beyond the city streets. We sat on the growing green grass on the shore of a large pond in a little suburban settlement and watched the Russians enjoying their day of rest and the sensations of brightness and warmth. Boys and girls flirted. Young ladies displayed their ample Slavic bosoms in swimming costumes consisting usually of ordinary panties and bras more or less translucent when wet. A young trooper of the MVD (police) forces in uniform played on his accordion and sang while a crowd gathered to listen. Across the way a picnic and celebration was under way with workers from a Moscow factory gathered about trucks from which they were served lunch and beer.

As we lunched we chatted with Russians next to us. As soon as they found we were Americans they began to question us eagerly about America. In a while we had assembled half a dozen or so and they were laughing with us and sampling our cigarettes. One of the boys from the Embassy decided to perform his favorite trick. He knotted his kerchief and put it on the ground in front of him, then stood up and took a water glass, filled it full of vodka and balanced it on his head. Slowly, as everyone watched, he started to descend, keeping the glass steady. Down, down, down he went. Finally he approached the ground, squatting. Out went one leg behind and he went down further. Out went the other leg. Finally he was spread out at length on his stomach on the grass and could grip the end of the kerchief in his teeth. The crowd of Russians, now increased to a couple of dozen, gasped. Slowly he rose. At one point it seemed as if his glass of vodka was going to fall but he balanced beneath it and saved it. Finally he stood completely straight and upright again. He took the kerchief from his mouth with one hand and the glass off his head with the other, tipped up the glass and drank it down. The Russians cheered and applauded. From all around others ran over to see what had happened. So the day passed—in play and horseplay, in small talk with Russians and among ourselves. It was wonderful. Then we went for a long walk and afterwards drove back into Moscow, so tired we could hardly talk.

I dropped the three young men at their residence on the Moscow River in the building known as "American House" on the Kropotkin Embankment. Then I decided to stop by at the office in the Metropole to see if there were messages from the AP. As I drove along I thought about this wonderful day we had spent among Russians, enjoying them and they enjoying us with friendliness and laughter. Things were getting better, I thought. The barren days were easing off, I felt.

In the office I found a telegram. I read: "North Korean troops invaded South Korea this morning in force. Want Moscow comment and reaction soonest. New York."

I stood for a moment in shocked surprise. How wrong I had been! Julie and I drove on to our apartment, quiet and sad.

*     *     *     *     *

Toward the end of the summer of 1950 the Soviet press announced, one after another, a series of gigantic construction projects, some already launched, others to be launched in the near future, and all to be completed in five or six years or so. Soon they were labeled "the Stalinist construction projects" and a great propaganda campaign was built on them. One of its themes was that while "American imperialists" massacred women and children in Korea the Soviet Union was engaged in peaceful construction for the betterment of the lives of millions.

Among the schemes embraced in the term "Stalinist construction projects" were the Volga-Don Canal, a big hydroelectric and reclamation project in the southern Ukraine at Khakhovka, a gigantic dam and hydroelectric station at Kuibyshev on the Volga, another, just as big, below Stalingrad, and a tremendous canal in Central Asia nearly seven hundred miles in length for irrigation and navigation. All these big projects except the Turkmenian Canal, have by now been built in their main parts. The Turkmenian Canal was abandoned as impractical as soon as Stalin died in 1953.

In 1950 as I reported these and other Soviet construction and development projects in my dispatches I thought what they meant. Take, for instance, the hydroelectric power dams at Kuibyshev and Stalingrad. Each was to be larger in hydroelectric capacity than the biggest American power dam—at Grand Coulee. When one thought of what the Grand Coulee and associated hydroelectric projects on the Columbia River had done for the Pacific Northwest in America, and realized that this kind of development, on an even bigger scale, was to take place in the lower Volga area of the USSR, one began to grasp what kind of economic might the Soviet Union had built for itself. This economic might was still in an early stage of its growth and was increasing year by year steadily at a rapid pace. There was, to be sure, an element of immaturity and childishness in the Soviet and Stalinist mania for the gigantic, the tremendous, the super-colossal type of project. But the heart of the matter was that the Soviet economy had become capable of creating, building, constructing, and doing super-colossal things.

# 14.    *Life in the Deep Freeze*

When I think of the time from 1947 to 1950 the feeling I have is one of desperate emptiness. I buried myself in my work to keep going and had with me all the time the consciousness Julie had no work because of me and must sit at home doing nothing, just waiting, and without anything to wait for. Of course in those years life had some wonderful moments too—but they failed to give the tone to things.

We lived not badly—for the Moscow of that time—by outward criteria. With the help of Julie's mother we managed to find and buy our way into a microscopic apartment to ourselves. We worked hard to make it livable and succeeded. We ate well with Julie's mother making all kinds of good things for us. In my car we could get about Moscow and outside it too a bit. We lived economically but we didn't have to pinch rubles or dollars, not too tightly anyway. We could get foodstuffs, clothes, books and many other things from abroad on a limited scale at least. Some of the best Russia had to offer was at our disposal too—and Russia had some things to offer those with the cash to pay.

So compared to Russians around us we had much and were glad to have it. But we didn't have freedom. Of course, we could go about Moscow without interference. We were not under house arrest. The sidewalks and stores which we could frequent were thronged with crowds. Live people were all around us. And this was, in a way, the tantalizing worst of it. For we were cut off from them. We felt like pariahs under some strange kind of invisible protective custody. One had the feeling that if one spoke to those Russians around us they

179

would suddenly run away. To have lived on a desert island and never to have seen anyone would have been easy by comparison, but to be there in a crowded capital with living human beings all around one and to be cut off from them, kept in isolation with a very few, so to speak, foreign cellmates—that was a real hell.

In those years, too, Julie and I experienced real hopelessness. To what could we look forward? Should we try to imagine and hope for the day, so improbable as it seemed then, when Stalin or someone else who followed him would permit Russian wives of foreigners to leave? How impossible that seemed in the political climate of those years! And even if it were to happen, could I imagine Julie, loyal like a lioness, leaving behind to the tender mercies of Communist totalitarianism her own mother, all alone with no one to turn to? Or could I do it myself, for that matter? For us there seemed no way out, no solution.

\*　　\*　　\*　　\*　　\*

In this situation it became important for us to keep busy, to be doing things together. Yet at the same time our possibilities for doing things were limited.

The Moscow theater, for instance, played a role in our existence. We became inveterate theater goers. We saw the latest propaganda and morality plays, the Russian classics, the non-Russian classics, everything. There was much to see. With two dozen or so permanent theaters in Moscow, all playing repertory, with new productions coming often, one could go to the Moscow theaters continually and not run out of things to see. And the marvels Russian acting and directing could perform, even within the limits of "socialist realism," were astonishing. Moscow theaters sometimes turned even propaganda potboilers into rather magical spectacles.

The Soviet theater told much about Soviet life, more than the newspapers, more than other forms of literature. And going as often to the theater as we did helped me increase my knowledge of contemporary Russia.

We went frequently to the Soviet cinema. This was nearly as interesting as the theater. Julie watched closely for all developments in the vaudeville and concert field and we saw everything worth seeing. This was a live and interesting art form and there also was much to be learned from it about current Soviet propaganda for the masses.

Julie and I, as time went on, came to lead an intense social life within the diplomatic colony. There were receptions, dinners, cocktail parties, day after day, year in and year out. The major problem was to avoid letting this sort of thing take up all one's time and energy—as some of the foreign diplomats, particularly the Americans, seemed to be doing. At such parties one saw the same pleasant people over and over. And after subtracting children and servants there were only perhaps one-hundred and fifty socially active adult individuals in the Western diplomatic colony in all. It was a small and ingrown society. The diplomats kept exchanging news and views with each other and with practically no one else. People in the diplomatic colony changed rapidly, particularly the Americans and British. By the time a diplomat had begun to learn in two or three years time something useful about the country and the language he was transferred out and replaced with someone who knew nothing of either. Some diplomats, particularly from smaller countries such as Sweden and Finland, were serious students of Soviet affairs. But they were exceptions. Of all the missions, the highest level of information and linguistic knowledge belonged to that of Israel. As time went on there came into increasing evidence a hard core of American diplomats in the Embassy well trained in Soviet studies.

Such, however, was the hostility then within the foreign colony toward everything Russian that it inhibited objective knowledge, the collection of objective information, and even active interest of diplomats in Moscow in the USSR. This was another aspect of the cold war.

As I watched my fellow foreigners there in the Moscow diplomatic colony I could not help noting how some—even including a few Americans—began to take their cue from the environment and take on decidedly Soviet characteristics—the worst ones. Living in this small group, one gradually began to feel that certain individuals were showing unusual, delving curiosity. One would hear later from friends about derogatory reports written for their Embassies by such amateur guardians of political integrity. It would have been amusing had not one time after time seen promising careers cut short during the period of McCarthyist frenzy by such "donosy," as the Russians would have called them—"reports."

Fortunately such individuals were in a very small minority. Not being in the government I could afford to observe their antics with some detachment.

Most American and other non-Communist foreigners whom we got to know in Moscow were, in fact, delightful people. Their warmth and hospitality was important to us. We made some close friends. There was among Americans and other Westerners in Moscow a permeating spirit of mutual helpfulness and democratic cordiality which I shall not forget. It made up for some other things. Yet, in another way the intensity of the Moscow diplomatic corps' social life only served to emphasize to Julie and me our loneliness and isolation. We were among our diplomat friends, but we were not of them.

There was much beside the theater, other public entertainment, and social life to keep us busy those years. Both of us read copiously. Julie in particular would devour two or three books a day. We constantly took excursions in and about Moscow, visiting all sorts of places— museums, churches, markets, stores. We spent a lot of time in stores, not so much as to buy as to see what was on sale and what Russians were buying. We had picnic and walking and swimming places outside the city which we used to visit.

\*    \*    \*    \*    \*

One day I came home from work at the Central Telegraph office. As I climbed the cold stairwell I heard music. I redoubled my pace up the stairs. Sure enough when I went into the apartment there was Julie playing away on the piano.

"Come on in!" she greeted me. "Listen to the new song I have just written."

I sat down on the divan. Julie began playing. It was a very blue blues with a plaintive, haunting appeal. Just the thing for a hot trumpet. Then she started singing,

"Tishina! Tishina!"—which is to say: "Quietness! Quietness!"

She had a set of complete lyrics, in Russian, done by herself.

"How do you like it?" she asked when she had finished.

"I love it!" I exclaimed. "Do you know how you could title it in English?"

"How?" she asked.

"The name has been used before by Duke Ellington but it's the only one that possibly fits it—*Solitude*. Try singing it." She sang it experimentally, "Solitude! Solitude!"

"You're right!" she exclaimed. "Why don't you help me do a set of English lyrics?" And so we did. When we finished she sang it over and was pleased with it.

"Just what exactly does 'solitude' mean?" she asked. I told her.

"I guess this will have to be our theme song," she said, only half laughing.

\*     \*     \*     \*     \*

I opened the door of the apartment one day and went in. As I entered the living room I saw Julie's mother get up quickly from her chair in the corner. She went to look out the window with her back to me. As she had turned away I had caught a glimpse of a kerchief in her hand.

"What's the matter?" I asked her. I went over to her. Indeed there were tears in her eyes. She said nothing and I put my arm over her shoulders. "Is it the same thing still?" I asked. "Are you crying about your son again?" I asked.

"I'm sorry!" she finally exclaimed with difficulty. "I know I shouldn't but I can't help it."

"You shouldn't cry about him," I told her. "He wouldn't want you to. You know that, don't you?"

So then, as often before, we sat down over glasses of tea and talked. I listened to her tell me once again how she couldn't forget for a moment the death of her only son, Julie's brother. She kept hoping against hope that he might somewhere, somehow, be alive, though she knew he wasn't. She couldn't forgive herself for not doing things which she felt might have changed it. It was more than six years since his death but time had not dulled the pain of it in the least.

Handsome and talented, Julie's brother, little more than a boy, had volunteered in the very first days of the war and had been sent straight to the front. His unit was surrounded by the Germans in their drive to Moscow in the fall of 1941 and he, like all the rest in his unit, was taken prisoner. But he escaped in a bold, desperate attempt and got into the forests of Western Russia where he found partisans and joined them. With them he fought his way back to the Russian lines. Missing for months, he had been mourned for dead by his family. But then he miraculously reappeared. Like so many other Russians who had escaped from German capture, he was, however, received with less than open arms by the authorities. Like many of the rest, he was subjected to merciless grilling for weeks. Why had he permitted himself to be taken prisoner? Did he not know this was treason, that he should have committed suicide? How had he escaped? Do you expect us to believe that story? Tell us the truth—it was the Germans who sent you back here to spy—but he stood up and finally he was believed and released and returned to the front, not with the medal he deserved, instead, with a black mark for having been taken prisoner. He was sent back as a member of a "penalty battalion" to go into the toughest sectors where death was virtually certain. And even that was not enough. In his unit his sadistic commanding officer hated him because he was intelligent, young, handsome, daring, bold and a success with the girls. And that officer sent him time after time into impossible places and refused to recall him, put him in the areas of hottest fire until in mid-1942 the inevitable happened and he was killed. And the family learned about it only from his friends, who sent word from the front —no official notification.

This was the tragedy which Julie's mother kept reliving day after day the rest of her life. It was always with her. Her son was dead but she could not accept it. Her being able to talk to me about it now and then was at least some help. And this was not the only thing we talked about. We became close over the years and there was much beside our mutual interest in Julie, though that was the heart of it, that we shared.

Julie's mother was not a sad or morose person, despite her obsession with her son's death. She had a delicate, well-developed sense of humor, and she used to tell me by the hour, laughing as she recounted them, of pranks Julie's brother played on Julie when they were children, of scenes from her own childhood, of incidents from her years studying abroad with her young husband, of happenings from their life together.

What would Julie and I have done without her? She looked over us with a vigilant eye, being sure we always had the right things to eat, doing all the many little and big things that we, two rather impractical young people, unconscious and neglectful of the chores of life, needed to have done for us. Day after day she walked from store to store and market to market, searching for things we would like, and then came home to cook them for us, any time of day or night when we were hungry. Both of us felt her constant attention and love and they helped sustain us.

*     *     *     *     *

One wintry day I looked up from the book I was reading toward the window. To my horror I saw a startling scene. Two snow-white cat's paws were desperately scratching for a grip on the down-sloping window sill and finding none. Slowly they slipped further and further down on the icy surface and then disappeared. I rushed toward the door, hollering to Julie as I went, "Charley's done it again. He's fallen from the window! Four stories!" I cleared the stairs, three and four steps at a time, down all three flights. But I had not been fast enough. Charley, our Siberian cat, with a bloody nose and a bedraggled, scared appearance, was up a small but quite big enough tree in the back yard. He was frightened and miaowing like mad—quite alive.

Fifteen minutes later with arms scratched up by a frightened Charley, my trousers torn from shinnying up the tree, limping from a sprained ankle received in dropping down out of the tree with clawing Charley in my arms, I climbed up the stairs with Julie behind me. It was not the first time. To be exact it was the fourth time Charley had fallen from the fourth floor down to the ground. It looked as if he would never learn. This was too bad. Charley was a principal feature in our life. We didn't want to lose him.

But he insisted on doing the most impossible things. He walked nonchalantly along the thin iron balcony rail and from there leaped four feet to the kitchen window ledge and from there leaped up onto the kitchen "fortochka"—the small ventilation pane in the window about three feet up which was often open. And then would sit, right there in the open "fortochka," with tail in or out depending on which end of himself he wished to air. He loved to go out through the "fortochka" and drop down to the sloping window ledge below and sit there for hours and then come back in by jumping back up. Once in a while he would miss in these acrobatics, as he had that day, and fall to the ground below. After such a fall he would quiet down for a few days but soon he would be back again at his dangerous stunts.

Charley, by sitting on our window ledge in the front of the building above the street where I had my car parked, performed an important function. He guarded my car against marauding young people. He really did. It was remarkable how it happened. It was our janitor's son who told everyone about it. One of the boys in the neighborhood once started fooling around my car.

"You better not do that!" said the janitor's son.

"Why not?" said the boy, continuing to unscrew something or other.

"Because that cat up there guards this car!" And with that the janitor's son pointed up at Charley, a magnificent orange and white tiger-like animal sitting out on the window ledge and watching intently. The janitor's son continued, "When anyone touches the car the cat jumps in through the 'fortochka' and tells his master. Then his master comes down and there's hell to pay."

"Nonsense," declared the small boy and continued fooling around my car. Just then Charley got up and jumped through the "fortochka." The meddlesome lad took one look, got an expression of horror on his face, and ran away as fast as he could scurry amidst the laughter of all the other children. They all believed the story. They *knew* that Charley, the Siberian cat, guarded my car for me, and that while he was watching, day or night, which he often was, there would be trouble if they so much as *touched* the "Americansky" car. From then on I could rest comfortably in my apartment, knowing that whether *he* knew it or not, Charley was in fact protecting my car. Legends are often as useful as truth. A most remarkable animal, that Charley!

\*     \*     \*     \*     \*

I sat on the step of the carved wood balcony of the private banquet room of the famous Aragvi Restaurant—named for a river of Stalin's native Georgia. I looked below. Fifteen feet down, stretching for seventy-five feet, was the main, thirty-five foot high restaurant serving room with several score customers, mostly men, at tables busily chewing at their "shashlyks"—shish kebobs—drinking copious glassfuls of red Georgian wines. The walls of the room, whose far end was rounded in a semicircle, were tiled in simple white except where in built-in panels hung ten feet high, colorful murals of dark and handsome Georgian knights in crusaders' armor fighting desperately with fierce tigers or carrying off on horseback beautiful brunette Georgian damsels. Directly across, in a balcony at the top of the room, just beneath the ceiling, sat the Aragvi orchestra, a quintet, busily strumming away at Georgian popular songs with strange little instruments, one of which looked like a grapefruit on the end of a stick, emitting the exotic sounds of typically middle-eastern music but in a rhythm showing the appreciation of the musicians for Western popular music. Behind them loomed a mural of a snowy mountain peak—the famed Kazbek of the Caucasus, a symbol of sunny Georgia like the Aragvi River itself. One of the swarthy, mustached orchestra members smiled at me. He knew me as a regular customer who sometimes requested favorite pieces. Behind me from the big, dark oak-paneled banquet room Julie called, "Come on in. The main course is here."

And so I went to sit down with a half-dozen other Americans, before a beautiful cut, oozing with red juice, of "Karsky shashlyk"— "shish kebob in the style of Kars"—the equal of which one can find nowhere, not even in Georgia.

The Aragvi Restaurant in Moscow stood out like a lighthouse of culinary art and gaiety in a city which has never yet been in competition with such cities as New York, Paris, or Rome in either of these departments.

\*     \*     \*     \*     \*

One early spring day when everything was thawing I returned to the apartment building in which we were living, a building erected not long before World War II. At the front door to our entrance I saw our Tatar janitor, Khariton, ruefully contemplating a huge hunk of cement which weighed, I suppose, one hundred fifty pounds, lying across the walk in front of the door.

"Where did that come from?" I asked. Khariton without a word pointed straight up and I looked where he was pointing. Up ten floors near the top of the building, there had been two large cement doodads on the front of the building. Now there was only one left. I looked where the chunk had struck, looked at the door, pictured Julie or her mother or myself or some other tenant stepping out just as that decoration came down!

Khariton watched me out of the corner of his eye.

"No one hurt?" I asked.

He shook his head. "It's thaw time," he said curtly as if that explained everything. And in Moscow it did. Thaw time in Russia was a time to keep one's eye peeled upward. What might be coming down —chunks of buildings, ice cakes, "fortochka" panes held in place all winter only by ice and ripe for falling, whole balconies—one never knew.

\*     \*     \*     \*     \*

It was a warm and quiet night at the very end of April. Julie and Harrison Salisbury of the *New York Times* and I stood within the walled enclosure of the Monastery of the Trinity of St. Sergius at

Zagorsk, thirty-five miles or so to the northeast of Moscow, and watched entranced. Thousands of men and women stood in the nearly breathless dark with flickering, glimmering candles in their hands, waiting for midnight.

This was Easter eve. Easter eve in Russia is a holiday celebrated almost universally throughout the land. On that eve every church in the country is crowded with throngs of believers and with curious people. On that eve women carry their Easter cakes to the priests to have them blessed so that they may be eaten at the Easter feast after midnight.

As the church bells chimed at midnight we stood, crushed in the Russian crowd inside the Assumption Cathedral. From outside we could hear the priestly procession coming nearer through the crowd. Then they were at the door.

"Christ has risen!" rose the chant.

"He has really risen," came the answer.

The procession, adorned in the richest golden robes, overhung with a cloud of incense from the swinging censers carried by acolytes at the rear, entered the cathedral and made its way slowly to the richly adorned altar screen—the ikonostas, covered with priceless, ancient ikons or holy pictures—which concealed the inner altar. A chorus of glorious music rose from the choir hidden in the upper reaches of the high church. A while later we left quietly.

"Look!" said Harrison as we stepped out of the cathedral into the night. There, where he pointed, red stars gleamed with ruby light atop the buildings of the Spiritual Seminary of the Russian Orthodox Church. They were the red stars of the Godless Communist Party of the Soviet Union, hung there to celebrate the international workers' holiday of May 1.

And around us there still flickered and gleamed in the night thousands of little candles of the faithful there in the monastery courtyard. Where else but in Russia could one see that!

Julie and I wandered about Moscow's most interesting market, absorbed. It was not the first time we had been there. We went back again and again, we found it so fascinating. This was the "Ptichyi Rynok"—"The Bird Market," once described by Chekhov. It was the Moscow market at which birds, dogs, cats, and fish were sold as pets. We stopped and looked at a gray bearded old peasant showing off a gray squirrel, complete with squirrel cage. The little animal was running, as if for his life, making his circular treadmill turn faster and faster.

A police dog puppy cocked his head at me and started to whine. I quickly looked the other way. I knew if I once reached out to pet him I was a goner—and would soon be his owner. I pulled Julie in the other direction too.

Along came a chap dressed in quilted cotton jacket with a tilt to his cap and a grin on his face. Under his arm he had a big cage full of little birds. "Four rubles each to let them loose," he hollered, chanting his wares. "Six rubles each if you keep them."

A customer came and proffered him eight rubles. As soon as he got the two birds in his hand he let them go and they fluttered over the market, delighted to be free. This supposedly brought good luck. Soon I let a pair go myself. I also wanted good luck—for us. One of them dipped down toward me as he tried his wings—as if to thank me. On the way home in the car Julie was very quiet.

"What are you thinking about?" I asked.

"I was thinking of those two birds . . ." she began.

"Never mind," I said. "I understand." Neither of us said anything else the rest of the way to our apartment.

\*     \*     \*     \*     \*

Four of us sat at a table in the dark and dingy but cozy upstairs tea room in the small village of Krasnaya Pakhra which cuddled in a valley in the landscape a score of miles to the south of Moscow. It was only early April and the tea room was unheated. We kept our coats on and shivered. We sipped eagerly at the hot, orange colored tea in glasses with glass holders which the waitress brought us. We munched at pieces of black bread and big chunks of fat and tasty Russian salami. At the next table a Russian air force officer, off duty, was solving his problem of keeping warm in more direct fashion. The waitress put in front of him "sto gram"—"one hundred grams of vodka" or, in other words, about three ounces. Up went his glass and down went the vodka. He followed it up with black bread and motioned imperiously to the waitress who came on the run. "Yeshche sto gram!" he ordered—"another hundred grams"—and she went to get it. Another waitress stood behind her counter where there were displayed miscellaneous candies, chocolates, cigarettes and sausages. She was dressed in an apron which was supposed to be white but by this time was a greasy gray. And she laughed. The air force officer looked over and started to engage us in conversation, the sort of alcoholic conversation one can get into so easily in Russia, which usually ends up with the Russian sitting at one's table with his arm over one's shoulder and talking to one with his mouth about two inches from one's face. So we parried politely, and he turned, disgruntled, back to his vodka and black bread. And we sat there drinking our tea, and drinking in also the Russian conversation rising like steam from tables all around us, where men sat and exchanged the time of day. I never could cease to marvel at just how far one could get away from the "diplomatic life" in just a few miles from Moscow.

*    *    *    *    *

I stood atop St. Isaac's Cathedral in Leningrad and surveyed the former capital from its highest lookout point, to which one climbed hundreds of steps up a narrow, perilous circular staircase. Here was a real capital! The breadth of the cold and gray Neva River rolling outward through its broad banks to the Gulf of Finland was a fitting centerpiece. On either side lay masterpieces of eighteenth century architecture planned to harmonize into a single, overwhelming, grand impression of majesty. And then over in the distance, on the other side of the river, lay the grandest sight of all—the Fortress of St. Peter and Paul with its tallest spire reaching far up into the heavens. It was worth coming a long way to see this city—and climbing high up to see this sight!

*    *    *    *    *

The road sign said "Bylovo" and pointed to the right off the black-top highway down a dirt road through the center of a wide, green and grassy meadow through birch and pine woods. We parked our car off the highway and went into the woods. Each of us had a basket under arm and stared intently at the ground. Julie and I were pursuing the ancient, most widespread Russian sport of all—the hunting of mushrooms. Each of us knew which mushrooms were good and which bad. We were hoping to find large, fresh "belye"—in other words, white—or "podberyozoviki," meaning, "the ones from under the birch trees." We knew there were many there. We had been there often and this was our favorite mushroom forest. After a day out in that woods we would return with ten or fifteen pounds of good mushrooms. Julie and her mother would pick them over. They would throw out the ones that weren't fresh and trim those left. Then they put them in the frying pan. In a short time a wonderful smell of frying mushrooms would rise. I would sit there, ravenously waiting. Finally dinner would be served—mushrooms and potatoes or perhaps rice—nothing more delicious in the world.

But the most delightful thing of all was walking through the birch and pine woods near "Bylovo" and feeling the touch of the Russian countryside.

*   *   *   *   *

"Don't be discouraged, Tom," said my friend, the American diplomat.

We were at the Fourth of July party at Spaso House given by Ambassador Alan G. Kirk and his wife. The party was continuing full blast even though it was very late and it looked as if it would go on to Moscow dawn which came at that time of the year around three A.M. Julie was dancing with a Secretary of the French Embassy who was flirting outrageously with her. I was not worried about that. "I'm not discouraged," I replied to my American diplomat friend. "But sometimes I do wonder what is going to become of Julie and myself."

"I don't blame you," said my friend and continued, "You just have to be patient. You'll have to wait and wait, maybe for years. I'm sure if you wait long enough it will all come out all right. The way I size up the situation is this. At one time or another Stalin went into a rage about the question of exit visas for Russian wives of foreigners, perhaps the last time it was brought up with him by the British Foreign Minister in 1947. He turned down the British Foreign Minister and told whoever happened to be around that he was sick of hearing about visas for Russian wives of foreign diplomats and journalists. He didn't ever want to hear about it again. And this, I suspect, is where the matter has stood ever since."

And then he went on, "You know we could make a big thing out of these cases. We could bring them up in the United Nations. We could try to get directly to Stalin with them. We could keep repeating demands for exit visas for the half-dozen wives involved on our side, but I'm against pressing the thing too hard. If we press too hard, or make it a propaganda issue, I'm afraid that all that will happen is that one way or another the Soviet government will manage to get rid of all of your wives and perhaps you husbands as well. How it will happen, I don't know, but I think it will. The only thing to do is to express at the foreign office now and then a continuing interest in all of you. The Ambassador is planning to do just that in the very near future when an opportunity appears. This will be enough to let the Foreign office know we have not abandoned you. And for anything more we have to wait till something changes. Then there could be an opportunity to solve the thing quickly. But I don't know how or when it will come. You just have to be patient."

The music got faster and faster and the dancing went on at a quicker and quicker pace. Pretty soon the first rays of light of the early July morning shone in through the big ballroom windows. Julie and I made our way home a little later in broad daylight.

# 15.    *Saltykovka*

On a gray, cloudy day in the late spring of 1950, with thundershowers suspended in the air ready to explode any moment and unload more moisture on an already drenched soil, we drove down a narrow cobblestone road with deep ditches on either side called by the impressive name of the Razinskoye Chaussée. We were in the suburban settlement of Saltykovka some dozen miles to the east of Moscow. For us this was new territory. Harrison Salisbury, Julie and I kept gawking out of the car windows while up in front Mr. Gavrilov, an engineer from the Soviet Administration for Services to the Diplomatic Corps, gave directions to Harrison's chauffeur. We turned down a gravel road, proceeded for a hundred yards or so, turned off to the left on a deeply rutted mud road beneath a forest of tall, straight pine trees and slithered with bated breaths, expecting to get stuck, another two hundred yards before coming to a halt in front of a tall, two-story unpainted house with a high peaked roof, constructed of solid logs squared with adzes on the downstairs and of boards upstairs, with a porch on the first story in the front and a veranda for the second story up above it.

"This is it," said Mr. Gavrilov in Russian.

We got out and approached the house. As we did, a small herd of young goats which had found shelter on the front porch, leaving traces of goat occupancy, scattered in every direction, bleating in dismay.

Our inspection of the interior was brief. Downstairs were a medium-sized living room, a small bedroom and a kitchen. Upstairs was one large room with its own entrance. Attached to the back porch was a privy. Mr. Gavrilov told us he was authorized to offer the downstairs to Julie and myself and the separate upstairs to Harrison. He doubted if his Administration, the only possible source of a "dacha" or summer home for us, had anything else it could offer. He named the rental. It was not cheap.

We looked over the lot. It was about sixty-five by seventy-five yards, maybe an acre altogether, flat, thinly shaded with pine trees sixty feet tall. Out in the front yard was one cleared portion which had at one time been a garden. The lot fronted on a broad grassy "street" through the middle of which a footpath wound its devious way and on which cows, watched by a herdswoman, were grazing. Across from the front door of the house the land was vacant except for the pines. Alongside it on either side were companion two-story homes exactly the same, one on the north occupied and the other on the south vacant. There were many other private homes in the settlement, some substantial two-story dwellings with fences about and others one-story cottages. Some were neat and others run-down. Most seemed to be inhabited, a fact indicating they were year-round homes. None were painted. Yet the impression in relative Russian terms was one of prosperity.

We asked Gavrilov some questions. Water supply? He showed us the community well, one hundred yards away. Electricity? During the day the current was usually normal but in the evening the voltage fell and the lights would be dim. Telephone? Not a chance, for that year anyway, explained Gavrilov. He added that the nearest pay phone was at the railway station, a mile distant. Was there any better road-way from the cobblestone road than that impossible trail on which we had come? Mr. Gavrilov indicated there was not. He shrugged his shoulders. This was the best there was.

We finished our tour in silence. We told Gavrilov upon arriving in Moscow we would let him know the next day. Over the supper table we discussed whether we should rent the dacha offered us or not. We knew it was the only one we would be offered. It had grave disadvantages—and yet. All three of us wanted a place outside the city. We felt acutely the need for a refuge from the stifling atmosphere of the Soviet capital. There were plenty of problems with the proffered dacha in Saltykovka but it seemed obvious it was worth a trial for one summer at least to see if we could deal with them.

*     *     *     *     *

We never regretted the decision to take the dacha. True, there were moments when, with my car sunk to the hub caps in the mud in vain efforts to traverse that short but impassable distance of just three hundred yards from the paved road to our country home, I cursed in Russian and English, both the Russian earth and Soviet inefficiency. Even such moments had the virtue of taking my mind off bigger problems.

The house in Saltykovka gave us a new lease on life, and gave me a more detached perspective on the things I had to write about. I could complete a dispatch reporting some new, macabre cold war development, and later that same day proceed to Saltykovka and sit quietly in the front yard in the long twilight with sounds all about me of Russians enjoying themselves in the open air and things didn't seem so bad. I could read in *Pravda* a vicious attack on the United States for "germ warfare in Korea" and go out to Saltykovka and be greeted by a pack of admiring Russian children as "Uncle Tom"—a term of endearment carrying humor with it because of the Russian fame of Harriet Beecher Stowe. I would realize that in the emotional heat of the vortex of the propaganda war between two systems, which in Moscow I inhabited, one could easily exaggerate the bad feelings Russians might be acquiring for Americans because of things printed in their papers. At the Saltykovka dacha I could relax. I could dig in my garden and grow a crop of vegetables which we could eat with gusto. And this made me feel that there was still much to be glad about and hope for.

Saltykovka was a world apart from Moscow. There was the railway for commuters with its frequent electric trains and hundreds of people—clerks, officials, officers, students, workers—traveling back and forth between Moscow and Saltykovka every day. But when they stepped out of their train at the Kursk Station in Moscow they were swept into the fast-beating tempo of the metropolis. When in the evening they stepped off their train at the Saltykovka Station they were once more out of the metropolis and a part of the lethargic leisurely life of Soviet suburbia.

*     *     *     *     *

We used the dacha as much as we could, but there were two serious limitations on our country residence—weather and work. It was too cold to live in our Saltykovka house on a full-time basis earlier than the last days of May and later than the end of September. We did go for visits or weekends before or after those dates. However, there were also chilly, rainy periods in the middle of the summer when on occasion we fled the raw country for the warmer city.

Communications at the dacha were so difficult at first that in busy news periods it was necessary to remain all the time in the city. Therefore we made desperate efforts to get a telephone installed. After a year or so of intensive letter writing we did get our landlord to put in several poles for us and install a phone. It cost a pretty penny and when it was at last installed we discovered that the total number of lines between Moscow and Saltykovka was so small that it might take as much as half an hour to get through in either direction. Still, the phone was a help.

Despite weather and work we managed to spend most of the summer in the country in 1950, 1951 and 1952. Julie would stay out all the time and I would come into Moscow each day for work and return later in the day.

There were even a few winter weekends in sub-zero weather at the dacha. They were adventures in endurance of cold on one side and heat on the other. There was a brick stove in the center of the house between the living room and kitchen. When well fired it radiated vast warmth—but the house was not tight and admitted a lot of wind. Also, it took a long time to heat up. So the three of us used to huddle close to the stove while from the kitchen there wafted the aroma of a stew made according to Julie's and Harrison's particular formula, involving beef, bacon, turnips, carrots, onions, bay leaves and much else. After a chilly day and a long tramp in the snow that stew was so delicious! By evening the house was so warm one could go about in shirt sleeves. Then by morning the only warm place was in bed—and it was a terrible shock to have to get up and get the fire going again.

\*　　\*　　\*　　\*　　\*

We used to wander about Saltykovka winter and summer and stick our noses into just about everything. We particularly enjoyed the local market. I never had any idea of the meaning of the English phrase about not being able to "hide a pig in a poke" until I lived in Saltykovka. It was a common sight and sound to see a Russian returning from market with a piglet in a sack squealing so loud it could be heard for a quarter of a mile. Russians often bought piglets in the spring to fatten them on scraps during the summer and slaughter them in fall for a winter's supply of pork. It was one way of beating the high cost of living.

The Saltykovka market was a place where one could buy more than piglets. In its own busy, noisy way it was a social-commercial center for the surrounding district. Peasants came from a distance to sell vegetables, poultry, dairy products and meat and to buy consumer goods. Gardeners found a vigorous market for seeds, bulbs, plants and the like. Pet fanciers bought and sold dogs and other animals. Housewives came to get the latest gossip. Handicraftsmen had a retail outlet for their merchandise where restrictions on the sale of such merchandise were not strictly enforced. Persons selling used goods or speculators seeking high prices for scarce merchandise might haunt the entrance of the market in a ghostly fashion, ready to disappear at the appearance of a militiaman.

Rarely did I miss my regular Sunday visit to the market. It was on that day that it was the most crowded, that there were the most things to buy and see, that there was the most noise, color, odor and life. I could pass the time of day with the gardeners who sold plants. I could pat the heads of the puppies there to find a new master. I could sample the sour cream of a peasant woman and shake my head sorrowfully, indicating that it didn't come up to my high standards, while all the while she was volubly explaining why her sour cream was the best ever produced. And I could watch with intense interest all the goings-on—of which there were plenty.

One day, I remember, a group was gathered around a tall man who had a large wooden wardrobe, made crudely though solidly and painted in an unpleasant orange brown. A militiaman was jabbering at him and there was a woman official taking part in the discussion. Nearly everyone of the dozen or so people about seemed to feel free to make comments from time to time and even to interrupt the militiaman. I listened and discovered that the militiaman and the female, a tax inspector, claimed the man with the wardrobe had brought it to sell without getting a permit.

"Show your passport!" insisted the militiaman.

The tall man was claiming he had bought the wardrobe himself and

was about to take it home. This was an old dodge, tried no doubt a
thousand times a year there.

"Who sold it to you?" asked the woman. "Point out who sold it to
you then!"

The tall man could not.

Finally he gave in and produced his passport. His name was taken.
That was that—except for the inevitable aftermath when another tax
inspector called on him at home to determine what income tax he
should pay on his revenue from this type of handicraft.

Many were the little dramas I saw acted out by Russians at the
Saltykovka market. Though I left many a ruble there I never regretted
a single one.

*     *     *     *     *

One reason I wanted to have a country house was to garden. It
was not unnatural, therefore, that the first thing I did in Saltykovka
was to get the garden plot spaded. That was the beginning of an orgy
of planting and growing things in which I indulged for all the remaining years of my stay in the USSR. My garden kept becoming
larger and larger every year. There were beds of flowers all over the
yard before I was through. Young bushes and trees, roses, lilacs, dog-
wood, raspberries, cherries, apples and many other things, flourished
and grew.

I worked hard at this and got immense satisfaction. In Harrison I
had a hard-working partner. Between the two of us we not only
reaped some good crops, but also gave the entire neighborhood amusement and some shocks.

The worst shock the inhabitants of Saltykovka got, I would guess,
was from seeing long-legged Harrison working away on a Sunday
afternoon in a pair of shorts. This type of garment had never been
introduced into the Soviet Union. As well-brought-up Russians knew,
it would have been much more proper for a man at a country house
on a Sunday to loll about in a pair of pajamas and also to let the
ladies of the house tend to the garden.

The thing that proved to our neighbors to their final, definitive
satisfaction, however, that foreigners were crazy, was my lawn mower.
This was, I gathered from the comments I heard from Russians from
over the fence, regarded as the end. A goat would have not only kept
the grass cropped for me but also fertilized the lawn, it was pointed

out. Or I could have let the hay grow and sell it—getting the lot mowed for free. The idea of keeping the grass short for the sake of appearance seemed outlandish. Russians liked their grass long anyway. Julie shared this opinion. She never approved of my lawn mower. Even my best friend, Harrison, deserted me. He said he had mowed enough lawns in Minneapolis in his youth to last him the rest of his life. If I wanted the lawn mowed in Saltykovka I could mow it myself. I did for a time, faced with universal disapproval, but finally my energies flagged. I put away the lawn mower and let the grass grow. Julie, Harrison and my neighbors all sighed with relief. So did I.

*     *     *     *     *

Gardening was not my only occupation in Saltykovka. Another pursuit was fixing up the house. We were only tenants, but if we wanted things done to improve the place it was up to us to get them done ourselves.

In early 1952 we decided to give the dacha a major face lifting. We wanted the front porch glassed in. We wanted the house painted— with oil paint. I set about getting oil paint from Finland where it was cheaper and sent out the word through the settlement that I was looking for a carpenter and house painters. It didn't take the word long to get about. One evening there stood at the gate a quiet, sturdy young man asking about the carpentry. I brought him in and showed him and asked his price. He named a reasonable figure and soon we had an arrangement. He would come every evening after work, get all the lumber, bring his own tools and do the work there. Dmitry—that was his name—promised to have the work completed in a month.

I had supposed that Dmitry, a professional carpenter employed at a construction job, would have access to cut and sized lumber and that he would have an assortment of modern tools. What was my surprise when he appeared with rough boards two and a half or three inches thick and from ten to eighteen inches across, and tools turning out to be a saw, a hammer, a simple hand plane of a type found in America only in antique stores, and nothing else.

Fascinated, we watched to see how he proposed to go about his job. Silent and serious, he set to it. Every single piece of lumber, big and small, that the job took, he cut out of his raw lumber with the saw and planed down to the correct dimensions. There were two sides and the front of the porch to be filled in—six large window frames with twelve panes each and a skylight with three more, making seventy-five panes in all, of which forty-seven were to be divided into equal triangles so a pattern of colored glass could be installed to line the edges of the frames. There were two doors and four large hinged panes for ventilation as well. Dmitry's skill and persistence were astonishing. He worked every night till it was too dark to see. He completed the entire job within a few days of the promised schedule, took his wages and departed, having said hardly a word to us.

It was also as a result of our home improvement campaign that I met the painters, Valentin and Pavlik.

One evening as the sun was setting there appeared on our front walk a short little man with an unshaven face and a twinkle in his eye. I went out to see him. "I heard you needed to have your house painted . . ." he led off. I took him around the cottage and showed him what I wanted. We reached an agreement on price.

"And now," he said, "how about twenty-five rubles in advance so that I can drink to seal this agreement?"

I laughed. "It's an American custom to drink only when the job is completed."

My new friend, Valentin, the painter, looked a bit disappointed till I reminded him that after all the price agreed on did include two bottles of vodka as a bonus. Licking his lips in anticipation he left. On the appointed day for the beginning of work Valentin showed up with another painter, a meek-looking chap named Pavlik. With a great to-do Valentin set to work. He made much show of bossing around Pavlik who, however, paid little attention and just painted. The two worked evenings. During the daytime both worked at a nearby factory. For a week or more the painting proceeded steadily. Things were going well and, in fact, I was becoming proud of both Valentin and Pavlik.

Valentin turned out to be quite a personality. One evening after the painting had ceased for lack of daylight I gave him a shot of whiskey and he began to talk. God had given him a silver tongue. He recited to me half a dozen verses of the famous Russian poet, Nekrasov. Then he began to sing for us old Russian traditional love songs. It was quite an entertainment.

One day Valentin came to me and announced that on the next day there would begin the "days of the Trinity"—a Russian religious celebration—and that Pavlik and he would not be working till after the holidays. So I endowed the two with a bottle of whiskey and instructed them to come back the day following the end of the Trinity days.

On that day Valentin did not appear, but Pavlik, looking tired and sheepish, did. He mumbled something about Valentin being fast asleep beneath a pile of lumber at the factory, so I didn't say more. For days Pavlik worked away by himself—no Valentin.

It was late and dusk was descending. I was dozing in my chair on the lawn when I was brusquely aroused by a burst of bright song from out in front. I saw in the semi-darkness a figure at the gate and went out to see. Pavlik continued, despite the lack of light, busily to brush away at the side of the house. There at the gate was Valentin. He was in a mellow mood. Wouldn't I be so good as to advance him fifty rubles? He needed something with which to wet his whistle. I, of course, turned him down. I warned him that if he did not show up soon to do his part of the work I would give the entire pay to Pavlik. At this Valentin began to pour out his life story. He had married a widow several years older than himself. She had a nineteen-year-old daughter. The widow did not understand him, he claimed, and would not give him money to get vodka, she was so stingy. He led a hard life, he declared. His wife did not love him, and therefore he had to have drink. He asked my sympathy with tears in his eyes.

From Pavlik I had heard a different story. Each night Valentin had been returning home in very high spirits externally because of the presence internally of a different kind of high spirits. He always had with him a half-empty bottle and each night the wife, not knowing how else to deal with the problem, swiped the bottle during his troubled sleep. In the morning when he awoke with terrible thirst there was nothing to drink. Since he had been in this situation before he was prepared. At the factory he had a cache beneath a pile of lumber consisting of several bottles. When he got there he would fuel up then proceed to fall into a drunken sleep in one of the factory sheds. It was a vicious cycle. Each day the fire within Valentin built up higher and would continue to grow until Valentin ran out of vodka and finally collapsed and slept it all off. Pavlik said it happened whenever Valentin undertook a painting job.

Finally, Pavlik completed our house by himself. The house gleamed in its new coat of white and blue. We inspected it and I agreed everything had been properly done. The time came for paying.

I was counting out the money into Pavlik's hand when from out of nowhere there appeared the exuberant Valentin. I pretended I did not notice him and ostentatiously handed to Pavlik the two bottles of vodka constituting the "bonus" agreed on.

"These," I said to Pavlik, "are for you."

I shook Pavlik's hand in gratitude for his good work. Valentin stood on the sidelines and watched. As I turned to go back into the house he shouted after me suddenly, "If you want your house painted again next year, let me know!"

\*     \*     \*     \*     \*

In Saltykovka we made no attempt to violate the restrictions on fraternization between Soviet citizens and foreigners. We didn't attempt to strike up acquaintanceships among the local people since we knew this could only hurt them and us in the unfortunate circumstances of the time. Yet, without trying, we soon began to feel at home among our Russian neighbors. They, on their part, seemed to feel at ease with us. The process by which this happened was as imperceptible as osmosis. We lived near one another. We saw one another at work or rest or play over our respective fences. We said hello to one another on the street when we met. We knew their children and on occasion had joined them in games. We stood together in line at the community well waiting our respective turns.

We, the foreigners, never ceased to be curiosities to our Russian neighbors, but we did at least become to them, with time, rather friendly people, and were certainly not regarded as evil "American warmongers." So far as we were concerned, they became to us real, live people with virtues and faults which, as time went on, we came to know.

Our Saltykovka neighbors and acquaintances were a varied assortment of people.

Some, like General Chernov, whose dacha stood a hundred yards across the way, we knew only at second hand. The important thing locally about General Chernov was that he had *two* bathrooms in his two-story home built for him by German war prisoners and Russian enlisted men. This in a community in which even one indoor bathroom was unheard of! This became the local standard of the height of conspicuous consumption—to have a house with *two* bathrooms. General Chernov also had an enormous ten foot high board fence surrounding his acre but this was not considered a luxury, since every Russian wanted as high a fence as possible about his home.

The Balakiryov family, that lived next door, on the other hand, we got to know rather well. There was neither cordiality nor hostility between us. We might exchange over the fence gardening information and chit-chat. On the other hand our fence showed a proclivity to break down at points next to our garden at times when their goat was tethered in such a position with his fifty foot rope to be able to invade our garden with disastrous results. One always had the uncomfortable feeling that if one did not nail things down they might suddenly move over onto the property of the Balakiryov family, consisting of a minor police functionary who wore the MVD (Ministry of Internal Affairs) uniform, his wife and three children. Yet they never stole a thing and worked like beavers to make their own dacha plot an extraordinarily productive little miniature farm.

With Nadya Petrov and her husband, Petya, a carpenter, we became even more closely acquainted. She was an attractive blonde, typically Russian, with a round face and a figure on the short, full side. Petya was a small, pleasant chap, ineffectual, with a weakness for the bottle. Nadya was energetic, responsible, hard-working with a touch of toughness and cynicism. Petya was not in the same league with Nadya. She ran the family herself. And there she was, at the age of thirty, in a little suburban Moscow settlement with no outlet for her strong urge for a fuller, more vivid life. The couple had three good-humored, well-behaved children, a boy ten, a girl nine, another boy five. Nadya also looked after her sister's two children, a girl nine and a boy five, while the sister worked. The sister was married to a militiaman and the two families, consisting of nine people, lived in two not very large rooms plus a boarded-in porch in a ramshackle barracks a few doors away from us. They were crowded, of course, and a heavy burden fell on Nadya. Not only did she do all the housework, look after the children, and do the gardening but she also worked part-time for us to earn money to buy badly needed things for herself and the children. Under these circumstances it wasn't surprising that now and then we seemed to detect in Nadya a slightly envious, discontented air while she worked in our relatively well-provided household. Yet Nadya and her family, in Russian terms, did not live so badly—and they had a share of good times and happiness. They deserved all they got.

It was a different kind of happiness that our acquaintance, Grandmother Varvara, found, but just as real. Grandmother Varvara was a nun. She had a little bit of a room which she rented in a home in Saltykovka where she kept her own little altar constructed of fine old ikons—holy images. Several days a week, partly as a fulfillment of her vows and partly to sustain herself, she sold ikons and prayer books at the Saltykovka market. The women who came to the market deeply revered her. And it took courage to live in this independent and lonely way.

Mikhail Petrovich, whose acquaintance I made at the market, also chose an independent path in life and not an easy one. He could, as he told me, have made more money working in a factory—but, as he said, "that would not be living." Instead he raised plants and took them to the market to sell to other gardeners. In exchange for accepting a more meager material scale of life he had the delight of doing what he wanted to do. He wheeled his little cart to market every morning and every morning he had the consciousness of being a free man who owned his own soul. More than most could say—in Russia or America or anywhere else.

There were also unpleasant people in Saltykovka. On the negative side, for instance, was Zaitsev, the head of the Moscow Dacha Trust in this area, who was supposed to look after the government-owned dachas such as ours, and keep them in repair. Zaitsev, however, was more interested in looking after himself. He considered his job had been given him by God and the Soviet government as a kind of special compensation for blessing the earth with his existence. He treated the dacha properties under his charge somewhat as if they were an endowment for his personal welfare. When the roof on our dacha leaked during a rain, Zaitsev could never be found to arrange repairs. But let there be a tall pine tree on the property which showed the least signs of losing its vigor and there was Zaitsev on the double, with axes, saws and a crew of workmen to take it down, cut it up and haul it off. Some of the wood may have gone for the needs of the Moscow Dacha Trust, but I have my suspicions where the rest went.

Dressed in a dirty, greenish-gray raincoat over a black, shapeless, shabby suit he wore a Russian "kepka"—a khaki-colored uniform-type cap with black visor fancied by some civilians. He had an alcoholic red nose and his eyes were shifty and impertinent. When he talked to me he avoided looking at me. He was middle-aged with a rapidly growing paunch.

Zaitsev manifested the most intense interest in the dachas in his care at haying time. He had a complex about hay. He considered that all the succulent green hay on each dacha lot belonged to him. He used to wait till we were out of the village and quickly have the hay on our lot cut and taken away—I presume, to his own shed. We wanted the hay to go to old Uncle Petya, guard of the Dacha Trust who guarded all the government-owned dachas in the area including ours and who was always helpful to us. One year we personally stood guard over the hay till Uncle Petya could harvest it and take it away, only to find later that Zaitsev had blackmailed him out of half of it.

Uncle Petya was a lovable, decent, friendly, honest old fellow who took pride in doing his work well and never failing in a responsibility. A former railway worker, he had a pension of some two hundred rubles a month. His salary as dacha trust guard gave him an equal amount. He lived a plain life but didn't go hungry. He supported his sick wife and helped give a home to his niece, forty, and her daughter, seventeen. All four lived in the same barracks which housed the family of Nadya Petrov and her sister. Altogether there were in it six families and sixteen people in six rooms. It was a broken down old place but inside in the winter when the stoves were burning merrily away it was warm and cozy.

I can picture Uncle Petya. Of an evening, a tall but slightly bent figure would unlatch the gate and come slowly up our walk. This was Uncle Petya and he had something he wished to tell me. He would come up and take off his dark blue cap. His brow was damp and he wiped it off. Though well over sixty-five he worked harder and more efficiently than many much younger men—in his garden, looking after his dachas, helping his neighbors. He was usually dressed in a loose gray cotton shirt which he wore with a wide belt over it around his waist. His trousers, like his cap, were of a navy blue. Removing his cap was a sign of friendliness and respect, for Uncle Petya was old-fashioned and believed in such customs.

"With your good health, Gospodin!" he would say. This was his habitual greeting. ("Gospodin" was the pre-revolutionary Russian equivalent of "Mister," used in the Soviet Union only in addressing foreigners.)

"Good evening, Uncle," I always replied. "How does your wife feel today?" His wife was chronically ill with what the doctors diagnosed as ulcers.

"She's ailing again today," said Uncle Petya. "It's bad. It's very bad." And then he went on with what he had to tell me, usually some minor matter concerning the dacha, maybe some small request.

Uncle Petya always had about him a sense of dignity. He was polite but never subservient. If he gave respect to others he expected it for himself. This was why it was such a blow to him when in a dispute involving a cow he was struck by one of the local inhabitants.

The cow belonged to a neighbor. The woman who owned it was uninhibited about where she pastured it. She used to let it into the yards of the dachas under the guard of Uncle Petya where it went to work on tasty tidbits in yards and gardens and left evidence of its visit all over. Naturally there were complaints. Uncle Petya went to the mistress of the cow. He respectfully explained things to her but she flew into a rage.

"My husband," she screamed, "is a member of the Party, and I will pasture my cow where I please."

Uncle Petya remonstrated with her, "But Anastasia Mikhailovna, your cow is eating things from the neighbors' gardens and dirtying up their yards."

"What do I care!" shouted Anastasia Mikhailovna. "When my husband gets through with you, you'll wish you had minded your own business!"

Old Uncle Petya listened to her further imprecations in silence.

All day long he was very worried. It was true Anastasia Mikhailovna's husband was a member of the Party. Uncle Petya began to get worried he might go to the Moscow Dacha Trust with some fanciful story and get him fired. But he was no coward. That evening he went back and took up the question with the husband himself. He had considered exactly what he would say.

"Panteilimon Zakharovich," he addressed the master of the establishment who came out angrily to meet him, "I am responsible to the government for guarding the dachas of the Moscow Dacha Trust. Your cow has been trespassing and the tenants are complaining. Your wife, however, refuses to listen. Therefore I have come to you with the request to keep your cow off the plots of the Moscow Dacha Trust."

Panteilimon Zakharovich, a small, heavy-set forty-year-old minor bureaucrat in a government office, hardly heard Uncle Petya out. He was dancing up and down with rage. He strode up and grabbed the old man by the shoulder.

"I'll teach you your responsibility to the government," he snorted through his clenched teeth. "You old good-for-nothing!"

And then he struck Uncle Petya. He did not hit him hard. Uncle Petya was not hurt. But the fact that he had been struck in fulfillment of his duties overwhelmed him. He was crushed. He turned and walked away from the still cursing Panteilimon Zakharovich in a daze. For weeks he could not come to himself.

As things worked out he had settled the question of the cow once and for all. Evidently Anastasia Mikhailovna and Panteilimon Zakharovich got to thinking the thing over and realized that being a member of the Party did not give a right to openly trespass on plots of other people—some of whom might be members of the Party more influential than Panteilimon Zakharovich.

Uncle Petya, however, kept dwelling on the incident for a long time. It had hurt him deeply. But he went on with his work for the dacha trust and its tenants as faithfully as before. Old Uncle Petya has long since gone on to another world where there are no dacha trusts, no Communist parties, and no trespassing cows—but warm memories of him live on.

\*     \*     \*     \*     \*

When I think of patience and perseverance I remember Colonel Borisov and the brick house he built across the street from us in Saltykovka. Colonel Borisov was not the only Russian building a house for himself in Saltykovka. The settlement was a forest of construction of individually owned homes being built slowly and personally by their owners.

It was far from easy in the USSR for a family to build its own home. It looked to me sometimes as if the Soviet government was deliberately doing everything to make it difficult for prospective private home owners. Lots could not be bought and to get an allotment of a suitable plot from a local government was an onerous, difficult negotiation. Most Russians wanting plots were unable to get one. There were no contracting organizations to build homes for the citizen. A Russian family had to do most of the construction work with its own labor. Carpenters, bricklayers, even electricians could be hired to work during their spare time but to an average citizen their services were costly. Construction materials were expensive and not always available. They had to be paid for in cash. Mortgages were limited. The few available went to workers in factories trying to tie down their workers tightly to their jobs. Their terms were burdensome by Western standards and the credit given was niggardly. When developments were laid out for private home owners no provision was made for running water supply, sewage disposal, or paved streets. The suburbanite usually had to be prepared to fish his water from a communal well, maybe hundreds of yards away, to use a cold and windy privy for his personal hygiene, and to wade through bottomless Russian brown mud many months of the year in order to get to and from his home. The suburbanite family was lucky to have electricity, and almost never had telephone services. Yet Russians went through extraordinary sacrifices to build themselves their own little cottages in which their families could live in privacy, by themselves.

Colonel Borisov and his family were an example, under our noses, of this form of unsung Soviet heroism in the face of obstacles. The Colonel kept his distance. He had no desire to have anything to do with foreigners. We never exchanged more than a few short words such as "hello" and "good day." Yet I feel as if I knew and understood him very well. From my porch I could watch him evening after evening, laboring away building his house, planting his orchard, setting out or cultivating his garden. Out of seeing him at work steadily, month after month, year after year, there grew in me an interest in his project and an admiration for him.

When we first went to live in Saltykovka in 1950 there was nothing on the Colonel's plot—a tract of about an acre—except a shed at the very back. Colonel Borisov, his wife, his daughter aged about seventeen, and his son, aged nine, were living in the shed for the summer. This shed was planned eventually to become a garage to house the Colonel's small Russian-made Moskvitch automobile which sometimes stood outside it. Meanwhile it housed the family.

The family devoted the entire spring and summer of 1950 to planting an orchard and garden, including a strawberry patch. During the autumn of the year building materials—bricks and timber, sand and sacks of cement—began to come in in truckloads. The Colonel knew the fundamental rule of home building in Soviet Russia. One must buy materials when they are available. Otherwise they may not be available when one needs them.

Actual construction began in 1951. The brick walls began to rise slowly but steadily toward the end of that summer. During the winter of 1951–52 the work went on, when the weather permitted. By the spring of 1952 the walls had been basically completed. In the spring of 1952 the Colonel made the first story of the house habitable and installed a temporary stove in it. He moved the family in. It was a great day when they left their shed for the house.

Gradually, during the summer and autumn of 1952, the Colonel worked on the upper story and in the spring of 1953 he was ready to put a veranda on the house. We watched him with interest as he executed this project in the month of May. In the late spring of 1953, amidst a wave of prosperity, the Colonel invested in TV. A "T" shaped mast rose up from his roof and all the neighborhood children used to go over on Sunday afternoon to see the weekly children's show with the Colonel's own young son.

So there stood the Colonel's home in the early summer of 1953 with a solid fence about his plot, a garden in the side yard and a flourishing orchard surrounding the home. It rose two stories with neat, well-laid, brick walls. There were three rooms on the ground floor and one large room upstairs. The roof was of good quality sheet iron and the windows double, like all windows in Russia, to protect against winter cold. Much remained to be done. Central heating was to be installed and an indoor toilet, according to the Colonel's plan. The home remained unfinished inside and outside. But the Colonel had conquered the major difficulties facing Russian home builders and raised a small but cozy little castle. In a few more years he would have everything done and own a home which not even an American factory worker would sneer at, one which the vast majority of Russians could not even dream about, not at that time.

That was the way things stood when we last saw the house in the mid-summer of 1953. But then something happened. Perhaps the Colonel died or perhaps he became ill. At any rate, up to 1959, six years later, the house remained in much the same unfinished state as in mid-1953. So we heard. So, as it turned out, he finished his project but he didn't quite finish it. But I am certain that no matter what happened the Colonel got from his home-building operation one of the keenest satisfactions of life—the satisfaction of creating and building something of one's own for one's own.

*    *    *    *    *

Whatever Colonel Borisov may have succeeded in doing or not he and the other patient, persevering Saltykovka home builders did succeed in making clear for me one emphatic point about human beings and social organization in the Soviet Union and elsewhere.

I used to sit on my porch and watch Colonel Borisov working, laying bricks, carpentering or gardening. Throughout the evening I could hear all around sounds of hammering and sawing as other Russians like him built themselves private homes. I used to ask myself: Why were the Russian home builders working so hard—almost with desperation—at overcoming obstacles put in their way by a government unfriendly to private home ownership in order to own their own homes? Part of the answer was obvious. They wanted more living space. But was that the whole story? I did not think so.

It seemed to me that the private home builders of Saltykovka, though they themselves surely didn't understand this in articulate form, were seeking more than housing. By constructing, despite difficulties, their own homes they were attempting, it seemed to me, to assert their dignity as human beings and in particular their human heritage of the right to own private property, their independence of the big organizations which dominate society, and their determination to seek an intimate, private, family, personal happiness in a society which seemed to frown on this, and placed the stress on sacrifice "for the public welfare" and on sweat and toil "for the glory of the Soviet state."

The man who owned his home in Saltykovka, it seemed obvious, would carry his head higher in his Moscow office and be more sturdily independent than the dependent official who occupied an apartment provided for him by the big organization for which he worked, and who would be evicted from his housing if dismissed from his job. It was this added dignity that the Soviet private home builder sought, it seemed to me, more than the extra housing space he needed so badly. This added dignity was worth windy privies, distant wells, muddy streets, crowded commuter trains, and all other inconveniences of life in Soviet suburbia.

But wasn't it perhaps precisely that added dignity and independence possessed by the private home builder and owner, the owner of private property, that the system begrudged him more than it begrudged him that little tract of land for his house? Didn't the system prefer to have employees dependent on their employing organization for their housing and everything else—so they would be more submissive?

And what does this line of thought suggest about the right of individuals to own private property in general and its importance for human beings?

In any society there are always two basic constituent entities—individuals (inside and outside organizations), and organizations. Modern industrial society, exemplified in the United States, the USSR, and developed Western European nations, is characterized by the enormous size, complexity and power of its big organizations, governmental and non-governmental. The big organizations possess great power over individual human beings working within them who are dealt with by ever more and more automatic impersonal methods en masse, and from whom the big organization demand stern discipline and meek submissiveness.

However, under Western capitalist social organization, as exemplified in the United States and Western European countries, the legal system still permits *not only organizations* to own and use property, including property in the means of production, but also individuals. The individual human being working inside or outside one of the big organizations in such countries can still have something of his own—property such as a home which he can use, property such as investments in real estate or securities which can produce an income, or ownership of a small enterprise of his own. The individual who for one reason or another does not wish to continue to work within one of the big organizations, particularly if he is foresighted and thrifty, or just plain lucky enough to have some property of his own—not necessarily very much property—can, if he so chooses, tell the big organization he works for to go to hell—and go and live on his farm or off his small business or off his income from his investments if he has any. The big organization, at any rate, certainly cannot, in such capitalist countries, deprive employed individuals of their housing. Even though under Western capitalist systems such as that of the United States things are, as time goes on, progressively more and more loaded in favor of the big organizations and against the individual "unorganized" human being, there still remains some open space in which the individual human being can operate and maneuver in his efforts to maintain his dignity and independence, in his efforts to avoid becoming merely a disenfranchised slave of the big organizations. This is important. And his right to own individual private property is a cornerstone of that dignity and independence vis-à-vis the big organizations—including particularly the government itself.

In the socialist Soviet Union, on the other hand, the rights of the individual human being to own private property, except things for strictly personal use, such as clothes, are severely restricted. The rights of the big organizations to hold and use property at the same time are virtually unlimited. The human individual has been almost completely disenfranchised in this vital respect, and the big organizations, which in the Soviet Union all partake of the authority of the government, whose branches they are, are freed of restraint in their dealings both with material wealth and with human beings employed in them. This, in fact, is Soviet socialism. This is what it is.

But the trend thus illustrated and carried to its extreme in the socialist USSR, where the organizations have almost everything and individuals almost nothing, extends outside the USSR. The big organizations in all modern, industrialized countries of the world seem to seek, perhaps as a law of their being, to deprive the human beings working for them of their individuality and their independence.

But even in the socialist Soviet Union there still remains that one foothold on the right of individuals to have and use private property, that one foothold on the dignity and independence that goes with it— the right to build and have one's own private home, and the private, personal, intimate happiness that so often is dependent on that. This is not so much—but at the same time it is everything.

And this is why the hammers and saws used to resound through the little settlement of Saltykovka with such vigor and gladness on Sundays and in the evenings of the Moscow summer.

# 16.    *Rule by Terror*

One always returned from suburbia to the metropolis. This was a basic fact of our life. I returned to Moscow every day to work. And in late September, we returned to Moscow to live. Saltykovka was an interlude, a respite—Moscow was the reality. And no matter how relaxed things were in Saltykovka, in those bitter cold-war years, things in Moscow were bleak and hostile. And the central element of life in the capital was the terror—stark terror. The terror was many different things.

The terror was overt and clandestine surveillance of foreigners and of Soviet citizens who dealt with them. It was tapped telephones, the bugging of walls with hidden microphones, the shadowing of individuals by auto or on foot, militiamen posted at the gates of foreigners' dwellings to keep track of entries and departures. It was clandestine opening of mail, the use of foreigners' employees to report on them. It was also the limitation on access to the USSR of foreigners, and the restrictions on access of foreigners to Russian citizens and institutions.

Terror was the silent arrest of citizens suspected of disloyalty or accused of political crimes. It was the holding of the arrested incommunicado, denial of release on bail, the denial of legal defense, subjection of the arrested to mistreatment or torture to secure "confessions." It was sentencing of the accused in secret and without fair trial.

Terror was the exile of prisoners to forced labor under noxious conditions in remote areas. It was the use of penal labor under unhealthy or unbearable conditions. It was the keeping of some prisoners in-communicado from families. Terror was the non-release of prisoners who had served out sentences, or release with cruel limitations on residence.

Terror was the liquidation or mass exile of national groups believed disloyal—the Crimean Tartars, Volga Germans, Kalmuks, etc. It was the suppression of the national cultures of certain minorities, as, for instance, the Yiddish culture of Soviet Jews. It was the subjection of whole population classes, such as former war prisoners, to forced labor at worst or at best, to civil and professional disabilities.

Terror was also the blanket of secrecy over this sector of life. Arrests and sentences were almost never announced. There was never discussion of the police or exile system, or any aspect of the terror. To talk about it was dangerous. Occasionally people returned from "there"—but they never talked about "it." In literature, in the papers, there was the pretense the terror didn't exist. Yet everyone knew it did exist. But it was kept as a terrible unknown.

More than anything else terror was the atmosphere created by all this. It hovered in the air. It was always there.

It is difficult to communicate the feel of this to an outsider. Fear was everywhere, yet Russians seemingly had come to accept terror as an element of life.

\*      \*      \*      \*      \*

I got my own acquaintance with terror. I saw it strike more than once.

There was Bill Oatis.

I used to telephone Bill, AP correspondent in Prague. I often dictated news stories to him. Sometimes there would be intervals while we waited for copy and Bill and I chatted. I had never met him, but we became friends over the phone.

Then one day I didn't call Bill Oatis any more. Bill had been arrested on a charge of espionage by the Czechoslovak Communist government.

There was Anatoly.

Anatoly was a valued Soviet employee of the American Embassy. As a general expediter he got things done which few others could have. Anatoly possessed a large book with hundreds of useful telephone numbers. He knew many people and many owed him favors. He was quick and brisk and efficient.

I knew Anatoly well and one day I asked for him at the Embassy. An Embassy Secretary took me aside. "Haven't you heard?" he asked.

"What?" I asked.

"Anatoly was arrested last night," he explained. "His wife phoned us to tell us. She is afraid they'll be coming back after her." And they did, a few days later. Both disappeared for many years.

Then there was Marusya. Marusya was an attractive girl. Her one-time husband, Misha, was a wartime ace with a dozen medals, who used to load up his plane with suitcases full of clothes for Marusya from Eastern Europe. Marusya would wear some of the things for a while, but mostly she would cart them off to the Commission Store to sell. Then she would give a party which might go on several weeks till the proceeds were gone.

Marusya had one important asset. She was a relative of one of the most famous figures of the Russian revolutionary movement. This for a time gave her protection. But finally, there came the reckoning.

Marusya's sin was that she ignored warnings to stop seeing foreigners when this had become a crime. I heard all about Marusya regularly. So when "they" came and took Marusya away I heard about it the next day. I had expected it. Still it came as a shock.

There was Fanya. Fanya was a pleasant person who worked as a correspondent's secretary for many years. She did some translating and she kept office records. Fanya was American-born and her tragedy was that her father had decided during the depression when he had no work to go back to Russia. As an auto worker he got a job at the Stalin Auto Works in Moscow. Fanya had American citizenship under American law. But Soviet authorities considered she had lost her American citizenship. As a person "without citizenship" she was, under Soviet law, denied the right to leave the USSR. This was tough. Fanya one day took a job with the American Embassy. The day she was to report to the Embassy she disappeared.

There was Feldman. He was a former American who worked in the Embassy. As time went on he seemed more and more nervous. One day he disappeared.

There was Raisa. She was the wife of an American waiting in America for her to join him. She got a visa to Poland where she apparently had relatives. She left Moscow. American friends from the

Embassy went to the Warsaw station to meet her, but she was not on the train. Official inquiries of the Embassy in Moscow elicited the information several years later that Raisa had "died" in 1952.

There was Valya. She was the wife of an American Embassy clerk waiting outside Russia for her to join him. She went out for a walk and didn't come back.

There was Abram. He was a boy, born in America, caught in Eastern Poland where he was visiting with parents when the war began. The area was annexed to the Soviet Union and Abram was still there. He came to the Embassy where he was given work. He was refused an exit visa by the Russians who claimed him as a Soviet citizen. He was sent a Soviet draft notice which, after consultation with the Embassy, he decided to ignore, since he knew it would mean the end of his hope to return to America. He was picked up on the street one day. Efforts by the Embassy to get information were to no avail.

All of these persons I knew personally. Some of them I knew rather well. And there were many others among those whom I had met or knew who got caught up in this thing. I once started counting them all in my mind. I got up to two dozen and stopped because there were so many. And there were so many others of whom I had heard at second hand.

Men's names would be in the papers. Suddenly they would be there no more. Nothing would be heard. One would wonder. Then would come the rumor. One would still wonder. But all too often it proved true.

The terror went on and on, devouring people, and it never seemed to stop.

\*　　\*　　\*　　\*　　\*

Julie had her acquaintance with terror. I wrote earlier that her father had died during the war. I did not say how.

It was in 1943. Julie, her mother and her father were in their apartment. The light was glimmering low. The iron stove, set in the center of the room to provide a little wartime warmth, was smoking away. There was silence in the room as there had been so many evenings before. Julie's father and mother were both in the depths of despair over the death of Julie's brother, their only son.

It was very late, but no one had gone to bed.

Suddenly there were stern knocks at the door. The father, with a feeling of alarm, opened the door. Two blue-capped security officers stood there. They came brusquely into the room. It was a nightmare. The three of the family stood watching numbly. It was a horrible dream. The officers told Julie's father he was under arrest.

Why? They gave no answers. Their faces told that they were used to such scenes, that they didn't care and that it wouldn't matter if they did. They had their job to do. They stomped out of the apartment with Julie's father between them. Julie shouted imprecations, then threw herself on the bed and sobbed. Julie's mother cried more quietly.

And then began the wait, efforts to find out . . . Letters to officials . . . Visits to acquaintances, to anyone who might be of influence . . . Everywhere there were frightened faces that said, so clearly, "Please go away and don't bother me with this. I am frightened myself." Friends suddenly were not friends. People who owed Julie's father much were no longer in when Julie called. Months passed. And then finally a postal card. "Come to such-and-such an address. Kuznetsky Most Street."

Julie went. It was a two-story building a few doors from the police headquarters on the Lyubanka. Up a dark stairway. Into an office. A long wait. Finally she was admitted. An officer informed her in curt language that her father had been sentenced to ten years at forced labor for political crimes. He would have the right to correspond with his family and receive food parcels from home. The officer refused any other information.

Julie and her mother wrote petitions for his release. They submitted them to office after office, to no avail. They sold, piece by piece, everything of value in the house. With the cash realized they bought canned foods which they did up in packages to send him. It was well known that survival often depended on such parcels from home.

Week after week Julie's mother used to take the train trip to the one postoffice way outside Moscow for such parcels. Dozens of other women were there performing the same errand.

Letters began to come from Julie's father. He was in Vorkuta, concentration camp center in the Arctic. The news was not good. His health was poor. Then he suffered a heart attack. He was moved to a camp for hospitalized prisoners in another northern area. Things were much better there.

The circumstances of his arrest became clearer. It turned out a colleague at work had written a denunciation to the police claiming he had made anti-Soviet remarks. For this he had been arrested, subjected to unbearable pressure, till finally, a broken man whose spirits had been undermined by his son's death, he had signed a "confession."

Once previously, fifteen years before, he had been arrested and charged with a political crime. But then he had held out, month after month, and refused to "confess." He finally won his release after seven months. Then, one could hope to get released if the investigators could not make a case. Later, a year after his release, he met on the street the investigator who had tried to make him confess to things he had not done. The investigator approached Julie's father, told him he was dying of TB, that he had his treatment of Julie's father on his conscience. The investigator admitted then and there he had known from the start that Julie's father was innocent, but had hoped to get a "confession" by force in order to advance his own career. So Julie's father knew the "system" and beat it once by sheer will power. But it couldn't be done a second time. He had been tried in secret in absentia by an administrative tribunal and sentenced. The "friend" who had denounced him falsely was also arrested and sentenced. Small consolation! Under the "system" both the false informer and the person falsely denounced could be "guilty."

Julie's father's health grew steadily worse in prison. One day came the news: He had died of a second heart attack. This was the reward of an able, hard-working non-political Soviet engineer and economist for his years of loyal service in the machinery of government.

*   *   *   *   *

Why was there this terror? It was so wasteful! Year after year it devoured tens of thousands of the most able and experienced Russians. They were seized and swallowed up. They lived out their meager days in prisons or camps and their services were lost.

The terror was obviously not needed to keep the Soviet regime in power. It was not needed to get people to work hard for a rapid buildup of the nation. The USSR had emerged from a war in which a burning patriotism had grown and rallied people behind the government as the conflict continued. In the postwar USSR there was patriotic devotion such as never before.

So why at this time the terror?

It is tempting to seek an easy answer. Many no doubt blame it on arbitrary power of police agencies and on the character of men who ran them. The security agencies, however, operated within the system established by higher authority on the instructions of the nation's political leadership, and particularly of Stalin. The personnel of security agencies doubtless suffered from the terror as grievously as any group. It is equally tempting to blame the terror on Stalin's character and neuroses. He created and master-minded the terror. He directed personally the terrible purge called the "Yezhovshchina" in 1937–38. He continued the application of terror throughout his lifetime. Of course, Stalin was a brutal, cruel man, a sadist. He had a persecution mania. No doubt in Stalin's personality there does lie one aspect of the terror. That is the official Soviet explanation for it.

One cannot, however, credit the terror merely to Stalin's madness. At least there was a method to his madness. I believe one can perceive a design linking all the puzzling phenomena of Soviet policy in postwar years, including the terror. This design, if I have understood it rightly, is frightening in its boldness.

It is worth a close examination. Vestiges of the Stalinist scheme still linger in Russia. Its philosophical foundations have never been wholly rejected. The basic concept seems still alive in more morbid forms in Red China. The whole scheme could be revived elsewhere some day.

Let's return to the terror. One obvious aspect of Soviet postwar life was the "iron curtain." It was a Chinese wall thrown up between the USSR and the outside world. It did not completely shut out outside influences—but it did subject them to the maximum extent to regulation.

Thus there was censorship to prevent unapproved foreign ideas from entering. There was prohibition on travel of citizens abroad and on foreigners entering the USSR and residing there. There was much more along the same line. There was, for example, the prohibition on fraternization between Soviet citizens and foreigners in Moscow.

In enforcement of the iron curtain the terror played a necessary role. Soviet citizens who had anything to do with foreigners or with the outside world fell into the view of the security system. Very many fell victims to the terror. The terror created an atmosphere of fear which hovered over everything to do with the outer world.

At this time the USSR was often compared to an enormous prison with a wall around it to keep the outside world out and Russians in. More appropriately one could make the comparison with a big experimental chamber kept by scientists in complete isolation from uncontrolled external conditions to permit experiments inside under controlled conditions.

A less obvious aspect of the terror was its role in isolation of individual citizens from one another.

Under the terror, as George Kennan once put it, people were arrested not for what they had done but for what they might do. If a person were regarded as a security risk, he might be arrested and charged with espionage whether or not he had ever committed it. He would even perhaps be forced to sign a confession—since the system demanded proof of its rightness as a part of its ritual. This might be regarded as a system of "preventive" justice aimed to prevent crimes by liquidating likely criminals. Actually, my view is that the system was not concerned with "crime" except incidentally.

The terror was creating an atmosphere in which people were afraid to share experiences, impressions, ideas with each other on an uncontrolled basis on essential matters. Even within the family there were dangers. Most perceptive Soviet parents, no matter what their own views, would hesitate before imparting to their children a point of view which could set them at odds with their environment and make life more difficult for them.

As a result of the terror every man had become, in effect, his own jailkeeper and was imprisoned in the little cell of his own soul. He was deprived of the possibility of sharing the experience and thoughts of his fellow men. The terror had disrupted communication between individuals. This was exactly what it was intended to do. Let's look further into the way things worked.

There was the requirement of absolute submission to the edicts of the Party. This was real. To emphasize it every now and then an example was made of prominent citizens. They were made to grovel in the dirt in an unseemly spectacle and confess "errors"—which illustrated to all there were *no* exceptions. There could be no talk of resistance. Resistance would bring down the thunderbolt of the terror. In the face of the terror there were no brave men. All were equal in submission. Who could be brave when that would bring the tortures of the damned not only on oneself but on one's near and dear ones.

There was no escape from this system. All exits were closed. No emigration was permitted. Few citizens were allowed to go abroad— only those on official business under careful supervision. Everyone should realize that there was *no way out* except feet first and underground. Soviet citizens *must* reconcile themselves to the fact that they had to get along with the system.

Let's return to the comparison of the Stalinist USSR to an experimental chamber kept by scientists in isolation from external conditions to permit experiments under controlled conditions. Inside the chamber the experimental animals, in other words, the citizens, were held in isolation from each other, were being kept by shock treatment in a state of submissiveness, and were held under total control. What kind of a scientific experiment was it that thus could involve an entire country?

If one talks of Stalinist science one immediately thinks of two scientific schools which stood out above others for the public attention devoted to them. The first was the psychology of Ivan Pavlov, discoverer of the conditioned reflex in experimental dogs. The second was Michurinist biology, which held that characteristics acquired by organisms during their lifetime could be passed on through inheritance to their offspring. The Soviet leadership evidently drew the conclusion that through use of propaganda it would be possible to alter the psychology of Soviet citizens. They could be induced to react in any desired manner, it was evidently concluded, to controlled and calculated stimuli—like Pavlov's dogs.

From Michurinist biology, seized on by Stalin, the conclusion was apparently drawn that changes induced in the citizenry by applied Pavlovian psychology could then be passed on to the new generation directly, without delay, through Michurinist heredity. This amounted to a pretty dream. Evidently Stalin felt the incalculable elements in human psychology could be brainwashed out by Pavlovian psychology, and then bred out for good by Michurinist biology. To accomplish this Stalin evidently considered it was sufficient: 1. to induce—through terror—a state of submissiveness and plasticity of mind; 2. to disrupt—through terror—uncontrolled communication between individuals; 3. then to subject the plastic citizenry to forced feeding with an intensive diet of propaganda through all the channels of mass communications—to produce desired conditioned reflexes.

Here the careful supervision of communications, also of arts, of science, philosophy and education, took on such importance. Even music was to be directed to remolding of human psychology. In the postwar period minute attention was given by the Party to day-by-day supervision of philosophy and literature, of biology, of philology, of cosmic science, and all other fields of intellectual effort. No aspect of creative or intellectual effort was too minute. There would be *total* control of thought and *total* control of communication. What was the goal?

This was talked about enough—particularly in discussions of literature. The New Soviet Society required, it was indicated, The New Soviet Man to populate it. Writers must depict him in their works, portray him in all his pathos and heroism, paint in lavish colors his sterling qualities. By depicting the new Soviet man, it was considered, writers would stimulate people to emulate him. The writers outdid themselves to create the new Soviet man. Gradually, out of the works of Stalin-prize-winning authors, out of the approved literary and dramatic works of the era, the much-praised and much-propagated works, there arose his image. He was a patient, durable, steadfast man, this new Soviet man. Often he was a dedicated Party secretary. He looked neither to the right nor left and trod a straight and narrow path of moral and ideological rectitude. He found his life exclusively in his work. Insofar as he had any personal life it was entirely incidental. His wife, if he had one, had to share his Spartan, barren existence, his long work day, his burning faith in the Party, his bottomless love for Comrade Stalin. Such he was. But strange to say, no matter how the writers would try, they could not make this little tin Communist God come to life. They could endow him with all the qualities in the dictionary—except humanity. He had everything—except a soul. And yet he was the goal of it all, of the whole system. And it was to create him—this new insipid papier-mâché Soviet man—that terror was held justified by Stalin.

Here we are again at the Stalinist slogan "the remaking of nature." Here we are at the "Canute psychosis" of the leadership. Stalin recognized no bounds to his own power. He would "remake nature." He would change the climate. He would alter the flora and fauna. He would make lemon trees grow on the Ukrainian steppes, watermelons on the cold plains of the Moscow Region, and tea bushes on the Karelian Isthmus. He would quell the dry drought winds from the South. He would make rivers flow backward. He would deprive human beings of their creative originality, their cantankerous dislike of confining authority, their love of freedom. He would make men into automatons—into new Soviet men.

The obsession with remaking nature, the Canute psychosis, had some of its foundations in Stalin's personality. But it had foundations elsewhere in the system which no doubt played their role in calling Stalin's dictatorial powers into being.

There was the claim of the regime to omniscience. It recognized no limits to the completeness of its knowledge of things and human affairs. It knew everything. Its pronouncements were, by definition, the only truth. It arrogated to itself the right to deliver final edicts on the most abstruse, even exotic, matters. Stalin's astonishing writings of 1951 on the origins and development of language, made into a central propaganda feature in the early fifties, are an example of the practical meaning of the philosophical claim of omniscience for the political authority.

Hand in hand went the companion claim to omnipotence. This went back to the origins of the system in revolution in which the Bolsheviks came into power with a program of destroying completely the old system and replacing it with a completely new, and revolutionary system.

The Party has never recognized limitations on its power, except those imposed by practical necessity. There were no checks and no balances. This claim to omnipotence long antedated the rise of Stalin.

Any regime that believes in its omniscience and omnipotence is by definition obliged to control everything, to manage everything, to run everything, and to leave nothing to chance. Otherwise it is shirking its duties. Furthermore, such a regime may also seek a personification of its omniscience and omnipotence in a dictator who is then deified as expressing these qualities.

This is why the "personality cult" of J. V. Stalin was never solely a chance matter of Stalin's own personality, why Stalin's personal penchant for the "remaking of nature" in a hurry struck a deep chord of response in the system. This is why the leadership considered itself obliged to control and manage and operate and run everything. To run things on this basis—and primarily in order to remake nature in a hurry—it is not surprising that terror was systematically used.

\* \* \* \* \*

There were a number of different results of the operation of the Stalinist system.

The concentration of power achieved was great. No man or center of political authority, unless perhaps in Red China, has wielded such a grant of power over so many as Stalin. It was not limited by local authority, social structure, by private property rights, by considerations of humanitarianism, or by any other of the common limitations on political power. Stalin's word was law and his whims were law too, but his power was not used primarily to satisfy whims.

It was used, first, to achieve a buildup at a pell-mell rate of the economic and military strength at the disposal of the Soviet state.

It was used, secondly, to induce in the population a state of semi-hypnosis in which there was vulnerability to certain types of suggestion from above. Thus the Soviet government was able to count on a measure of belief among citizens in the truth of the charges of use by Americans of germ warfare in Korea.

It was used, thirdly, to establish submissiveness to authority, founded on the terror. There was even a measure of apparent success in "progress" toward the Stalinist goal of remaking human beings in a hurry.

There were other results—of a different kind. Let's begin with specific examples. Take, for instance, Soviet agriculture. In his speech on the "personality cult" of February 1956 Nikita Khrushchev revealed that Stalin knew nothing of the farm problem. He cited one instance, ascribing to Stalin a plan to raise taxes on the farmers (in 1952 or early 1953) by a colossal sum which exceeded the total income realized by farmers from sales to the government in 1952 by about 50 percent. Khrushchev called Stalin's proposal "the fantastic ideas of a person divorced from reality." He said Stalin had never visited a farm village for twenty-five years.

To take another aspect of the farm problem under Stalin: Soviet crop statisticians used to report grain harvests by a system estimating the crop not as delivered, after harvesting losses, to storage and distribution points—but as on the stalk in the field. This resulted in continual exaggeration of estimates of grain harvests by a margin of at least 10 or 15 per cent. The exaggeration may have been even larger because this system of crop reporting was adopted because of heavy pressure by the leadership on statisticians to report bigger harvests. The statisticians reported them, having in mind their predecessors had been purged for "sabotage" of statistics, but the grain they reported was not there.

It isn't necessary to give a detailed picture of the Soviet farm problem under Stalin. Suffice to say that in 1952 the citizens were still getting much less animal protein and fat in their diet, per capita, than they had received a quarter century before—before collectivization of agriculture. The peasants themselves were overtaxed, overexploited, and lived on a miserable level. Most significantly, there did exist in the growing power of industry the resources to begin to correct this. But there existed in the leadership a psychological block against acceptance of the facts.

Let's take as another example literature. On one hand the leadership demanded of writers that they produce "great" works, the equal of those produced by Tolstoi, Chekhov, Pushkin, Turgenev, Gogol, and the rest of the Russian classics. At the same time the leadership was continually looking over the shoulder of Soviet writers to see that everything they produced was "ideologically" correct. Every significant work was examined by authorities under a microscope to detect flaws. There were lengthy meetings discussing questions of literature—as, for instance, "bezkonfliktnost"—or "absence of conflict"—for a time advocated as the only correct line of treatment of character, then subsequently equally vehemently denounced. There were lengthy discussions of "tipichnost"—of what was "typical" for the new society and how far a writer could go in the depiction of negative characters in novels and plays. All this did nothing to produce "great" literature. And in the close and repressive atmosphere of the time there wasn't the slightest possibility for the production of great literary works.

In the leadership, however, there existed a block against recognizing the conflict between strict Party supervision of literature and a flowering of great art. Soviet writers understood this. They also understood it was useless to explain this to the leadership and remembered numerous Soviet writers who had fallen victim to the terror.

One can take as another example of the results of the Stalinist system, the Soviet break in 1948 with Yugoslavia.

Khrushchev said in his 1956 speech on the "personality cult" that "the 'Yugoslavia affair' contained no problems which could not have been solved through party discussions among comrades." He said, "There was no significant basis for the development of the 'affair'; it was completely possible to have prevented the rupture of relations with that country."

Laying the blame on Stalin, he quoted Stalin: "I shall shake my little finger—and there will be no more Tito. He will fall." Khrushchev commented, "But this did not happen to Tito. No matter how much or how little Stalin shook, not only his finger but everything else he could shake, Tito did not fall."

Khrushchev's disquisition on the Yugoslav affair was no doubt accurate as far as it went. But there was more to it. The dispute involved a basic question for the Communist movement. Before World War II in only one country—the Soviet Union—was the Communist Party in power. The Soviet Communist Party had on this basis established a position as the sole, undisputed center of the movement. After World War II a new situation arose. There were other countries with Communist governments. Most were under Moscow's control and rested on Soviet bayonets which had put them in power in Eastern Europe. But one—Yugoslavia—had achieved power on its own. This government soon developed an independent internal policy at some variance with Soviet practices. Could there be tolerated in any Communist Party any deviation whatsoever from Soviet-established norms or, for that matter, any genuine independence from Stalinist Moscow?

Long-established Soviet Communist habits of thought were opposed to acceptance of the fact of Yugoslav Communist independence from Moscow's domination. Yet this independence existed. A new situation called for a new approach. But there was a psychological block in the Soviet leadership against a new approach. Consequently, there took place a break between Yugoslavia and the Soviet Union.

Taking these examples—agriculture, literature, and relations with Yugoslavia—one sees elements illustrating workings of the Stalinist system. In each there was a serious situation. There was nothing obscure about what was happening. There were, no doubt, Russians at various levels with insight into these problems. But, nevertheless, because of the submissive atmosphere of the times and, in particular, because of the terror, they probably kept their feelings to themselves. The particular situations were allowed to become aggravated. Taken together with a whole series of other such situations, they added up to an impending crisis for the country. The common element in all such situations was existence on the top levels of a psychological block against facing the facts of a particular problem. In subordinate echelons of the political apparatus of the nation there was simultaneous unwillingness to bring to the attention of the top facts not in accordance with the top's prejudged opinion.

There had taken place an atrophy of the regime's central nervous system. It was unable to recognize or respond to certain types of warning signals. There was a breakdown of communications. And one of its symptoms was the incapability of the system to distinguish between actual fact and its own propaganda.

For the leadership, as one aspect of its claimed omnipotence, arrogated to itself the right to slant, distort, use and abuse truth as it pleased, for political advantage. This was propaganda, most important weapon of the Party, field of the most important department of the Party's Central Committee which ran Soviet mass communications. But the Party never did evolve a system for drawing a distinction, for those officials for whom it might be necessary, between propaganda and the actual situation. Some officials might understand that there was a difference, but they had to pretend they did not notice. Some officials might, in order effectively to carry out assignments, employ a "double-think" which enabled them to use that portion of the truth they had to use and still not deviate from the Party line. However, even on the top level of the government there was inability to distinguish between propaganda and the facts.

For example, Soviet economist, Eugene Varga, an expert on business cycles in the West, was attacked by the Party leadership after World War II for predicting that there might not be a major crisis in the United States for years. Varga obediently changed his predictions and from then on every year predicted anew a crisis in the United States. The Soviet leadership actually apparently came to believe in the imminence, on the basis in part of Varga's predictions, of an economic crash in the United States.

One could cite many examples. There was, as a different case, the failure for years to pay adequate attention to Western scientific progress because Soviet propaganda was continually spouting off about the "superiority" of Russian science.

Stalin was personally to blame for these things. But Stalin was more than an individual political leader. He was an image which the system had made—and in extraordinary degree the Stalin image was the system. The faults were faults of Stalin personally, but also of the system that had made him so all-powerful.

And here lay both explosive power and danger. There was the contrast between the economic-military might the system was piling up and the atrophy of the regime's nervous system which was preventing the economic power from seeking outlets in solution of the country's extraordinary problems and crises.

Domestically the nation desperately needed an improvement in its low living standards. Soviet citizens were ill-housed, ill-clothed and ill-fed even though the Soviet Union was already the second most powerful industrial nation of the earth. The farm situation was acute, and the peasantry needed to be relieved of its back-breaking load and get a fair share of the national income. Creative artists needed more freedom and less direction.

In foreign affairs there was an equally difficult state. The Soviet-inspired Korean War had led to bitter hostility between East and West. The Soviet government had succeeded in antagonizing most of the newly free Asian-African countries of that time by regarding them as still colonies. The Kremlin had lost its vitriolic propaganda war with Yugoslavia hands down. Foundations seemingly were being laid by Stalin for an even bigger fiasco of the same sort with Red China. Revolts could conceivably have begun in oppressed and badly-mismanaged Eastern Europe, run from Moscow. The Soviet Union was approaching the danger of being left in complete isolation from the entire rest of the world, Communist and non-Communist.

Three problems stood out.

First, there was the need to reduce the enormous Soviet military establishment which, since no one intended to attack the Soviet Union, was an anachronism.

Second, there was the need to abolish the bane of penal, forced labor which hung over the whole Soviet Union like a black cloud, undermining standards of living, frustrating modernization of entire branches of the economy, and consuming people in the most inefficient, cruel manner possible.

Third, there was the need to abolish the terror, as inconsistent with the requirements of social, political and economic life in a developed, complex, modern industrial nation. The terror was the source of more waste than any other single factor in Soviet life. Humanitarian reasons aside, it was necessary to end the terror for sound managerial reasons. But none of these problems could be attacked with Joseph Stalin still running the Soviet government. Stalin was too closely identified with the aggravation of foreign relations in order to justify his internal regime. He was, above all, too closely identified with the terror itself. It was his alter ego. If it went he would have to go too. But in 1952 Stalin was still running the Soviet government with a firm grip and there seemed no chance at all that he might for many years step aside, die or be removed.

# 17. *Year 1952*

An evening in early November, 1951. Outside, night had descended on the busy, chilly city. Julie and I, both with grimy hands, sat down heavily in armchairs facing each other in the small, somewhat barren living room and smiled wanly.

"Thank God we're finished!" I exclaimed.

"I will never move again all the rest of my life!" Julie declared wearily.

For days we had been toting things from our old apartment to this, our new apartment on broad Sadovaya Boulevard, a mile or so away. Today, finally, the movers had come and shifted all the heavy furniture. And once they had been given their traditional bonuses of stiff drinks of vodka and cash tips and departed Julie and I had been left to move everything till we were satisfied with the arrangement. Then there was so much more to do. Finally we had done as much as we could that evening.

I got up and went about the place giving things a once-over and taking pride in all we had done. It was a queer, ill-arranged little apartment we had acquired, with nearly as much of its floor space absorbed in a long, broad corridor as in rooms for living purposes.

The yellow plaster-faced building in which it was located was an eight-story structure in stultified "Stalinist classical" style containing seventy-two apartments or so, and had been christened by foreigners with the title of "the diplomatic ghetto." The name was given because of an effort by the authorities to concentrate here many diplomats and

230

journalists previously in apartments scattered all about the city—to permit their being kept under observation more easily.

The structure was new, completed in 1951. Typifying the state of Soviet housing were two facts any new inhabitant quickly discovered. If one put a pencil on the floor along the wall and released it, it would roll towards the center of the room. In the second place, it was another feature of the dwelling that there was no running hot water. The only hot water was from a fearsome instantaneous gas "geyser" heater in the bathroom which provided hot water only for baths or showers, not for wash basins or the kitchen.

Julie and I were not, however, complaining. We had begged the Administration for Services to the Diplomatic Corps to rent us an apartment there. We had been waiting years. Our need had been nearly desperate. It was with pride and pleasure that we set about turning our new apartment into a comfortable home.

*     *     *     *     *

Maria Ivanovna entered our lives on an afternoon in January 1952. There was a knock at the door. Julie opened it. There stood a heavy-set Russian woman of forty-five. She wore a black wool overcoat, a dark gray woolen scarf around her head, and carried in her hand a large black "sumka"—a "purse," more properly a satchel. She introduced herself and presented a document. Julie invited her in. The two of them sat talking for twenty minutes or so in our living room. I looked at the woman's face. It was rotund, motherly and had about it an aura of warm affection. The interview was soon over. The visitor departed. Julie sighed with satisfaction.

"Maybe we'll have a cook at last!" she said. "I hope so. It's time we gave my mother a rest from looking after us. And I'm sure this woman is a good cook. She's old-fashioned and kind. I like her." Our efforts to get a servant had been as long and drawn out as our attempts to get an apartment. Nothing came easily in Russia.

"Maria Ivanovna . . ." I said aloud. "That's about as Russian a name as one can have." We were not disappointed in her. She was a good cook. Her "borshch" was rich and succulent. Her "kasha"— buckwheat groats baked with mushrooms in butter or chicken fat— was delicious. She could produce wonderful roasts and make the tastiest "kotlety"—Russian meat patties with bread added, broiled or fried and eaten with sour cream. The only problem with Maria

Ivanovna's cooking was to keep one's waistline from growing, growing, growing.

She was more than a cook. She looked after us assiduously. She mended our clothes and picked up after us; made me wear overshoes when it was wet outside, and even induced Julie to wear something on her head when it was cold.

Promptly at 11 every morning Maria Ivanovna would enter our rear door with her shopping bag full of purchases for the day. And she would start to get us our lunch. Promptly at seven every evening, after dinner had been served, she would leave. She went home to her own apartment to look after her husband and teen-age daughter.

One night Julie and I lingered over our coffee after dinner.

"Well now we finally have a proper household. We have an apartment with at least a little bit of room. We have Maria Ivanovna. We have good furniture and pretty china and just about everything else we need for the house. We can even entertain guests now and then and it's all very comfortable. I'm glad."

I thought for a minute. I remembered the cold toilet at Malovlasevsky. I remembered before that when we were on the Moscow streets in the chilly autumn. I counted how long it had taken to reach this modest comfort . . . Seven years! Truly in Russia patience was the most important quality, patience and perseverance.

*     *     *     *     *

It was four o'clock on a cold February morning. The wind howled across broad Pushkin Square. Snow flurries whirled in my face as I stepped out of my car and entered the *Izvestia* building. I approached a small window at the end of a corridor labelled "Expeditsiya." Behind it stood a sturdy, burly, cordial Russian woman of uncertain age. She looked at me and smiled.

"Just a minute," she said. "I'll go and see if it's ready." I waited in the corridor for five minutes, contemplating the fact that the Soviet government deemed it necessary to have at the inner doorway leading into the *Izvestia* printing plant an aged guard in a big sheepskin coat with a rifle in hand which looked to be from World War I. What state secrets were concealed in this newspaper plant, I wondered?

After a time the friendly Russian woman came back with a copy of the morning's newspaper, *Izvestia,* the official organ of the Soviet government. I took the paper, opened it right there, took a hurried glance to see if there was urgent news. There was. I saw the full text of a new diplomatic note on the second page. I strode out, got into my car, and drove three minutes further to the Central Telegraph Office.

An hour and a half later, after having transmitted by telephone my dispatches to the AP, I packed up my typewriter and returned bleary-eyed to my apartment. It was light outside when I wearily climbed back into bed to resume the slumber interrupted by my alarm at three-fifteen.

My visit to *Izvestia*—a daily event—was one aspect of changed working conditions for me arising from a re-organization of the AP work. The former AP office in the Hotel Metropole had been abandoned. Henceforth my office was my apartment or wherever else I could find space to put down my typewriter. My files were the information in my head. I worked by myself, at the strangest, most inconvenient hours.

There was good reason for this. The reason lay in the eight hour time differential between Moscow and New York—which meant that important stories breaking as late as six or seven A.M. or, at the latest, even at eight, could still make late city editions of morning papers in the United States.

By dint of personal exploration I found that copies of at least one Soviet morning paper—*Izvestia*—could be had sometimes as early as three-thirty or four in the morning. I had also discovered that often important stories in the morning paper were not broadcast on Moscow Radio until much later. By getting up early and going to get the morning paper myself, I could occasionally secure major beats.

This happened not so often. Maybe only once during two weeks I might get a substantial "scoop" this way in my reporting work. For this I had to disrupt my sleep every night, turn our household upside down, and put myself under a considerable strain. But it seemed worthwhile. One never knew. The big story of the year might break in just this way.

\*    \*    \*    \*    \*

In the damp April of 1952 there gathered in Moscow a strange assemblage. It was called "the Moscow Economic Conference." The sponsoring body was the Soviet Chamber of Commerce, a non-governmental organization which fronted for the Ministry of Foreign Trade.

No expense was spared, in preparation for the conference, and in entertaining lavishly at Soviet expense the delegates who came from all over. Provision was made for a propaganda fanfare to spread the news of the conference abroad. It was planned as a big deal.

In going to the enormous effort involved in holding the first "international" gathering in Moscow since the Council of Foreign Ministers session in 1947, the Russians apparently hoped to achieve several aims: 1. To have a platform for a propaganda attack against tight restrictions on trade with the Soviet Union erected by Western European countries under American leadership; 2. To entice with prospects of profits Western businessmen eager to do business with the Soviet Union and get them to bring pressure on their governments to relax or abolish the trade restrictions; 3. Lastly, perhaps the Russians did actually hope the conference might open up new trade opportunities.

However, the concept of broadened economic ties with the non-Communist world ran counter to the whole spirit of Stalinist times. This was one of isolation from the outside world. Anyone could hardly help but be struck by this in Moscow at the time. The conference seemed an exercise in building Potemkin villages in the center of the capital. It was a sort of expensive and painful farce.

With no little amusement our rather cynical little group of American journalists watched the delegates stream in. There were Communists and fellow-travelers from the satellite states and elsewhere. There were sleazy fly-by-night types in search of a quick buck. There were some absurd characters who seemed to have emerged from special woodwork for this occasion. Some types came for a free ride on the caviar circuit. Some came for the sake of publicity or curiosity. There were—and this provided the contrast—even good solid Western European and British businessmen interested in prospects of trade. The British—always alert for trade prospects and not about to miss a good chance for information or contacts—sent a strong and able group. The Americans, of course, flubbed the rather remarkable opportunity, and such few Americans as did come were strangely assorted and most of them frightened of their shadows. There was an aging but erect middle-western businessman with a beautiful young American Indian wife perhaps forty years his junior. There was a curious camera-laden traveling salesman who planned to use the material and film he collected for a year of lectures to Kiwanis Clubs or the equivalent. An ex-American Jamaican leftist trade-unionist, who had been expelled from the United States, came in from Commie labor headquarters in Vienna at the last minute to "bolster" this United States "delegation."

The most important Westerner attending the conference was Lord Boyd-Orr, former head of the Food and Agriculture Organization of the UN, and a Nobel Peace Prize winner. He is also, one might add, a businessman extraordinary, and a man for whom no iron curtains exist—quite as much at home in Peking as in Paris. Lord Boyd-Orr, with his bushy white eyebrows, has been scouting out the prospects and possibilities of world peace many long years, and he's not afraid to go anywhere in the search. He was even willing to go to Moscow in 1952—which not many men of his caliber were courageous enough to do. He thought it worth a try.

For Julie and me the Moscow Economic Conference was a howling success for one particular reason. As a result of it we secured our copy of the new Russian cookbook—the first published in decades and in such desperate demand that ordinarily peaceful housewives were ready to riot to get one. The cookbook, as it happened, was on sale for conference delegates—even there on a strictly under-the-counter basis. I managed to buy one. And it is still a treasured possession.

\*    \*    \*    \*    \*

It was a summer Sunday afternoon. The sun was still high in the heavens. Four of us sat amid tall grass at the back of our large yard at the dacha. We talked and laughed. We discussed serious and not-so-serious subjects and we exchanged observations on life in Russia and America.

Julie, Harrison Salisbury, and I were chatting with the new American Ambassador in Moscow, George Kennan. He had dropped in unexpectedly, as he occasionally did, in order to spend a quiet hour or so in the countryside, away from Moscow's stifling atmosphere.

"How would you like to go and pay a visit to our little market here?" I suddenly asked.

"Why not?" replied the Ambassador. We got up and went out the back gate, walking up toward Saltykovka market.

One of the inevitable features of a visit by the Ambassador was the presence at our front fence of a squad of four Soviet security guards. These tough but not unfriendly plainclothesmen accompanied the Ambassador everywhere. They always stayed outside the entrance of whatever establishment he was in. Ostensibly they were there to protect him. They also served the function, more important in Soviet official psychology, of being a human wall between him and the people. They were under strictest instructions to keep as close to him as possible wherever he might go.

On this occasion when we started walking toward the market, the guards were caught unawares for several minutes. They had been standing, gossiping with each other, paying little attention to us. We walked past Uncle Petya's garden and the barracks in which he and his wife lived. Not till we got one hundred and fifty yards up the road did one of the guards notice our departure. We turned and watched the sudden flurry with great amusement. All four guards started running. They knew their very lives depended on obeying their instructions and sticking to the Ambassador like flypaper.

Panting a bit from their exertions they caught up with us. The four then spread out on either side of us on our left flank and on our right flank and marched abreast of us. This was the way we entered the crowded market on that Sunday. Like the Army football team in a "V" formation, we swept through the center of it with Russians scattering in fright in every direction on either side.

Ambassador Kennan got a look at the market. But under these circumstances he did not have much chance to talk with the local citizens. All this was amusing, and when we got back to the dacha we laughed about it. But it had its sad side too. Kennan had always taken considerable delight in even quite limited contacts with Russians from all walks of life. Keenly observant, he gleaned significant impressions from his chats with Soviet citizens. Returning as Ambassador even knowing everything about the isolation of foreigners from the populace, it was nevertheless a source of keenest frustration to find how thick was this wall the Soviet government had built.

Kennan's return in 1952 was an event. Though his stay was not to be very long, his presence meant that during his stay, in a crucial period, there was a flow from the Embassy to Washington of penetrating reports and telegrams.

\*   \*   \*   \*   \*

"What do you know about the recent purge in Georgia?" Ambassador Kennan asked me one day when I was in the Embassy for a morning chat. I knew nothing and told him so. The pressure resulting from my unusual new schedule had been such that for many weeks I had been far behind in my reading of the Soviet provincial press.

Kennan gave me some of the published details. And when I got back to my apartment I started combing through piled-up copies of the newspaper, *Dawn of the East,* published in Tiflis. Soon I found an account of the meeting of the Central Committee of the Georgian Communist Party. I read the reports and speeches carefully. There had been a purge of the leadership. Most of the long-time leaders of Party and Government in Georgia had been swept out of office and unknown personalities put in their place. Near the end of the account it was reported that L. P. Beria was present.

I started to think about this. Lavrenty Beria was one of the three or four most important men in the USSR. He was a Deputy Premier, a Politburo member, and one of Stalin's closest collaborators. Like Stalin, he was Georgian in national origin. Beria was believed to have three areas of responsibility. He was considered to be in charge of police and security activities. He was thought to be in charge of Soviet nuclear weapons development. And he was thought to be in charge of the Republic of Georgia.

Now, as it appeared, he had gone to Georgia and was present at a purge of the Georgian leadership. But the leadership he had purged was a leadership he had installed. It included many of his friends and cronies from pre-1938 days when he himself was the Party and government chief in Georgia. And an attack on that leadership could be in effect an attack on Beria himself. Or so, at least, it seemed to me.

Yet Beria had been present, and presumably it was he who transmitted the orders from Moscow on which it was based. It looked as if he had been sent to oust his friends. This could be interpreted on the one hand as a sop to his ostensible continuing authority over Georgian affairs. But it could be interpreted as a deliberate humiliation—rubbing his nose in his own dirt in public.

This was interesting. Whoever had lashed out at Beria must have been sure of Stalin's support. Beria was not a man to be struck with impunity unless he had previously been disarmed.

It was then that I heard another rumor which indicated that even more serious things along the same lines were afoot. Said the fleeting rumor, Minister of State Security, Victor Abakumov, had been fired; his replacement was not known. The rumor could not, of course, be verified. The particular post was one of the most important in the

Soviet government, but everything about it, including even on occasion the name of its occupant, was a carefully guarded state secret.

If this story were to prove true—and eventually it did—it might mean there had been interference with Beria's control over Soviet security and secret police activities. The Ministry of State Security had charge of intelligence, counter-intelligence, and state security measures in general. It was the most sensitive link in the Soviet apparatus. Free of Party control, possessing a broad scope of police authority, it had great power. In a struggle among groups or factions in the leadership, it was a key position. The Ministry of State Security was Joseph Stalin's own baby and the key weapon he used to infiltrate and terrify the Party, the government, and the armed forces, and keep them all submissive to him.

The apparently ousted Minister, Abakumov, was a former subordinate of Beria who had worked under him as head of counterintelligence during the war. As Minister of State Security he had been under Beria's direct supervision. If Abakumov had now been fired, this could mean there had been another heavy blow dealt to Beria.

By whom? Why? What intrigues were going on at the heart of Soviet power?

\*    \*    \*    \*    \*

On the mid-July afternoon the steam engine chugged into the Finland Station in Leningrad and came to a stop. I looked for the ancient "International Car" with its well-weathered wooden frame. I went up to it eagerly. Julie waited behind while I climbed aboard past the conductor who let me on. I looked anxiously down the passageway. There, all of a sudden, I saw her—my mother.

She smiled from out of a wan countenance. Behind her loomed the familiar rotund face of my father. I shouted greetings down the corridor and waited where I stood until the preceding passengers disembarked and my parents came abreast of me. We embraced with feeling and at length. How long it had been since I had seen them!

I escorted them out of the train. Julie came up briskly to meet them. This was the first meeting of parents and daughter-in-law and they looked at each other with interest. I could read the thoughts in my parents' minds as Julie kissed them. So this was the girl who had kept their son away so long!

A few minutes later we marched off and packed ourselves into the

Intourist limousine ready for us and ordered the chauffeur to take us to the Hotel Astoria. As we drove along Julie and I plied them with questions about their journey on the slow train from Helsinki, which took about a day and a half for a distance of a couple of hundred miles. They had been the only Americans on the train and objects of curiosity to the other passengers. In this era the only Americans entering Russia, aside from a rare fur buyer now and then, were diplomats. Mother and father, in fact, had to receive permission from the State Department to make the journey to Russia. American travelers were not generally allowed to visit the USSR.

The project of the visit had begun long before this happy day. Dad and Mother wished to meet Julie and to see me. Julie could not leave the Soviet Union and I refused to leave her behind. So we invited them to visit us. They accepted. Friends begged them not to go, such was the fear surrounding travel to Russia in those days. But they refused to be scared away. The Press Department at the Ministry of Foreign Affairs had agreed, when I asked their aid, to help expedite issuance of entry visas through the Soviet Embassy in Washington.

So finally they had actually arrived. It was hard to believe. The days of their visit went quickly. There was the train trip to Moscow on the Red Arrow Express. There were tours about Moscow in the car seeing the city's sights. There were hours at our apartment with tasty and calorific meals served lovingly by Maria Ivanovna. There were bright, noisy diplomatic corps receptions and a scintillating ball given by Ambassador and Mrs. Kennan at their residence. There were trips out of town to the dacha, and an excursion to the monastery at Zagorsk.

One day we walked through the Kremlin. Special permission had been given for the visit. Before us marched three blue-capped, burly security guards. A similar threesome brought up our rear. We walked from one object of artistic and historical significance to another as a guide explained the rich sights.

Mother from time to time glanced behind at father. It had always been a point of complaint with her that Dad lagged behind. He was slow and deliberate and refused to be hurried. But there in the Kremlin when he got a bit behind us the three Russian security officers quietly caught up with him till they were not quite stepping on his heels. Dad would finally become aware of their proximity and move faster. Mother whispered in my ear, laughing, "This is one place that I don't have to worry about losing your father!"

The visit came to an end too soon—on a wharf in Leningrad where mother and father boarded a Soviet ship taking them to Helsinki. Julie and I kissed them goodbye. When would we see each other again, we wondered?

*    *    *    *    *

Rainy midsummer Sundays in dacha settlements can be dismal. One has gone to the country to indulge in the out-of-doors and sunshine. One is conscious of the evanescent character of Moscow summers. But down pours the rain, churning dirt walks into sticky Moscow mud. One stands on the veranda nervously, looking out at the wet day. One feels as if God is short-changing one deliberately. One is so very sorry for oneself. As the Sunday wears slowly on, one's mood becomes fouler and fouler.

Such a Sunday was August 17, 1952. After lunch I went listlessly upstairs. I picked out a book from the shelf. I lay on the bed to read, but I had no enthusiasm for reading. I dropped the book on the floor and fell into a doze, then into a sleep. When I awoke I continued to lie there. I listened with ennui to the rain falling on the roof. I looked up at the brown boards on the ceiling. I smoked one cigarette after another.

Charley, the cat, was miaowing at the veranda door. He was also in an ugly mood. Twice I had gotten up, at his insistence, to let him out onto the veranda, and both times he was miaowing to be let in again within a few minutes. Something painful was evidently gnawing at his insides. I looked at him with a surge of sympathy. But suddenly I grew angry at his discontent, reached for a soft slipper, and tossed it at him, missing him by just an inch or two. Yipping, as if he had really been hit, he scampered out of the room. I sank back on the bed.

Had the weather been fine on such a midsummer Sunday there would have been all sorts of joyful sounds in the air. There would have been a gay party down the road. Young people would have been laughing and singing there. Couples would have been wandering slowly arm-in-arm down the lane in front of the house, talking with one another quietly. Families would have been returning from picnics at the pond, flushed with sun, vodka and good fellowship, chorusing some familiar song, maybe the vivid tune whose refrain ran, "I waited for you the whole war long . . ."

But not that Sunday. The only sound I could hear beside the rain on the roof and the wind in the pines was the roar of a car motor several hundred yards away, stuck in the mud, with the driver racing the motor in a hopeless effort to get out while his wheels spun deeper and deeper into the morass. How well I knew his feelings!

I felt a bit the same way myself—frustrated. It was the weather, but more than the weather. There were things to be frustrated about. Sometimes they came to the surface. What, for example, was to become of Julie and me? How long would the uncertainty of our fate go on? The visit of my parents had, I guess, brought home to us our apparently hopeless situation with particular force. They had left, and we stood there saying goodbye to them knowing we could not follow. I looked at the ceiling there on the second floor of our dacha. But what good did thinking do? What was there that could possibly change?

Julie and I were caught in something so big that it was difficult to envision. The picture that came to mind was of a tremendous log jam in a torrential river in flood. For miles and miles the logs piled on each other in an unbelievable tangle. The river boiled and swirled and gushed behind the log jam and the pent up power of the raging waters sought a way out—and there was none. It seemed hopeless that it would ever break up and flow downstream. Yet it is said that in every log jam there is some key log which, so long as it stays in position, holds back the entire accumulation behind it, and when it is blown out by a perceptive lumberjack armed with dynamite the whole jam tumbles swiftly down the torrent. The raging river, as I saw it, was the constantly, rapidly growing physical strength of the powerful Soviet economic-military machine. The log jam was the traffic pile up, the constipation, the stagnant mess of unsolved problems of all sorts caused by the atrophy of the political system on the topmost level, the breakdown of communications in the system. The dichotomy was frightening. The pent-up forces seething and boiling, seeking an outlet, were unimaginable in their magnitude, volatile and dangerous in the extreme. So it seemed to me. But I could not see anyone or anything capable of mining that key log in the jam and blowing it to bits, letting the river—and perhaps us with it—flow its unhindered way.

I heard the telephone ring downstairs. I went down. Julie had already answered. It was one of my colleagues. He told me TASS, the official Soviet news agency, had released an announcement of the arrival of a top-level Chinese government delegation. He advised me to come to town to work on the story and its ramifications.

Before we were back in Moscow it was already completely dark. I drove through the night, Julie by my side. I was still thinking about the same thing.

\*        \*        \*        \*        \*

As I approached the Telegraph Office that night of August 17 I began worrying about more practical and immediate problems: whether I was late with this story, whether there would be a text of the announcement at the telegraph office, whether there was a telephone line to London available, and about a dozen other things.

As it turned out there was a copy of the TASS release waiting for me. I sat down and hammered out my article. A little later when it got on the wires of the AP it began:

"Moscow, Aug. 17 (AP)—A top-level 15-man Chinese government delegation headed by Premier Chou-En-Lai arrived in Moscow tonight for very important talks with Soviet leaders in the Kremlin. The Chinese party, which came by air from Peiping, included military, diplomatic and economic leaders. Chou and his colleagues were met at the airdrome by a group of top Soviet leaders headed by Deputy Premiers V. M. Molotov, A. I. Mikoyan, N. A. Bulganin and Foreign Minister A. Y. Vishinsky. It seemed obvious that closer Soviet-Chinese military ties are on the agenda along with economic and political topics."

After two hours of work I had completed my story. I picked up my things and drove home. Julie had already gone to bed and was sound asleep. I went to the kitchen to get myself a cup of tea. I sat at the little table in the corner next to the window watching the trucks go roaring by on the boulevard outside.

Why had the Chinese Communists sent a new delegation to Moscow, I wondered? The composition of the delegation made it clear that the Chinese had come with requests for a big rise in Soviet aid. The Peking regime no doubt needed such increased aid desperately. It was barely three years of age. It had not completed crushing resistance pockets inside Red China. It had enormous economic task needs in order to get started on industrialization. Mao had been drawn into the Soviet-inspired adventure in Korea. Peking was pulling

Moscow's hot chestnuts out of the fire. So Peking had come with demands for more help. This was a reasonable hypothesis.

Ordinarily when a Communist delegation flew to Moscow for "talks" basic questions had already been decided. The delegation came for a round of receptions and for the formal ceremony of signing the agreements. That was that. It was a formality. Was this the situation of Chou's delegation? Remembering Mao Tze-Tung's visit of 1949–50 when over two months had gone by before agreement was reached on a series of pacts, I doubted it. Nothing between Peking and Moscow seemed to be simple and clear-cut. Somehow the Chinese revolution seemed to pose for Moscow insoluble problems. Moscow's attitude toward Peking was, I felt, permeated with conflict.

I remembered how *Izvestia,* in January 1952 had gone to the special trouble to elucidate the true nature of the Chinese revolution. It was, said *Izvestia,* "a bourgeois democratic revolution," and "a revolution of national liberation directed against foreign imperialism."

"At the present time," declared *Izvestia,* "the tasks of building socialism, its direct tasks, are not being raised and not being undertaken in China."

This put the Chinese revolution in the same category as the American revolution of 1776. It also kept the October Revolution of 1917 in Russia something apart—for that was not a "bourgeois democratic revolution." The Soviet Union had not only undertaken the tasks of building socialism but had already built it—so the Soviet dogma ran. All this seemed to put the Peking government in very much the same ideological category as the bourgeois democratic governments of the West.

How had the Soviet Union treated Communist China? Pretty roughly and pretty stingily. This was obvious. When Mao came to Moscow in 1949 Stalin insisted on keeping, for the time, the Soviet position in Port Arthur. Stalin had given Mao only a niggardly loan. There had been agreements on sending Soviet technicians to China and formation of joint Soviet-Chinese companies to exploit Chinese resources. Both of these devices looked like Soviet weapons for imperialistic penetration of Red China.

And then in late 1950 the Red Chinese got themselves into the Korean debacle—which the Russians had started through North Korean puppets. So, it might seem, the Soviet Union had Peking over a barrel. Peking could not get along for long in Korea without Soviet aid. Chou En-Lai had come for more. I was sure that Stalin would drive a hard, hard bargain.

Yet Moscow also took pride in the Chinese revolution. This was the other side of the coin. The Soviet Union, allied with Communist China, was no longer internationally isolated as before 1950 with only East European satellites as "friends." The Russians were exhilarated so much by the triumphant declaration, so frequently made, that the Communist nations were nine hundred million strong. But six hundred million of these were Chinese.

One thing was clear. The arrival of the Chinese delegation once more put the basic question of Red China on the agenda for the Kremlin. And the question of Red China involved the leadership of the international Communist movement, a point of which the Soviet leadership was, no doubt, acutely aware.

I looked at my watch. It was already one forty-five A.M. and I had to be back down at work by about five-thirty. I sighed and went to bed.

*    *    *    *    *

"Shall we go back to the dacha today?" Julie asked me at the lunch table the next noon. I had done my early morning work and caught a mid-morning nap before rising in time for the noon meal.

"I don't see why not," I said. And so we made a brief effort to resume our country life. I worked in the garden that evening till late. Only the animal sounds broke the still of the warm dusk, cows mooing, dogs barking, goats bleating. Julie and I sat on the porch, absorbing the calm.

The next day I wrote a letter home: "The dahlias are blooming. They are beautiful. We have had nearly a dozen cauliflowers from the garden as well as regular wax beans, peas, carrots, summer squash, lettuce and the like. We have cleaned things up a bit. There aren't so many weeds. Charley, the cat, got into mortal combat the other morning at about five-thirty after I had already left for the city. The battle took place beneath the house, right below the bedroom where Julie was asleep. There is a gray cat that insists on invading the yard and Charley took him on. You can imagine how Julie enjoyed the early morning yowling. Charley got a wounded ear but is walking around proudly and aggressively."

I looked up from my letter writing to watch Charley perched high up on a box in the back yard, keeping a vigilant guard over his domain. It was a lovely and a quiet summer day. But in Moscow big things were cooking.

* * * * *

The next morning I arose at five. I drove fast into town in the dawn's rosy light. I cut down along the Moscow River embankment into the central area of the city and the sun's rays struck St. Basil's Cathedral as I climbed rapidly up the hill onto Red Square and drove through the square and up broad Gorky Street. The city was beginning to stir. I parked my car at the telegraph and went inside for my copy of *Pravda*.

Across the top of the page was splattered in large bold, headline type—in Russia a rare thing—the announcement of a new Communist Party Congress to meet in Moscow Oct. 5—the first Party Congress since 1939.

The announcement said, as its first item, that the "otchotny doklad" —in other words the "keynote report"—would be delivered by Georgi M. Malenkov, Secretary of the Central Committee. Other than the Malenkov report there were to be two main subjects. One was a new Five Year Plan to run through 1955. The report on this was to be delivered by the Soviet planning chief, Maxim Z. Saburov. The directives took up two pages of the paper. The other was proposed changes in the statutes of the Party on which the report was to be delivered by Central Committee Secretary Nikita S. Khrushchev. *Pravda* carried a page and a half of text of the proposed New Party statutes.

Finally, the congress was to elect a new Central Committee which itself would presumably elect or reelect other ruling organs of the party.

I read through parts of the lengthy documents and filed a first story in which I merely pointed out highlights. I telephoned it to London. Then I went home to get a cup of coffee and think it over. It needed study. There was a lot of material.

I sat in the kitchen reading *Pravda* carefully. I glanced through the Five Year Plan directives. Emphasis obviously was on heavy industry development, coal, steel, chemicals, machinery. There was nothing unexpected here. From the economic plan I went on to the changes proposed in the Party Statutes. The name of the Party was to be changed—from "All-Union Communist Party (Bolsheviks)" to—

"Communist Party of the Soviet Union." The famed Politburo—top policy-making Party organ—was to be replaced with a "Presidium of the Central Committee." What did this mean? One could only wait and see.

And there was much else of interest in the documents in *Pravda*. But the most important thing about the coming Congress was that there was to be one. It was twelve years since the last congress. Under Party statutes a Party Congress was supposed to be held once every four years. But Stalin had ignored this. Why? I could not help remembering an occasion when a Party Congress was scheduled to take place. In 1949 there had been held a series of regional Party Congresses intended to lead up to a general Party Congress. But nothing had happened.

Why? I recalled another scheduled event which had not taken place. It was during the election to the Supreme Soviet in March 1950. The tradition was that the last speech on election eve was to be made by Stalin. And so things were left ready for this great event. All channels were clear and open for the "great leader and teacher." Everyone else had already spoken. It remained for him to utter the final word. Workers gathered around radios in factories waiting to hear the words of wisdom. But the leader never spoke.

Why? The answer was probably simple in the extreme. The aging Stalin, contemptuous of the public, didn't want to deliver long speeches. But, as the General Secretary of the Central Committee of the Communist Party, if there were a Party Congress Stalin was expected to make the keynote report—the "otchotny doklad." This by tradition must be a long declaration of accomplishment and policy.

Stalin could, if he chose, delegate this function to one of the other secretaries. But here was the real dilemma. If he delegated this function this would be, in effect, the naming of an heir apparent. This touched on the most delicate Soviet political problem of those years —the problem of succession. So now a Congress had been called and Georgi Malenkov would make the main report! Very interesting indeed! This certainly put the spotlight on Malenkov.

That was the main significance of the coming Congress. Yet I had a vague but strong feeling that the last word on the subject of succession had not been spoken. There would be a Party Congress and Malenkov would make the main report, but it seemed to me that old Joseph Stalin probably had a few surprise aces up his sleeve which might still leave things up in the air and unsettled. I doubted very much that he felt the need for any crown prince.

*   *   *   *   *

In my work I had to range from the sublime down to the diabolic and back to the ridiculous—constantly. That was the way it was. The ridiculous made up a good part of my work. The Soviet Press took itself and what it said seriously. To some people in the rest of the world it was so silly as to be sometimes funny. Better than the comic page. More Lower Slobovian than Lower Slobovia, alas! Good copy though.

One afternoon in September 1952, a little before World Series time, Harrison Salisbury of the *New York Times* strolled into my apartment with a magazine in his hand.

"Look at this!" he said with a laugh. The magazine was *Smena*, official illustrated journal of the Young Communist League. It carried a photograph of a baseball scene in America. I began to read the article. I was amused. I looked up at Harrison.

"This is a hell of a story!" I exclaimed.

"You're damned right," he replied. I sat down at my typewriter and pounded out an account of the *Smena* article which later, when it was put on the AP A-wire across the length of the United States, looked like this:

"Moscow, September 15 (AP)—The Soviet youth magazine *Smena* told Soviet young readers today that 'beizbol' is not American in origin but just an American distortion of the Russian village sport 'lapty' which was played in the Russian countryside hundreds of years before there was any America on the map.

" 'American "beizbol",' the magazine said, 'is a "beastly battle, a bloody fight with mayhem and murder." '

"*Smena* is the organ of the Young Communist League. 'Players of "beizbol" in the United States,' said the magazine, 'are slaves who are bought and sold like sheep. When they are worn out, and usually cripples, as the result of the injuries they have suffered on the playing fields, they are thrown out on the street to die of starvation,' *Smena* added.

"The article entitled 'Beizbol—Big Ketch' was written by a pair of authors named A. Kuleshov and M. Kremnev.

"It gave Soviet readers some real inside details of the American national game. One of the pictures, for instance, showed a player knocked out on the field with the caption: 'An episode in a game between "Sen Luis" and "The Rodgers"—Del Rios, having received a blow on the back of the head is being carried unconscious from the field!' "

The article continued in the same spirit for several more paragraphs. I have never had such fun writing an article. I don't suppose I have ever written an article which got such play either. It made the Russians the laughing-stock of America. All over the United States the story was splash-played. Hardly an editorial writer in the country could avoid the temptation to take up his pen and write an editorial. The word "beizbol" became for a time a byword in America. Americans perhaps realized from it, as never before, the lengths to which the Soviet press was going in its hate-America campaign.

*   *   *   *   *

September 18th I stood in the Chancery of the American Embassy between desks of two secretaries and looked out of the window. The view was one to which I had become accustomed. Below lay Stables' Square, several hundred yards across. Beyond it was a park, the Alexandrovsky Garden, which had a monument in it resembling Cleopatra's Needle. At the other side of the park were the brick Kremlin walls, and over them, inside the Kremlin, were yellow-painted buildings making up the Kremlin offices, churches, museums and palaces.

I was waiting with other American correspondents in Moscow to see Ambassador Kennan. He was going away the next day for a visit to Western Europe. He planned, as we had been informed, to return to Moscow in early October. Kennan had invited us in for a brief farewell visit before his departure.

Soon Dorothy Hessman, the Ambassador's secretary, came out of his office with her stenographic notebook in her hand. She motioned us to go on in. We filed through the door.

Kennan talked for more than a half hour. He spoke calmly, in a low tone and seriously. I would not even wish to try to recollect in detail the things that he said. But I do remember the mood of his remarks with a great deal of clarity. Kennan spoke with what seemed to me to be a strong emotional undertone. He was pessimistic and more than once he was caustic. One could not feel from his analysis of Soviet affairs that he saw any chance for any improvement of the strained relations between the United States and the Soviet Union for the near future. Yet, startlingly enough, for the longer range, one gathered, he was not without hope. There might be a change. It might come suddenly. There was little that the outside world could do at this juncture to bring about this change. One had to be patient and wait. But, for the meanwhile, things were very bad.

All of us present in Kennan's office that day had felt keenly the seriousness of the steady deterioration in relations between the Soviet Union and the West ourselves. Day by day as we reported the news from the Soviet Union we could watch it. Kennan had articulated many of our own impressions in his own wise way. We left his office in a mood of deep gloom. It was the last conversation we correspondents were to have with Ambassador Kennan in Moscow.

Several weeks later the Soviet government declared Kennan "Persona Non Grata"—no longer acceptable to the Soviet government. As a pretext for this action the Russians cited remarks Kennan had been quoted as making in Berlin after his departure from the Soviet Union.

On an October morning I called on Mrs. Kennan at Spaso House to say goodbye for Julie and myself. As I left Spaso House I thought what a fearful thing it was that, at this moment, with a desperate need for a conciliatory voice between the USSR and America, when everything seemed headed toward catastrophe, that Stalin, in a fit of calculated rage aimed at setting the scene for the coming Party Congress with an act of brazen defiance of America, had chosen to remove from Soviet-American relations the one man who, given a chance, could have done so much to bring about a lessening of tension.

\*      \*      \*      \*      \*

There were many questions about the coming Congress, but perhaps the most important was what role Joseph Stalin intended to play at it. The official announcement, signed by Stalin, had said the congress keynote report would be delivered by Malenkov. This put Malenkov in the position of a seeming heir apparent. But Stalin was not dead yet. Far from it! And therefore the question remained.

I got my answer just before the Congress was scheduled to open. On the morning of October 2, *Pravda* announced the contents of the latest issue of the official magazine of the Soviet Communist Party, *Bolshevik,* due to appear that day. Included among them was an article by "J. Stalin" entitled "The Economic Problems of Socialism in the USSR."

I waited for the magazine to appear. In the late afternoon I got my copy. The Stalin article was several score pages long and the material was complex. I went through it quickly and picked salient points of the article. I phoned my story to London as quickly as the censor passed it. I concentrated on the obvious aspects, particularly those concerning foreign relations.

Later that evening I reread the article more leisurely. There was much in it. There was, for instance, a declaration on the key question of "the inevitability of war." The question had been raised, wrote Stalin, of whether in view of the enormous growth of the strength of the Socialist countries in the world the Leninist formula of inevitability of war remained in force. Concluded Stalin: It did.

I thought about this. If one thought war was inevitable then one must prepare for it and assume that it would come. The assumption that war must come was likely to lead to war itself, if even one big power were to act on that assumption. This was not the last to be heard of this question.

Then later in the article there was another formulation of Stalin touching on quite a different subject, the subject of policy toward Soviet collective farms. Should they be nationalized in order to end the "contradiction" between state-owned industry and cooperative-owned collective farms? No, answered Stalin. He went on to propose a queer system whereby, in his view, the collective farms would be brought into a state of adjustment with the state-owned and operated sectors of the economy by means of "product exchange." This would apparently be a very complex system of contractual barter between industry and agriculture introducing, on the basis of the examples Stalin suggested, a multiple price system and other complications into economic life. This was his suggested program for farm development. Even at that crazy time this seemed queer.

I went through the article a third time. I was looking for things I might have missed. I was also trying to get a view of it as a whole. What emerged was this: Stalin had presented here his blueprint for the future of the USSR. This answered the question of what role he was going to play at the Congress. He had undercut the whole thing ahead of time.

*     *     *     *     *

The Congress opened in the Kremlin October 5 and closed October 14. It heard a long keynote report by Malenkov. Changes in the Party statutes and a new Five Year Plan were adopted. There was much verbiage but little of significance was said. There was much bluster against the "American warmongers." There were lavish tributes to Stalin and his newest contribution to Leninist-Stalinist theory. There were the inevitable predictions of a worldwide victory of communism. Many foreign communist leaders were present and spoke. At its end the Congress elected a new Central Committee.

At its very close the Congress heard a speech delivered by Stalin. It was a curious thing. Here was the most important public confab of Soviet and foreign communists since before World War II. Stalin was the recognized leader of the world communist movement. Stalin had not delivered a public address of any sort since February, 1946. One might therefore have expected that Stalin would have gone to some pains to honor the meeting with an important statement to the delegates in person. He delivered, however, a brief, almost curt, little off-the-cuff statement. He addressed it not to his own Soviet Communist Party at all but to the foreign communist delegates. And it was all in a slightly contemptuous tone.

He thanked the foreign communist delegates for their trust in the Soviet Communist Party. He said "it would be a mistake" to think that the Soviet Communist Party "no longer needs such support." Support by foreign communists for the Soviet Communist Party, he avowed, is actually support for one's own people. The Soviet Communist Party—in its role as "the shock-brigade" of the working class —had had a hard row to hoe, he noted. Communist Parties in countries where they had not yet come to power were having an easier time than "we Russian Communists"—partly because these foreign communists can learn from the Soviet Communist example, partly because the bourgeoisie is not what it used to be. "Down with the warmongers!" he proclaimed in conclusion. It were as if Stalin had decided deliberately to show all the delegates and guests at the Congress just how little he thought of them.

Stalin reserved his real surprise for after the Congress. On October 17 the Soviet press announced the election, by the new Central Committee, of its Presidium and its Secretariat. The new Presidium replaced the old Politburo. Lo and behold, instead of the dozen members of the old Politburo, the new Presidium had twenty-five members and eleven alternates. It was tripled in size.

The Secretariat was doubled from five to ten. Among the multitude of men newly elected to the enlarged Presidium and the enlarged Secretariat there were many unknowns, some of them former obscure party secretaries from the provinces. Obviously the new Presidium could not be an operating body. It was too big. What then was it for? And why the enlarged Secretariat?

I thought about that for a time. And the conclusions I came to were two: In the first place, it seemed to me to be a deliberate public blow struck by Stalin at the authority of those who for years had been his chief lieutenants and members of his Politburo. In the second place, I felt the enlargement of the Presidium and the Secretariat could—if that were what was desired—be an ideal smoke screen or cover for an approaching removal from the leadership of a number, or even all, of these old "comrades-in-arms" of Stalin.

Very interesting indeed!

*    *    *    *    *

December 25. I ran through my Christmas morning work at the telegraph office and by eight o'clock was ready to leave. There had not been much to report. I drove to the American Embassy Building. I went up to the fifth floor and opened the door of a private apartment. I sneaked in quietly. I was doing it with permission of the sleeping occupants. I tip-toed into the kitchen where I was greeted by a wiggling, tail-wagging, little black dog who jumped up at me as I stooped down and gave me a great big lick on my face. I found her leash hanging nearby, hooked it to her collar and absconded with her the same way I had come.

I drove back to our apartment on the broad boulevard and took the little black dog upstairs to our apartment. Julie was still sound asleep and I quietly tip-toed down the corridor to the kitchen and shut the door and sat there sipping my breakfast coffee and watching the dog—whose name was Candy—conduct a systematic search of the kitchen.

Candy was an English cocker spaniel and had been brought to me with infinite difficulty by two wonderful people in the Embassy who wanted to help me give Julie a Christmas surprise which she—and I —would love. They purchased her in Berlin. She had arrived with them by plane just a few days before Christmas and they had agreed to keep her in an Embassy apartment for me till Christmas Day itself.

Inevitably, the problems of bringing a dog into Moscow gave rise to mysterious phone calls from the Embassy. I could not conceal that something unusual was afoot—that some kind of exotic Christmas present was on the way. Julie guessed and guessed. She imagined it might be a new piano, a new accordion, or some new huge piece of furniture which she was afraid would not fit into the flat. She worried about it all a good deal but she never got a hint of what it really was.

So there I was in the apartment with Julie's surprise Christmas present, a super-active little present too, and she was asleep! After a long while I got up and opened the kitchen door. I heard from the bedroom at the other end of the corridor a plaintive call, "Tom!"

I went down to the bedroom and sat on the bed beside Julie. "Merry Christmas!" I said.

"Where is my Christmas present?" she asked, insistently. Just at that precise second there shot into the room a black streak. The black streak jumped up on the bed, snuggled up beside Julie, and started frantically to kiss her all over her face. Julie drew back for a second in fright, but then she suddenly grasped what it was.

"That's your Christmas surprise!" I said. Julie threw her arms around Candy's neck and hugged her close.

"What a surprise!" she exclaimed.

We had a good Christmas that day. Maria Ivanovna roasted a goose for us. Julie's mother and Harrison came as our guests. There was a big Christmas tree and many presents under it.

We went to sleep that night early—tired, well-fed and happy. Affectionate little Candy—already rechristened with the Russian diminutive nickname of "Keshka" which has stuck to her ever since—lay quietly at the foot of the bed.

\*     \*     \*     \*     \*

On the last day of 1952 I sat thinking over events of the past year. The Party Congress had been over two and a half months. There were things in the wind. But what? The only way to get a glimpse of the shadowy future was to be alert.

The November holidays had come and gone. Portraits of the leaders went up on public buildings. They were the same old portraits as before. The men arrayed alongside Stalin were the old Politburo members. There were a few changes in precedence. Beria had been shoved down the line two or three places. But one could only conclude that, regardless of the enlargement of the Party Presidium and Secretariat, the old guard was still in the center of things—for the time being, at least.

In the first days of December I came on the first real signpost to coming events. I picked up a copy of *Pravda Ukrainy* from Kiev from the mail. It was dated November 29. It reported an unusual trial. The individuals tried were heads of the Chief Light Industry Marketing Administration in Kiev. Their crimes were not unusual crimes. They allegedly had diverted merchandise in short supply into speculative channels, pocketing the profit. This was typical of the black-marketing activity widespread in Russia then because of the underpricing of certain goods in the retail network.

What was unusual was not the alleged crime but the way this case was treated. The particular defendants were tried in a military court, in other words, a court-martial. Military courts or courts-martial were reserved, so far as jurisdiction over civilians was concerned, for only the most serious offenses such as treason or espionage. And herein lay the second unprecedented aspect of the case. The court equated speculation or black-marketing with "counter-revolutionary wrecking" —in other words sabotage, making it equivalent to treason. This was a queer twist! The sentences were cruel. The three leading defendants were executed without appeal. This was at a time when, under Soviet law, the only crimes for which capital punishment was prescribed were treason and espionage.

Several of the defendants, including at least two out of three of those executed, were, judging by their family names, persons of Jewish origin. The full significance of this was not immediately clear, but somewhat later it became apparent the Kiev case was being used throughout the Ukraine in a burgeoning campaign to stir up public indignation. The slogans of this campaign stressed these family names. Here again was that sinister red thread.

I began to ponder. Somewhere in the back of my mind there was a recollection that I had seen a suggestion that speculators and embezzlers should be treated as "enemies of the people." I began to look back through things I had read. Finally I found it.

". . . every Party and Soviet official, every honest Soviet citizen, must regard pilferers of socialist property not only as enemies of the state but as their own personal enemies as well. Comrade Stalin has pointed out that '. . . a thief who pilfers public property and undermines the interests of the national economy is a spy and a traitor, if not worse.' " It was in a speech at the Party Congress by A. N. Poskrebyshev. Its relevance was pointed up by the fact that in the next breath the speaker declared that Party organizations in Kiev had "under-estimated" the danger. Poskrebyshev was head of Stalin's personal secretariat.

Here in his speech was the directive which had led to the Kiev trial. There could be no doubt. I read the rest of the Poskrebyshev speech, a remarkable document. There was in it a touch of authority. Poskrebyshev spoke with the air of one giving orders. Yet he had no important Party position.

But, as I had had occasion to observe in the developing events, his words at the Party Congress were being treated with that same reverence reserved for Stalin's own statements. He proposed a legal reform. Soon there was a meeting to discuss this project. He criticized Soviet jurists. Soon this criticism was echoed in one publication after another.

Then, almost at the end of December, Alexander Poskrebyshev spoke out again. This time he was author of an editorial in *Pravda* on the "Great Multinational Soviet State." The editorial said nothing one could pin down as a new departure in the party line, yet there were in it two interesting points of stress. One of these dealt with "enemies." In his Congress speech Poskrebyshev had said bluntly, "We have enemies." Here in *Pravda* at the end of December he said it again in a somewhat different way. The victory of socialism in the USSR was attained, he declared, in "implacable struggle against Trotskyites, Bukharinites, bourgeois nationalists and other enemies of the people, agents of the capitalist encirclement." He went on to attack "bourgeois nationalism, chauvinism and cosmopolitanism" and in his next breath delivered a bitter tirade against agents of the "American imperialists." None of this material was new but, repeated so insistently and vigorously by such a person, it seemed to be pointing in a particular direction.

There was also a second point of stress in this editorial. The article lavished praise on the Russians, "the great Russian people" which was, said Poskrebyshev, "the cementing force which holds together the friendship of the peoples." He devoted extravagant encomiums to the Russian language which, he said, had become "the means of commu-

nication between nationalities, the means of most effective maintenance of contact and mutual relations with each other."

Given the habitual care of Soviet leaders in expression of anything
singling out the Great Russians from other Soviet nationalities or open
proclaiming a special historical role for the Russian language, such
remarks seemed to savor of Great Russian chauvinism. This had had
its other manifestations elsewhere.

So there at the year's end I began to think about the evidence coming to the surface during the crucial past year and some of the in-
gredients for the broth abrewing.

Trouble for the old guard in the leadership and the sudden emer-
gence of new, mostly unknown, men . . . Trouble in the Ministry of
State Security . . . The possible setting of the scene after the Congress for a dramatic shift in leadership . . . Stalin's personal secretary, Poskrebyshev, emerging into a post of unofficial but enormous
influence . . . Increasing outcroppings of anti-Semitism . . . Great
Russian chauvinism and xenophobia. Above all, the continuing contrast and conflict between Soviet economic and cultural progress on
one hand, and political and ideological stagnation and decay on the
other, was being increasingly accentuated month by month. Here was
a recipe for cataclysm! What a beautiful prospect for the coming
New Year!

# 18.    *An End*

Often, after finishing work in the morning, instead of going home for a nap I would pay a visit to Julie's mother. We would sit over coffee chatting about anything that came to mind. We enjoyed these visits together. On January 5, 1953, I went to see her. She did not open to my knock. I opened the door myself and called her and there was a muffled answer from the bathroom. After a while she came out.

"I'm not feeling very well today," she said. "I am dizzy. I feel very weak." I got her to sit down in an armchair and went to make some strong coffee. She sipped a bit of it and went over and lay down on the divan. Since she had diabetes and did not take insulin she occasionally had spells. At first I was not particularly worried. But after a while when I found she was not improving I called up Julie and told her to call a doctor and come over right away.

While I waited I looked out the windows at the street below. Snow was piled deep along the sides of the cobblestone street. Russians walked hurriedly by emitting little clouds of frost into the air. The temperature was far below zero. The janitor and his son were out, dressed in gray aprons, wielding twig brooms, cleaning off the street and sidewalks. The morning was gray and gloomy.

Julie's mother felt ill again. I grew afraid.

I went back to the window. A "Pobeda" taxi drew up. Julie got out and ran into the apartment house. A few seconds later I opened the door for her.

"Where's Mother?" she asked.

I pointed to the bathroom. Julie went in. Soon the two came out and Julie's mother lay on the divan again. Julie got on the telephone. Russian first aid service is generally prompt. But on that day it was impossible to get a doctor. Julie called everywhere. At every place they insisted "the patient must come in herself." This was out of the question. In desperation, Julie ran to a clinic down the street to try to get a doctor to come.

I decided I'd better try myself, through my own connections. There was a polyclinic reserved for use of foreigners. It had excellent physicians. Julie and I had been treated there frequently. I decided to try there. I got the head physician on the phone. He listened to my explanation of the symptoms. He told me he would come immediately. I was grateful for the prompt response.

Julie came back in tears. She had encountered a peevish snip of a doctor who had refused to come. Under the stress she lost her temper, told him what she thought of him and ran home. I told her help was on the way.

An hour and a half later, after a thorough examination, the doctor who had come told us Julie's mother must immediately go to a hospital. He made several quick phone calls, then turned to us and said, "We can go now. I think it would be best not to wait for an ambulance."

Together we managed to get Julie's mother, who was feeling worse, bundled up warmly and into my car, on the front seat beside me. I drove to the hospital. She rested on a divan while they prepared a cot for her. After an hour we left her in good hands. We kissed her goodbye and told her we would be back later that evening. We did go back to see her. She felt better but exceedingly weak and there was no diagnosis.

The next morning I called up the woman physician who was the head of this section of the Botkin Hospital to ask how Julie's mother had passed the night. She listened to my questions in silence and answered after a bit of hesitation.

"The news I have for you is very bad. Your mother-in-law has had a severe heart attack. We do not know how much chance she has. Right now she is resting comfortably and we are doing our best. You can come and see her this afternoon but please be careful not to excite her. It will be several weeks before we know how things are going to work out." I told the news to Julie and Julie wept.

*    *    *    *    *

Then began the waiting.

The doctors said the initial heart attack had been severe, and that it was a miracle Mother had survived. But, they warned, there was great danger of a second attack in a short time. If Mother went a month without a second attack, then it might be assumed that she was on the way to an initial recovery. But, they warned, a second attack in the immediate future was almost certain to be fatal.

There was nothing we could do. At the hospital they were attentive. Mother was receiving excellent care. Specialists were called in for consultation. We could bring things to eat which were not available at the hospital. We could call and see her as often as we pleased. They set no limit on visiting hours. But all of this made it little easier for Julie. She slept fitfully. She was constantly nervous. She jumped whenever the phone rang. She spent most of her time at the hospital, sometimes with me, sometimes without me.

"Isn't there anything we can do, Tomochka?" she asked me for the fiftieth time one day in the middle of January. "There must be something we can do!"

"I'm afraid there isn't," I answered. "There's just one thing to do —wait."

*    *    *    *    *

Julie's period of personal trial coincided with a period of trial for the whole nation.

January 13 I drove down to the *Izvestia* building in the early morning while darkness lay over the city. I got my copy of the paper from the usually friendly woman at the "Expeditsiya" window. This morning she had a grim face. I glanced through the paper and found an official announcement on the last page. I read quickly the first phrases: "Arrest of a Group of Saboteur-Doctors . . . Some time ago agencies of state security discovered a terrorist group of doctors who made it their aim to cut short the lives of active public figures of the Soviet Union through sabotage medical treatment . . ."

It took a second for this statement to sink in with all its enormity. I shook my head. What nightmare was this? No, it could not be! I went back and re-read it word by word. But I had read correctly.

With mounting alarm I read further. The announcement named nine doctors. The announcement claimed they had "confessed." It said they had murdered Politburo members, Andrei Zhdanov, in 1948, and Alexander Shcherbakov much before that. It said the accused doctors had deliberately diagnosed incorrectly the illnesses of these and others and prescribed fatal treatment. It called the doctors "monsters" and claimed they were agents of foreign intelligence services.

Then came the real shocker. The announcement said that five of the accused were in the employ of an international Zionist organization which "conducts extensive espionage, terrorist and other subversive work in many countries including the Soviet Union." The announcement ended with the ominous words: "The investigation will soon be concluded."

I ran to the car and drove on the icy streets to the telegraph office. In a short time I was dictating this news story to the AP Bureau in London. A little while later I was reading the lead editorial in *Pravda* which singled out for bitter attack Soviet state security agencies which, it charged, had failed to uncover the alleged plot. The editorial said there were in the Soviet Union "bearers of bourgeois views," *"living persons,* secret enemies of our people" who "with the support of the imperialist world, will continue to cause harm." It ended with the wrathful demand that "gullibility" among Soviet people should come to an end: "To end sabotage it is necessary to put an end to gullibility in our ranks." So this was the thunderbolt that had been presaged by the developments of the previous year!

I sat in the stuffy phone booth, waiting to dictate more of this story as it came back to me from the censor. And I thought about the gloomy prospects for the future.

One thing was obvious: a great new purge was scheduled—under way. Stalin was going to resort once more to the same violent mass terror he had used in 1937 in order to instill in the nation an atmosphere of fear and horror in which resistance to his unquestioned rule would be impossible. Millions of the best people in Russia would be tortured, abused and killed off in a new awful "Yezhovshchina."

Why? There was no evidence that there existed in the ranks of the Soviet government and Communist party any capability for resistance to Stalin. No matter how absurd or how damaging to the interests of the country his edicts might turn out to be, they would be executed unquestioningly. There was no evidence in any form that there was any possibility of organized opposition to the Stalin system of dictatorship through terror. The entire Soviet leadership from top to bottom was permeated with a spirit of abject submission to the wishes and the caprices of "the great leader and teacher." Why then a new purge?

This I thought about. The only real answer I could come up with was that which was given by the peculiar direction of the coming purge campaign. Modern anti-Semitism had deep roots in Russia. The word, "pogrom," is a Russian word. Anti-Semitic manifestations in Tsarist Russia in the late nineteenth century had shocked the entire civilized world.

Nor had outbursts of anti-Semitism entirely ceased with the Revolution. From time to time this ancient curse of Russia kept popping up under the Soviet regime which had always maintained resolutely in public that racial and national equality for all was a foundation stone of the Soviet system and which at its beginning had actually set out to try to abolish discrimination against Jews and other national minorities.

During and after World War II anti-Semitism had more and more come to the surface. In 1949 the anti-Semitic drive against "the homeless cosmopolitans" had had its swift upsurge. From then on, anti-Semitism continued to lurk in the background. And now in 1953 Stalin was resorting to anti-Semitism as a basis for a new purge.

*    *    *    *    *

The snowy days went by. Mother improved day after day. The head physician of this section at the hospital, a competent, attractive woman of about forty, was encouraging.

On January 23 at eleven A.M. I had been in the courtyard taking the dog, Keshka, for a walk. I took her back into the building. From up the stairwell I heard Julie calling. There was a note of fear in her voice. I ran up the stairs. Keshka followed, barking furiously. I ran into the apartment.

"What is it?" I asked.

"It's the hospital!" she cried. "They say to come quickly. Mother's worse!"

She threw on her coat and we ran down the stairs. We got in the car and I drove as fast as I could out the busy Leningrad Highway.

Each successive stop light seemed to last forever. We sat in silence all the way.

Twenty minutes later we pulled up in front of the familiar one-story building in which we had spent so much time during the previous two weeks. We got out of the car and hurried into the building. We were both trembling. A nurse met us at the doorway.

"The head physician wants to see you right now," she said to us. And she took us into the office. The tall brunette doctor looked at us with feeling. We waited. We knew what she was going to say.

"I'm afraid I have bad news," she started.

I heard Julie sobbing beside me. Yes, Julie's mother was dead. The attack had come quickly. She had lost consciousness within minutes. I looked at Julie and realized. A few years before there had been a family. There were four—husband, wife, daughter and son. Now only one was left. Each died in a different way in a different place. This was the fate of one Russian family. How many families there were throughout that land who had suffered tragedies no less poignant!

\*     \*     \*     \*     \*

January 26. The blue bus rumbled over snow-clad cobblestones in Moscow's eastern reaches. Julie and I and half a dozen others sat huddled on the side benches and stared at the wooden, flower-decked coffin which lay between us. The bus rattled and shivered to a stop. We clambered out the back door.

I went into the cemetery entrance. I found the chief grave digger inside the gate and asked him to help us with the coffin. He did. It was twenty-five degrees below zero. There was a thick frost in the air and one's breath seemed to turn to frost crystals before one's eyes. The gaunt, barren trees of the cemetery seemed to form a kind of arched passageway over the cemetery walk. Microscopic snow flakes drifted slowly down on us as we passed. Mounds of snow covered many of the monuments, and those monuments which remained exposed, bore, some of them, foreign names. This cemetery had long ago been a traditional burying place for foreign residents. Most of the minuscule plots had little iron fences around them. There were some graves roofed over with enclosures made of screen. Inside them there were even a few shrines in which candles burned, kept lit by faithful relatives.

We bore the coffin slowly on our shoulders. Behind us there followed those who had come with us. We arrived at the grave plot and the grave diggers lowered the coffin into the icy earth. Julie went forward and took up a handful of earth from the pile and threw it on top of the coffin. The others who had come followed suit—all except our cook, Maria Ivanovna, who stood behind. She had brought with her a small bottle of vodka. It was not to drink. She had been at Russian winter funerals before. She knew that tears would be shed and that they would freeze on mourning faces. So she was prepared, with her vodka and a small towel, to wipe away the tears before they froze.

The grave diggers went to work with their shovels as we stood and watched. Soon the coffin disappeared from view.

*   *   *   *   *

Meanwhile in political life things had been moving fast. Following the announcement of the "doctors' plot" the entire Soviet press took up the shrill cry of "vigilance!" Article after article appeared. Typical titles were: "Zionism—an agency of United States and British imperialists"; "Heighten Political Vigilance!"; "Be Watchful and Be Vigilant!" Buried in these articles there were often citations of cases involving "exposure" of spies, traitors, thieves, embezzlers and "bourgeois nationalists." Often the names of the exposed "criminals" turned out to be non-Russian. The suggestion constantly made was that the "enemies" were disguising themselves as patriots.

Declared *Izvestia* on January 15, "The spies . . . operate by 'sapping.' They mask themselves in the guise of Soviet persons to penetrate our institutions and organizations, to worm their way into confidence and conduct their vile work." The natural effect was to make everyone suspicious of everyone, and evidently that was what was intended.

The youth paper, *Komsomol Pravda,* in its editorial of January 15, expanded the "vigilance" campaign to include entire categories of "morally unreliable" young people. Declared the paper: "If your friend blabs too freely, check him. If you learn that a friend has fallen in with bad company, get him out of it. Expose unworthy persons. Do not be afraid to speak up . . ." In other words: "Be an informer!"

When *Ukrainian Pravda* of January 16 arrived in Moscow it became apparent how serious the unfolding purge was. The newspaper put on a par with the ruthless November case, in which three were executed for treason on the basis of speculative activities, a series of other cases. Some of the names of the "criminals": Grinshtein, Perse,

Kaplan. Two secretaries of the Party in Kiev Province had been fired for "gullibility" and "protection of criminals." Other leading officials elsewhere had also fallen victim.

The campaign took a particularly sinister turn January 21 when leading newspapers published on front pages a decree awarding the Order of Lenin to Dr. Lydia F. Timashuk "for assistance rendered to the government in exposing the murderer-doctors." Dr. Timashuk's "assistance" consisted in informing on the alleged "saboteur-doctors." Here was an open invitation to envious and neurotic characters to denounce whomever they disliked as a "spy." Names and more names —non-Russian mostly—kept piling up in article after article: Izrailit, Blokh, Lumer, Levitas, Kerzhner, Khanin, Levin, Khanovich, Meilman, etc.

*Pravda* on January 31 finally turned up a case of a supposedly honest-to-God spy. His name was A. I. Orlov. It was said he had been caught stealing a secret document. This was the first actual new "spy" case cited from the beginning of the campaign. This same editorial began to reach into high places citing "former" Deputy Minister of Non-Ferrous Metallurgy, S. P. Petrov, who was said to have lost a number of secret documents.

When one studied the mass of material on the "vigilance" campaign and analyzed the type of individual caught in the purge and the "crimes" involved, it became apparent that, for all the desperate effort being made, practically no cases of actual political crimes such as espionage, sabotage or treason, by any reasonable definition, were involved. Almost all cases cited concerned merely those most ancient of Soviet crimes: embezzlement and speculation. A high proportion of the "criminals" turned out to be employees in wholesale and retail trade.

What the authorities were clearly attempting to do was to create a link in popular psychology between minor crimes of thievery, speculation and embezzlement, and the major anti-patriotic crimes of espionage and treason. Time and again the "vigilance" campaign articles quoted Stalin's statement of 1926—that a statement cited by Alexander Poskrebyshev at the Nineteenth Congress equating theft of public property with treason.

It was on February 6 that *Pravda* turned up a case with possibly serious implications. Wrote the paper, "Some time ago an inveterate Trotskyite and agent of a foreign intelligence service, S. D. Gurevich, was arrested by the agencies of State Security. He was brought up in the family of a Menshevist Bundist. In 1914–17 he was in the United States and there made friends with Trotskyites. After his return to Russia, Gurevich became himself an active participant in an anti-Soviet Trotskyite group. In 1927 Gurevich gave the Party organization a declaration of withdrawal from Trotskyism. This was deceit and double-dealing. Remaining a covert Trotskyite and sworn enemy of the Soviet people, Gurevich in 1939 established a tie with a foreign intelligence service and for a number of years supplied it with espionage information."

The same day *Pravda* cited three other spy cases but the Gurevich case was the interesting one. Gurevich—if we correspondents had identified him correctly—was an individual who had at one time worked for a number of American correspondents in Moscow and also for one or another of the Western Embassies. He was an intelligent person and he had made many friends and acquaintances. I knew him, and I think every other American correspondent in Moscow at that time, with possibly one exception, knew him equally well or better. It was our impression that he had, in fact, been more recently employed by the Soviet news agency, TASS, and that on occasion he was the individual deputized to telephone news agency correspondents, including myself, about important Soviet announcements.

The importance of the Gurevich case was this: If his activities were to be linked in some kind of a public show trial, with that of the "saboteur-doctors," then things might be handled by the Russians so as to bring in the names of any number of American diplomats and journalists who had known or merely met Gurevich.

Here was something to think about. And as the "vigilance" campaign raged on and people in Moscow looked at one another with fear in their eyes, I did think about it.

*    *    *    *    *

On a February night, long after midnight, I lay in the darkness of our bedroom staring at the invisible ceiling. Julie was asleep and breathing softly and I was still and motionless so as not to disturb her. This was not the first night I had lain awake for hours staring up into the dark.

I was following the same train of thought so disturbing on previous wakeful nights. There was in preparation in Russia a big show purge trial. Of this there could be no doubt. There had to be a show trial, like the trials in Moscow in the thirties, like the trial of Cardinal Mindszenty in Budapest, like the other show trials in the East European satellite countries in the past few years.

This trial was now a necessity for the Soviet government. Otherwise why any announcement of the "confessions" of the "doctor-murderers"?

The trial had to be a good one. It had to have some verisimilitude. There would be abject confessions. One could count on this. There had to be raging denunciations by a prosecutor of the type of Andrei Vyshinsky, prosecutor in the Moscow purge trials of the thirties. The confessions would no doubt depict a "foul conspiracy" for the assassination of Soviet leaders with instructions coming straight from such Western leaders as my former boss, Ambassador Walter Bedell Smith, onetime Chief of the C.I.A. in Washington, from Allen Dulles, Smith's successor, from David Ben-Gurion of Israel, and perhaps even from Winston Churchill and former President Truman. There would have to be supporting evidence for the thesis of a conspiracy involving the intelligence services of America, England and Israel. Some of this would come from hapless Soviet citizens like S. D. Gurevich, who had been caught in the web of this purge.

But there was something else needed, as it seemed to me. The Russians needed, it seemed to me, a real live foreigner like the unlucky Israeli citizen the Czechoslovaks had dragged into the Slansky trial. Such a foreigner who would become well nigh the chief defendant would be the only thing that could give this trial the appearance of possible verisimilitude.

What foreigner?

I wondered. And then there began the real nightmare. What better than a correspondent—like Bill Oatis in Prague? Correspondents had no diplomatic immunity. Obviously an American correspondent in Moscow. There were only five. I went down the list, name after name, once again. Who had the "qualifications" in the eyes of the Russians? Here again I came up against one unforgettable fact. I had worked for an American intelligence agency, the OSS. This was a matter of record and the Russians certainly knew about it. It wasn't so very secret. The OSS had long since been disbanded and all my connections with that type of work had ceased. But what difference did that make? I had also worked in the U.S. Embassy in Moscow—another relevant fact from this point of view. And I was the only American correspondent in Moscow with those particular "recommendations." I lay there in the bed still silent. My heart pounded. There was a pressure in my temples. I thought I would burst. Eventually I would go to sleep from sheer fatigue, I knew. I had gone to sleep from sheer fatigue every night that month. And I would have to arise at three or four or five—in just a short while—to go to work. I knew that when daylight broke these nightmare visions would disappear, even seem silly, but then when night came again they would come back. And, as I knew too well, these fears were not so silly, not at that insane time.

"Eenie, Meenie, Meinie, Mo . . ."

* * * * *

February 12 the Soviet government announced a break in relations with Israel. The excuse was a bomb thrown into the Soviet Legation in Israel. The real cause was "the doctors' plot." So Israeli diplomats trooped out of Russia.

Then there was a sort of final, particularly vicious, fillip to the "vigilance" campaign. Typical of it is a quotation from *Izvestia*, describing the trial of a citizen caught speculating in government bonds: "And now this underground millionaire—Senka-nose—stands before the court, unmasked, in his true light. His long fleshy nose points mournfully downward, his puffy eyes tremble with fear, his small rat-like eyes roam uneasily."

And so it went. Articles on "vigilance" continued to appear. But somehow the drive had gone out of the campaign. It had turned into a routine propaganda hullabaloo. No more "spies" were turned up— only petty and not-so-petty speculators and embezzlers. One got the feeling that the authorities had already reached the dregs of the barrel before the thing got off the ground. Nothing more was left. The "vigilance" articles themselves lost their punch—began to appear less frequently. So it seemed, at any rate. One wondered. Yet this thing hung over the Soviet Union.

Toward the end of February an interesting event became known. A new Chief of Staff of the Soviet Army was appointed. He was the war hero, Marshal V. D. Sokolovsky, who had played a distinguished role as Marshal Zhukov's Chief of Staff during the final campaigns of World War II. He replaced a wartime unknown, Army General S. M. Shtemenko, who had occupied this key position for a time and who seemed to have been a political appointee of Stalin. Why did Marshal Sokolovsky take over the Soviet Army at that particular time? A very interesting question—but the answer may well never be known. And so there things were—hanging in midair. Something had to happen.

*     *     *     *     *

The obvious imminence of big news led other correspondents to follow my lead in morning work. During February we all organized for speedier coverage. I myself formed an alliance with Harrison Salisbury and one other correspondent for collaboration on early-morning duty stints.

March 4, at about six A.M., it was Harrison Salisbury who aroused me with a call. This was his morning for protection. "You better come down now," he said. "The newspapers are late. There's every indication they have been held up for an important announcement."

I dressed and drove to the telegraph office. Three other correspondents were there. Typewriters were open on the table in the center of the room. Orders were being placed for telephone lines with London. No one knew what was up but everyone was certain something big was coming. What we really expected was some further announcement about the "doctors'-plot."

We waited. I paced the floor. The telephone rang on the desk of one of the girl telegraph clerks. She answered it. She put down the receiver and called to Andy Steiger, the third member of our collaborating trio, "Your wife wants you to call her immediately." Hardly had the clerk put down her phone when it rang again. The telegraph clerk gave an identical message to another correspondent.

Andy called his wife on the pay phone on the wall in the corner. He listened to what his wife had to tell him and came over quickly and quietly. "TASS just called my home," he said. "They told my wife they will soon have for us the text of an official announcement 'on the illness of Stalin!' "

We looked at each other in dismay. This was something! What a story! TASS had given all the other news agency correspondents one after another, the same information—a noncommittal general statement without details.

All of us there that morning knew we were close to one of the biggest news stories of modern times. But it was just beyond our reach.

Chauffeurs sent to the TASS office for the official text of the announcement did not return. They had not yet been handed the text. Initial
telegrams reporting the TASS communication to correspondents were
held in the back room by the censor. The minutes passed by one by
one, each an eternity. Somewhere an official announcer in a Moscow
radio station was getting ready to read this shocking news in a broadcast which would be instantly picked up and translated in London and
flashed throughout the world by the big news agencies, including my
own AP.

Our big break had come. But yet it hadn't. We had near to us a
tremendous news story. In between us and the mass communications
facilities of the press and radio of the free world there was that eternal
barrier, the censor. One official Soviet government agency—TASS—
was going to give us our text. Another official Soviet agency—*Glavlit,*
the Soviet censor—was going to prevent us from reporting the news
contained in the text. A third Soviet agency—Moscow radio—would
report the news first while we gnashed our teeth. That is precisely the
way it all worked out.

Some minutes after the Moscow radio announcement, shortly after
eight A.M., the censor began to pass copy.

Stalin had had a stroke. He had lapsed into a coma. This had happened, according to the official announcement, during the night of
March 1–2. Two whole days—some forty-eight hours or more—had
passed before this news had been made public. The reason the news
had now been made public was obviously that it had been decided it
was necessary to prepare the public for the coming announcement of
Stalin's death. And this was something which was almost too big to
grasp.

\*      \*      \*      \*      \*

The announcement of Stalin's death came at four A.M., March 6.
Successive medical bulletins issued had pictured Stalin as rapidly sinking. By midnight March 5, after phoning my story on the latest of
these bulletins, I reread it carefully. I was not a doctor but it was clear
the old dictator couldn't last more than a few hours. He might already
be dead. I settled in for the night at the telegraph office.

At about three-thirty I went out for an early morning ride to see
what was stirring. I drove around the Kremlin. The ancient brick-
walled fortress lay quietly under the Moscow night while a cold wind

blew across Red Square. Above the dome of one of the Kremlin palaces there flew the crimson Soviet flag, as always, with a floodlight on it. The ruby glass illuminated stars glowed from the crenelated towers. There were no signs of unusual activity.

I returned to the telegraph office and sat in a telephone booth awaiting a connection with London. My chauffeur, Dmitry, came in quietly and opened the door of the booth to whisper something in my ear. He had been listening for me on my car radio. Stalin, he said, was dead. The official announcement was being broadcast to provincial newspapers at dictation speed.

I went to ask that my phone connection be expedited and handed in my already prepared bulletin. But there at the telephone board stood a Ministry of Communications official. He had torn out all the connections and was giving instructions:

"There will be no telephone calls abroad until further notice."

I listened amazed. The Moscow Radio was telling the world but American correspondents in Moscow could not telephone their stories. I shrugged my shoulders. Once more the frustration of being an American correspondent in Moscow overwhelmed me. At any rate, however, I did not need to worry about any competition from my colleagues. We were all completely incommunicado. I went back into the other room and typed out my story at leisure. A few hours later, after telephone communications had been restored, I had completed delivering it to London. Then I went out to see what was happening in the city.

*    *    *    *    *

When I emerged from the telegraph office at about seven A.M., March 6, I observed a fascinating sight.

Truck convoys were rolling into the city. They were military trucks. They were loaded with blue-capped troops of the security services. They were proceeding, not aimlessly, but with precise plans. I watched.

In my presence a detachment of trucks occupied the entrance of Ogaryov Street onto Gorky Street—right in front of me. The chauffeurs unloaded their troops and then maneuvered their trucks to form a wall several trucks thick across the entrance of Ogaryov Street. They completed this movement in about twenty minutes. When they were finished the security troops formed a living line, arm in arm, locked together, down Gorky Street. An opening had been left at the Ogaryov Street blockade along the sidewalk between the wall of the Central Telegraph and the trucks, a few feet away. This entrance was controlled by security officers who, for the time, admitted anyone who wished to pass, but who would close the entrance whenever the signal was given. This identical maneuver was being carried out, I could observe, at the entrance of every side street onto Gorky Street. Elsewhere, as I later found, the same thing had been done along every main artery and around every square in the entire central area of Moscow inside the "B" ring—an area of many square miles containing all the central institutions of the Soviet government. Within this center of the capital all movements were completely under control, to whatever extent desired, and every block shut off from every other block and from every main artery, to whatever extent desired.

Meanwhile, as we correspondents also soon discovered, train traffic into Moscow from outside the city was totally halted. Moscow, in other words, was under siege. The siege was carried out by security forces. It lasted for three days and nights until Stalin's funeral on March 9.

To attempt to give the Russian emotions a well controlled outlet, without endangering order, the authorities placed Stalin's body in its flower-engulfed bier in the Hall of Columns in the center of Moscow and let Muscovites form immense lines reaching in all directions like endless snakes through the capital's streets, the people in them waiting hour after hour and day after day to file past Stalin's bier. Some of them, certainly, never did get there.

It was a chill and silent city in those days. People were quiet. They kept their thoughts to themselves. But I suppose their predominant emotions were shock and fear. Only faintly and fleetingly, I suppose, was there an evanescent sense of expectation of better things. The fact was that so effectively had Stalin impressed on the popular mind the image of himself as an omniscient and omnipotent indispensable God-the-Father that there was something apocalyptic about his demise. There was an end-of-the-world flavor to it all. It was hard to believe that he was mortal, that he could die, and that the country could go on without him. Hence the shock. With Stalin gone the future was a black unknown. Hence the fear. Hope for things better? All of their history has conditioned Russians to feel that whatever happens to them is bound to be for the worse, for it almost always has been.

I marched through the Hall of Columns with the Russian mob. There he lay, waxen, amidst a bank of flowers that emitted a sickly sweet smell of death. Chopin's funeral march blared through the familiar hall, scene of so many public meetings and concerts. An honor guard of leaders stood at attention on either side of the bier. We were all of us driven through the hall and out a back exist into a dirty unkempt courtyard off Gorky Street.

Even in death the old man was awe-inspiring.

\*    \*    \*    \*    \*

I stood in the middle of Pushkin Square in the murk of the night of March 6. There were few lights. It was almost as if there were a blackout. The damp cold was penetrating and I shivered. About me stood a scattered, careless crowd of Russians. We listened as the big loudspeaker on the square blared out its official decree, paragraph by paragraph. Unable to take notes in the dark I listened and tried to memorize the most important facts.

Here was I, caught by the announcement of the makeup of the new government of the Soviet Union, little more than half the distance between my apartment and the telegraph office. I was not happy about being caught this way but by this time I was fairly philosophical. One could only do one's best and I had been doing that.

I had managed to get home earlier that evening, dead tired, for a short nap. No sooner had I got my head on my pillow when I was awakened by TASS calling to tell me that the decree announcing the new government was to be broadcast in a few minutes. I was a mile and a half from the telegraph office. Between me and that point lay a score or so of security troop barriers. To drive down was impossible. Afoot there was a chance. I could argue with every security officer at every cordon and maybe get through. And so I set out, half-walking, half-running, for the center of town. I remember it now as if it were a dream. I broke through two of the cordons, slipping under the locked arms of the blue-caps and fleeing into the dark. Fortunately they were under instructions not to shoot. I trekked through a series of back courtyards and over three or four fences, working my way steadily toward the center block after block. At one or two points I was passed through control points on the basis of my correspondents' documents. At others I was refused passage and crawled beneath trucks. And thus it was I had reached Pushkin Square when the decree was put on the public address system.

Georgi Malenkov—Premier. Lavrenty Beria—a First Deputy Premier and Minister of Internal Affairs. V. M. Molotov—Minister of Foreign Affairs. The list went on and I listened carefully. I did not hear anything about the key post in the country—General Secretary of the Central Committee of the Party. What about that? Only one phrase seemed to have implications. N. S. Khrushchev, it was said, had been released as head of the Moscow Party to "concentrate" on his duties in the Central Committee. This was noncommittal in the extreme. One phrase in the decree struck me as shocking. The first sentence called for "the greatest unity of leadership and prevention of any kind of disorder and panic."

"Disorder and panic"—such words did not sound like those which might be expected from a self-assured government.

So this was the new government. I pondered its composition after I had filed my dispatches. The fact that stood out was that the levers of power in the nation were in the hands of the old guard, the members of Stalin's old Politburo. They seemed, for the time being, to have formed a committee to run the country.

*     *     *     *     *

March 9. A bright, sunlit but cold, day, ten-fifteen A.M. The funeral cortege began moving slowly from the Hall of Columns into the Stables' Square and across it. Chopin's Funeral March played often enough in the preceding three days for the whole country to be sick of it, blared again. Stalin's casket lay topped by a Plexiglas bubble. It was on an artillery carriage and draped in crimson cloth. A big group of leaders of the Soviet government and heads of other Communist governments trailed behind the caisson. With measured pace they mounted the incline past the Historical Museum and up into Red Square.

I watched them intently. At ten-forty Stalin's bier entered Red Square.

Khrushchev, in charge of funeral arrangements, opened the ceremonies. Then three of the leaders spoke. Georgi Malenkov delivered a well rounded little oration. Beria followed him and then came V. M. Molotov, the only one who sounded very sad.

I listened to what was said and how it was said. I hoped there would be clues to the future. There were. The first clue lay in Malenkov's speech, not in content but in style. It was a balanced, well written, smoothly delivered address. And it was a type of speech which could never have been delivered during the lifetime of Stalin. Anyone who had heard many Soviet speeches knew this. The dead hand of the obligatory forms of the Stalin era had, it was already clear, been removed. Then too its tone seemed to auger well for a possible relaxation of international tension. It contained a certain amount of bluster. But it lacked that familiar vitriolic anti-Western bitterness of the preceding months. It held forth not an olive branch —just a bit of a twig. But this, at such a time, was a very interesting thing.

Beria's speech contained a different kind of a clue. He undertook to recommend Malenkov to the public as a "talented disciple of Lenin" and a "loyal comrade-in-arms of Stalin." These were almost patronizing words. One could almost see the twinkle in the eyes of the ruthless Georgian police chief whose security forces still controlled Moscow. Bundled in his great coat with the collar up to his ears and his black felt hat pulled down over his forehead, he apparently fancied himself a kingmaker. Perhaps he had been just that.

At eleven-fifty-four Khrushchev declared the "funeral meeting" closed. The Soviet leaders descended from the Lenin Mausoleum which now bore also the name of Stalin and carried the casket down into the depths of the tomb.

Thirty volleys were fired in a final salute to the dictator. The Kremlin chimes rang twelve. For three minutes throughout the Soviet Union steam whistles blew while everything stood still. Then the Hymn of the Soviet Union resounded across Red Square. The leaders climbed again to the top of the Mausoleum. Overhead there roared the motors of a fleet of war planes driving from north to south in parade above the square.

The funeral was over.

On Moscow Radio and the Moscow Public Address System there was a brief moment of silence. And then, as if there had been no death and no funeral at all, there came a burst of jolly, merry, rollicking music which poured over the squares and boulevards and byways of the country.

Stalin's body was in cold storage. Stalin's era had come to an end and a new era had begun.

\* \* \* \* \*

More than eight years have passed since the death of Stalin. Time has resulted in some additional information on this event. The interesting thing, however, is how scanty that additional information actually is. Stalin's death and the events leading to it remain today, as much as they were on March 9, 1953, a fascinating mystery.

What is known now that was not known then? At that time there was merely the suspicion, based on circumstantial evidence, that Stalin was planning to purge part or all of the members of his former Politburo. Now there is an authoritative assertion—from Khrushchev's secret speech of February 1956 at the twentieth Party Congress on Stalin's "personality cult."

Said Khrushchev, "Stalin evidently had plans to finish off the old members of the Politburo. He often stated that Politburo members should be replaced by new ones. His proposal after the nineteenth Congress, concerning the selection of twenty-five persons to the Central Committee Presidium, was aimed at the removal of the old Politburo members and the bringing in of less experienced persons so that these would extol him in all sorts of ways. We can assume that this was also a design for the future annihilation of the old Politburo members and, in this way, a cover for the shameful acts of Stalin . . ."

We now have the assertion, from the same Khrushchev address, that in a talk to the new Central Committee after the Congress in October, Stalin hinted that A. I. Mikoyan and V. M. Molotov, two of his closest associates, were "guilty of some baseless charges." Khrushchev said that if Stalin had lived a few months longer he probably would have finished off Mikoyan and Molotov.

We know, from Khrushchev's speech, that Stalin also had "toyed with the absurd and ridiculous suspicion that" aging Marshal Klimenty Voroshilov "was an English agent."

We know that Khrushchev declared that Stalin himself initiated the investigation of the "doctors' plot." Khrushchev said Stalin personally gave orders for the doctors' arrests, and that he gave personal instructions on getting "confessions" from them by torture.

We now know that behind the purge of the Georgian leadership in early 1952 lay another fabricated case similar to the "doctors' plot." This was the case of the "Mingrelian nationalist organization" in which, according to Khrushchev, thousands fell victims to fabricated charges of conspiracy to detach Georgia from the USSR. The actual main target of this case—an aspect not brought out by Khrushchev—is indicated by several facts. First, the erstwhile Soviet police chief, Beria, was himself a Mingrelian, a tribe of Georgians. In the second place, numbers of Beria's associates in Georgian affairs were among the victims. In the third place, when Beria regained control over police affairs in Moscow after Stalin's death, one of his first acts, after denouncing the "doctors' plot" as a frame-up, was to jail the persons regarded as responsible for the "Mingrelian nationalist case" and free the remaining victims.

If the "Mingrelian nationalist case" was aimed against Beria by enemies who had gained Stalin's confidence, the same is apparently equally true of the house-cleaning in the sensitive Ministry of State Security in late 1951 and early 1952. This overturn saw the dismissal of Beria's former subordinate, V. S. Abakumov. The man eventually appointed Minister in Abakumov's place was Semyon D. Ignatiev, an expert on grain procurements, who had apparently never had police experience. He was evidently a mere stooge for others. These are just some of the links in a chain of intrigue running through the last year or so of Stalin's rule.

We know that Stalin was masterminding most of this conspiracy from the Kremlin. There was, however, more to it than mere palace intrigue. Through it there ran leitmotifs—including anti-Semitism and Great Russian chauvinism. Stalin was by no means alone in this macabre drama. Through it there flit the shadowy, sinister figures of two little-known men who have since disappeared. One was Deputy Minister of State Security, Mikhail Ryumin. He was accused of fabricating both the "doctors' plot" and the "Mingrelian nationalist case." He was executed after Stalin's death. The other was Stalin's head of his personal secretariat, Alexander Poskrebyshev. The enormous influence which this man accumulated during Stalin's last months disappeared like dew on a hot summer morning when Stalin died. He disappeared. There has never been a public announcement of what was done with him.

Here is how Nikita Khrushchev characterized Stalin in the last years of his rule:

"His persecution mania reached unbelievable dimensions."

"Stalin was a very distrustful man, morbidly suspicious . . ."

"Everywhere and in everything he saw 'enemies,' 'two-facers,' and 'spies.' "

This goes to make up a fairly clear picture. Stalin had turned on his closest associates. He was preparing a new mass purge or "Yezhovshchina" grounded in anti-Semitism and in Great Russian xenophobia. He had suspended swords of Damocles over the heads of his old Politburo colleagues, but he had not yet removed them from their positions, or deprived them of all of their authority. He had left them to wait, with no doubt on their part as to their impending fate, till he got good and ready to finish them off. That was the situation when Stalin died. On the morning after his death the old guard, the men scheduled for liquidation, turned up in the possession of the plenitude of power.

No one will ever know the answers to all the questions which can be asked about Joseph Stalin's demise. What one can say is that because Stalin died when he did there are many people alive today who otherwise would not be here. Julie and I are perhaps among them.

# 19.    *And a Beginning*

What kind of a new government would the Soviet Union have? This was a crucial question to which I eagerly sought an answer. Experience had given me a certain amount of ability at interpreting things in the press and elsewhere. I set to work assiduously observing.

The March 6 announcement, listing appointees to major positions, had answered some questions and left others unanswered. Malenkov was the new Premier. The way the whole March 6 decree had been worded made clear he was being given precedence over his colleagues. He was the new head of government. Yet I could not forget this was the Soviet Union ruled by the Communist Party, in which control of the Party was the key to power, in which, for years, Stalin had been the dictator without the title of Premier, holding the position of General Secretary of the Party, which was enough.

Malenkov's considerable authority before Stalin's death had rested on his position as one of the leading Secretaries under Stalin of the Party. What about that job? Did he still hold it? One had to assume he did since nothing was said to the contrary. But then what was his relative rank among the other secretaries who numbered, so far as could be determined at this point, apparently seven in all? And why had nothing been said about this decisive point?

I watched the papers for signs of the role Malenkov was to play. On March 8 in *Pravda* the lead editorial quoted two men in black face type. The first was Stalin and the second Malenkov.

This same paper carried a photo on its second page. It was a

278

picture of Malenkov speaking at the Party Congress. Directly behind him sat Stalin. The photo had been clipped so only these two were shown. This was seemingly an effort to depict Malenkov, in photographic form, as the chosen disciple of Stalin. In this sense it seemed analogous to the famous photo of Stalin showing him seated on a bench with V. I. Lenin not too long before Lenin's death. So here was the beginning of a Malenkov build-up. How would it develop?

The next indication came March 9 at Stalin's funeral. That day three men spoke. Khrushchev presided and introduced Malenkov. Malenkov was introduced as "Premier and Secretary of the Central Committee of the Communist Party." Yet he was not described as "First Secretary" or "General Secretary." Besides Malenkov two others spoke, Beria and Molotov. Malenkov spoke first, giving the "keynote" funeral address. His speech was front-paged in all newspapers—printed ahead of the other two. And the photographs of the leaders on the mausoleum showed him speaking, not Beria and not Molotov. However, he had not been the only speaker. His colleagues were evidently not prepared to permit him to appear as sole spokesman of the government.

On March 10 the papers appeared, reporting the funeral ceremonies. They contained a strange photo. It appeared on Page 3 of *Pravda*. In it there were three persons—Stalin, Mao Tze-Tung and Malenkov. The caption indicated it had been taken at the signing of the Soviet-Chinese Treaty on Feb. 14, 1950. I checked the original photo of this event in *Pravda*. Indeed, these three men were actually in this photograph. But so were sixteen others. Looking at the original photograph it turned out that there four other men who had originally been in the field encompassed by the new version. It was clear that a special photomontage had been manufactured for this issue of *Pravda* of March 10 to show Malenkov alone with the two other leading Communists of his time. Here was a rewriting of history to provide a build-up of the new Premier.

One felt, at this point, that here was the launching of a propaganda campaign to make Malenkov into the new "great leader and teacher" of the Soviet peoples. But Malenkov's build-up ceased on March 11 as quickly as it had begun. No more pictures of Malenkov were published. Quotations from his "works" generally ceased.

The Supreme Soviet met briefly on Sunday, March 15, to approve the changes in the government made following Stalin's death. At this session Beria nominated Malenkov as Premier. Malenkov presented the list of appointments to his government with a brief speech. That was all. Nothing was said about the Secretariat of the Party.

The first news on this subject came as a thunderbolt in *Pravda* eight days later on March 21. It was a brief announcement. It said that on March 14—one day before the Supreme Soviet session— there had been a meeting of the Central Committee of the Party. The meeting, it said, accepted the resignation of Malenkov at his own request as a Secretary of the Central Committee and named a five-man Secretariat consisting of Khrushchev, Mikhail Suslov and three others.

Malenkov was no longer in the Secretariat. And the names of the five party secretaries had been listed out of alphabetical order—and the first one named was Khrushchev. He was not given the title of "First Secretary." But he was the first in precedence among the five secretaries thus factually occupying the post of First Secretary without the title. And the First Secretary of the Party was, as I well know, the chief executive of the Soviet Union.

What events lay behind this curt announcement? Why was this announcement of top importance held for eight days? What kind of discussion or to-do had resulted in Malenkov's resignation as a Secretary? What else was said and done at this Central Committee Meeting? The new announcement was then—and remains—an intriguing riddle.

So here was the situation at the end of March: 1. Malenkov was Premier and first in precedence among the leaders, but he had lost control of the Party apparatus. 2. Beria was the powerful Deputy First Premier and head of the police apparatus, but he had no control over the Party. The Party also had no control over him apparently. 3. Khrushchev was factual but not titular head of the Party. 4. The ruling organ in the country appeared to be the ten-man Presidium of the Central Committee of the Communist Party—similar to Stalin's old Politburo, and composed for the most part of the same men— without Stalin. 5. There had been the beginning of a build-up of a new "leader and teacher"—but it had been stopped in mid air. Yet so far there were no ideological underpinnings promulgated as a theoretical foundation for what appeared to be a type of committee rule. These ideological foundations appeared only later. They came in two important press articles.

On April 16 *Pravda* published an editorial entitled "Collectivity—the Highest Principle of Party leadership." It attacked "one-man rule." It said that "one-man decisions always or almost always are one-sided decisions."

Said the editorial, "The principle of collectivity in work means first of all that the decisions of all important questions of principle adopted by Party Committees are the result of collective discussion. No matter how experienced are the leaders, no matter how much knowledge and talent they possess, they cannot succeed in replacing the entire collective."

The editorial did not attack Stalin by name but everyone knew that his had been the prototype of "one-man rule." So here there made its appearance one of the key slogans of the post-Stalin era—"Collective Leadership."

Not until June 8 was this line carried one step further. On that date the magazine *Kommunist* carried an editorial attacking undue stress on "the role of heroes in history." *Kommunist* said that "the personality cult" was a serious mistake which must be overcome. The editorial said that outstanding personalities and leaders have sometimes been pictured as the determining force of history. This, said the magazine, is a "distortion of Marxism." Again the magazine did not attack Stalin by name. But everyone knew to whom the term "personality cult" referred. This phrase—a euphemism for "one-man dictatorship"—was thenceforth repeated over and over in the press and became another of the slogans of the era.

Thus it was that the post-Stalin regime acquired its "new look." These at least were the principal surface manifestations of the carefully concealed inner workings of the leadership which led to the formulation of a new style of operation.

\*      \*      \*      \*      \*

In the last days of March the new government began to announce, one after another, a series of steps in foreign and domestic affairs. In them came the first indications of new policies.

On March 26 the Soviet Union announced new agreements with the Chinese Communist government providing for increased economic aid to Peking. The significance of this was that it apparently represented a move by Moscow to shore up relations with Peking which had probably deteriorated seriously during the last months of Stalin's rule. Emerging from the official announcement was the fact that the Chinese Economic Delegation which concluded these agreements had been in Moscow ever since August 17, 1952. Having now by these agreements evidently compromised with Peking's demands, the new Soviet government had committed itself to dealing with Peking on a different basis than that hybrid of delay, pressure and blackmail which Stalin had apparently been using ever since Mao Tze-Tung had first come to Moscow in December, 1949. In the long run—even in the short run—this was to be a very expensive venture. But for the time being at least, it took Soviet relations with Communist China out of the blind alley into which Stalin was driving them.

On March 28 I reported in my dispatches a broad amnesty for minor criminals. The measure freed from confinement many petty offenders and also stopped prosecution of most pending cases. Scores of thousands of ordinary criminal cases begun during the last months of Stalin involving petty corruption and thievery were dropped. The immediate effect on political prisoners was minimal. But it was obvious, even right then, that this could be the possible first step in a lengthy process of gradual shut down of the Stalinist system of mass use of forced penal slave labor. At any rate, it was a move in the right direction.

On March 31 the government announced a new and broad price reduction. It embraced a series of important foodstuffs—bread, meat and sugar. It also contributed to the gaiety of the nation by cutting prices on vodka and other liquors. It included a certain number of textiles, articles of clothing and footwear. The general reduction on a number of basic items ranged from 5 to 15 percent. Altogether over one hundred classifications of goods were embraced. This price reduction, though no doubt more significant than whatever similar step might have been taken had Stalin been alive, did not represent a new departure in policy. Price reductions had been regularly proclaimed about once a year at this time since 1947.

On April 1 the Soviet government made a statement on the Korean armistice negotiations which had dragged out so many exasperating months. In its declaration the Kremlin expressed readiness to assist agreement in Panmunjon. This was something which could mean much or nothing, depending on what the Russians had in mind. It was apparent that the Russians could do much, if they wished, to bring about a Korean armistice, and the continuing conflict in Korea was the single most important factor in international tension.

Things seemed to be looking up a bit—but it was still too early to tell.

\*    \*    \*    \*    \*

March 31 the first post-Stalin breath of fresh air from the outside blew into Moscow. It came in the form of a strange and interesting collection of American news people headed by publisher James Wick of New York and Washington. The Wick group was an annual journalistic tour designed for editors of small town newspapers. It was on its way through Europe when Stalin died. Wick immediately applied for visas for all his party. The Russians promptly granted the visas.

Not since 1947, despite innumerable applications, had any group of American journalists been allowed into Russia. So the Wick party came, wide-eyed and a little frightened at all the implications of this unexpected enterprise. All of them had managed to get special assignments from the host of news organizations and magazines eager for special reports from Russia. They besieged all five permanent American correspondents in Moscow with questions, and requests for advice and assistance in filing dispatches. On our side we were glad to see colleagues from home.

The group was given modest publicity in the Soviet press and excited a bit of public attention. It was astonishing and frustrating for us permanent correspondents to see how the red carpet could be laid out for visiting correspondents and how burdensome restrictions to which we were subject could be lifted in order to make a good impression.

The American editors wandered about Moscow with their cameras ready. They took as many shots as they pleased. Occasionally a militiaman approached and asked who they were. And then, greeted with the term "Amerikansky Zhurnalist," would salute, grin and spread his hands out in a gesture of hospitality. And they filed their dispatches, sometimes through the censorship, on occasion by telephone direct from their hotel rooms. The censor did not bother them much. For us the red pencil was as vigorous as ever.

\*    \*    \*    \*    \*

The new government had begun taking its initial steps in domestic affairs in the last few days of March. There had been the amnesty and the price reduction. Both seemed to be moves toward an easier and better life, but they were almost routine for a new Russian government and weren't in any sense definitive signposts of new domestic policies. When would such a signpost appear? I wondered —but not long.

I read the announcement April 6 in *Pravda* carefully and then went on to read *Pravda*'s lead editorial. Their subject was the "doctors' plot." The official document was a communique of the Ministry of Internal Affairs. It said the accused doctors, after a thorough investigation, had been freed. The charges against them had been dropped. They had been restored to their official positions. It said, in an obvious reference to the use of torture, that the "confessions" had been obtained "by means of impermissable and illegal methods." It said that the documentary materials on which the accusations had been based were faked. The announcement named fifteen Russians among those accused—in comparison with the original nine names announced January 13. But among those listed as released, two of the original names announced on January 13 were missing.

*Pravda* carried an editorial entitled, "Soviet Socialist Legality is Inviolable." Whoever wrote the headline did not have a very keen sense of humor. *Pravda* laid the whole fabrication at the door of the former Minister of State Security, Semyon D. Ignatiev, and his Deputy Minister who was in charge of the Ministry's Investigatory Section, Ryumin. The editorial revealed that Ryumin had been arrested as a "secret enemy of our state and people." The paper, needless to say, did not comment on what role Stalin played in it. It was not for three more years—in February 1956 at the twentieth Party Congress—that this question was finally discussed. However, despite this lack of frankness in the discussion of the case, the salient fact was that the "doctors' plot" had been discredited in such a decisive way that it would not be practical for the Soviet leaders of the Soviet Union to proceed further with this particular Stalinist technique of plot and confession, which was so essential to the purge system and the system of rule by political terror, which Stalin had maintained. And it followed that, if the purge system and rule by terror on a mass scale were no longer to be, the foundation of the Soviet system, other means of rule, based in some more significant part on satisfaction of the crying needs of the country and the people for change and a better life, would probably have to be devised.

But this was just the bare beginning. And could one imagine, for instance, such a man as Lavrenty Beria, the living symbol in the popular mind of Soviet police terror, carrying out the liquidation of that aspect of the system? Hardly—and yet he stood there obviously as a king-maker and strong man in the new regime. How would that dilemma be solved?

*     *     *     *     *

On the heels of this first sign of a real "new deal" in domestic policy, came the revelation that there would also be a "new course" in foreign affairs. But it came in a different way.

To be sure, from Stalin's funeral on, the new government had repeatedly emphasized its desire for peace and the settlement of problems. Western ambassadors making protocol calls on Foreign Minister V. M. Molotov found the atmosphere in the Ministry seemed to be much more pleasant and relaxed than formerly. Then too the Soviet government had made its interesting démarche of April 1 on Korea. This was interesting, but would there be a real change? The answer came quickly and, as it happened, I played by accident, a personal role in arranging the setting.

The American journalists were about to end their stay in Moscow. Julie and I had made good friends among them. We decided we would like to give them a farewell party. I engaged the private banquet room at the Aragvi Restaurant.

I included in the list of guests not only the visiting journalists but the Chargé d'affaires of the American Embassy, Jacob Beam, his wife, and several other Embassy friends. As I was completing arrangements I had an afterthought. Perhaps I might invite some of the Soviet officials from the Press Department. I had, to be sure, invited them on occasion before and they had refused. This was routine since in Stalin's time few officials ever accepted invitations from foreigners.

Well, I would ask them anyway, I decided. They might refuse but it was polite to invite them for such an occasion. So I called the Press Department and issued my invitations—and then forgot about them. On the day of the party I received a phone call from the Press Department telling me that Acting Chief of the Department, Mr. Kartsev, and his Deputy, Mr. Vavilov, would attend. And I was told that Mrs. Vavilov would also be coming. This last was a particular surprise since Soviet wives of diplomats usually did not attend social functions in Moscow with their husbands.

The party assembled at the Aragvi. There were more than two dozen guests. The crystal-clear Moscow vodka had been well iced, as requested. Large dishes with lovely gray Astrakahan malosol caviar were on the table, along with toast and chopped green onions. Small glasses of vodka were poured by the busy waiters and the veteran Muscovites gave instructions to the neophytes on how to down a small glass of vodka "do dna"—"bottoms up"—and then chase it down with a big mouthful of toast and caviar. The atmosphere was gay. The journalists had had an excellent day and were prepared for an excellent evening.

The door opened and the Russians from the Press Department appeared. The two men were resplendent in their light blue Foreign Office uniforms, complete with gleaming shoulder boards. I went to greet them with some slight misgiving. I knew my Russians, or thought I did. And I did not think these officials would be prepared to let down their hair and have a good time. Kartsev grasped my hand in a warm salutation and shook it vigorously.

"We're delighted you invited us to this friendly party!" he said. He was beaming with cordiality. I lost my misgivings quickly. I took them over to the table where the vodka was being poured and proferred them drinks. Soon they were chatting gaily with other guests.

A little while later I went over to listen to the conversation which Kartsev was having with Chargé d'Affaires Beam.

I could hardly believe what I was hearing. Kartsev was doing most of the talking.

"There have been many mistakes in the past," he said in a firm and friendly way. "The important thing is that we must forget the past and start out anew. I do not mean, of course, that mistakes should not be corrected. They should be. And I imagine that we are ready to correct them. But we have to forget the animosities of the past and make a new start—now." This was a new kind of talk for Moscow!

Kartsev had come to this gathering with the knowledge of his superiors, including Molotov himself. If he was saying such things to the American Chargé, it was because he had been instructed to. He was holding forth a clear promise that many aspects of Soviet foreign policy would be subject to review—and negotiation. He was making an admission there had been mistakes. This was not the kind of an admission that the Foreign Minister could make. But an official on Kartsev's level could, on instructions. By so doing he "got the message" to the American government without committing the Soviet government to anything specific. But no one could doubt its seriousness.

The party went on and on. There was one surprise after another mostly from our Soviet guests, who were not only fulfilling their official mission but having a good time. Mr. Kartsev rose to make a toast. "I want to drink to the health and success of President Eisenhower!"

That was the first time that toast had been uttered by any Soviet official in Moscow. We all knew this was something startling. Some of my journalist colleagues present gulped down their dinners and rushed to the telegraph office to file stories. I had only thought to give a party. But it was a big news story—and more than that.

\*        \*        \*        \*        \*

A familiar handsome figure sat in the easy chair in the Blue Room on the first floor of Spaso House. He chatted with fluency. He gestured with animation with his agile right hand in which he waved a cigarette. This was Ambassador Charles E. Bohlen. He had arrived earlier on that windy sunny day, April 11, for a long stay.

At that moment Ambassador Bohlen was reminiscing about his first sojourn in this same house. He recalled how he had come there in early 1934 to assist the first American Ambassador to the Soviet Union as translator and factotum. He told how one of his tasks had been to accompany the French cook to Moscow stores in a futile effort to purchase spices. It was futile because he did not know the names of most of the spices, even in English, and because Soviet stores were not known for their selection of spices. Becoming more serious, Bohlen told us we could quote him as saying he did not intend to anticipate in this interview instructions he might receive from the Department. He stated he would ask for an appointment with Foreign Minister Molotov in accordance with protocol.

Having thus given us the noncommital statements we could use in our reports he relaxed a bit and talked "off the record"—expressing feelings and concepts about his new post. He expected to have an interesting stay. He was convinced the time had come when many problems might find a solution.

I left Spaso House with hope. The American representation in Moscow was in good hands. Bohlen had made the study of Soviet affairs his life's work. He had come to Moscow at a time more favorable for the settlement of outstanding issues than any time since the War. Things were looking up. If the Russians wanted to talk turkey, Bohlen was the man who would listen.

*     *     *     *     *

Four of us—American correspondents who had been in Moscow many years—sat in Ambassador Bohlen's office in the Embassy and listened. It was a matter of concern to each of us. It concerned our own fates and those of our wives.

"I have decided," Bohlen was saying, "to ask Molotov at an interview tomorrow morning for exit visas for the Soviet wife of each one of you. I am going to bring up the two similar cases in the Embassy and other visa problems. The Secretary of State has given me clearance."

The Ambassador smiled gently and uttered a soft warning.

"Now, don't get your hopes up!" he emphasized. "You know how touchy a subject this is. You may be once more disappointed. Don't take it too hard if that turns out to be the case. The question is going to be pushed. The time is right." He went on, thinking out loud, "In relations with the Russians there are times when one can get things for nothing. The Russians want to make a gesture. Then is the time to ask. This is such a period."

*     *     *     *     *

During April and May new developments showing changed directions of Soviet policy piled up on each other in profusion. Every day there would be some surprise in the papers. Or I would make a call at the American Embassy to find that something new had happened there. Or I would drive around town and I would see something new.

Spring came to Russia in those days and it was a wondrous spring. The snow and ice thawed on the streets of Moscow and at the same time it was thawing in the hearts of a country. The sun was shining down on the bright cold spring days and it was warming the souls of a people who had lived under the shadow of fear, people who welcomed it, hesitantly at first, and then joyfully and happily. There has never been such a spring in Moscow as there was in 1953!

I can read the history of the times in my telegrams. They tell the political side of the story. But there is that other side, the human and personal. Nevertheless, they make their point.

On April 8 I reported that the Soviet Union would send a cruiser to take part in the Coronation Naval Review in June in England. It had been unheard of previously for the Soviet Navy to send naval vessels to foreign countries.

On April 10 I reported that seven British civilians interned in North Korea since the beginning of the Korean War had been turned over to Soviet representatives for repatriation and return to their homelands.

On April 21 I reported the presentation by American Ambassador Bohlen of his credentials in the Kremlin and the unusual reporting in the press of official remarks by Bohlen and, in reply, by Chairman of the Presidium of the Supreme Soviet Klimenty Voroshilov. It was noteworthy that Voroshilov expressed the hope, so frequently expressed at the time, that all difficult problems between the Soviet Union and the United States could be solved.

On April 30 I reported that two Soviet scientific delegations would go abroad in 1953 to attend international scientific meetings. For many years Soviet attendance at international scientific gatherings had been sparing indeed.

May 1 was the national Soviet spring holiday. This year the emphasis was away from the displays of massed military might typical of some previous years and slanted toward the lengthy and colorful "workers' demonstration" which followed the military parade. The brand new feature this year was that Soviet militiamen made no attempt to interfere with foreigners who went out to take photographs in front of the American Embassy.

*Pravda* carried this day an article by Ilya Ehrenburg entitled "Hope." Ehrenburg, who in the past on the occasion of important holidays had delivered some of the most strongly-worded diatribes against the "American imperialists," wrote in a gentle, warm and optimistic tone.

May 1 the British Embassy had been told by the Russians that a young British Embassy clerk, confined to the Embassy for several years in order to avoid serving a jail sentence imposed by the Russians, would be free to leave the Soviet Union.

On May 6 I reported the award of a Soviet government decoration to G. I. Petrovsky. Petrovsky in the early days of the Soviet regime had been one of the leading men of the Party. In the mid-thirties, like so many other Old Bolsheviks, he fell into disgrace. He had been dismissed from his posts and nothing had been heard of him for years. Now he had been given a decoration. Here was perhaps a sign that some of the distinguished Communists who had fallen under the shadow of Stalin's jealousy might once more be honored—those few who had not perished.

On May 9 I reported that the "Stalin prizes" in science, technology, art and literature for 1952 had not yet been awarded. They never were again.

On May 11 I described the arrival in Moscow, on their way home, of seven American civilians, liberated through the good offices of the Soviet government from internment in North Korea.

May 15 I reported that my AP colleague, Bill Oatis, was being freed from prison in Czechoslovakia.

May 17 I reported that there had been visible tendencies in Soviet policy in the direction of normalization of the previously acutely hostile relations between the Soviet Union and President Tito's Yugoslavia.

May 22 I reported that, for the first time in over two decades, there were on regular retail sale in Moscow the most popular grades of wheat flour. Previously flour had been made available only on certain holidays in very limited supply. Here was a development which would mean more to the women of the Soviet Union than all political developments taken together.

May 24 I reported that rumors were circulating that the government was preparing to open the Kremlin to the public. The Kremlin, a national monument, had been kept closed, with the public excluded, for two decades, because Stalin used it as his headquarters.

On May 29 I reported an attack in *Pravda* on Soviet economists who had been taking seriously Stalin's proposal for a system of "product exchange" between collective farms and cities in the Soviet Union. The newspaper said that the important thing for the present in the Soviet Union was the development of the existing system of retail trade. Here was the abandonment of another one of Stalin's key platforms for the Soviet Union.

Day after day the reversal of the policy lines of Stalin was becoming more pronounced.

\*    \*    \*    \*    \*

June 6. The phone rang. I answered. It was Harrison.

"I'm at the Embassy and I've got news," he said hesitantly. "It's about the visas . . ."

"Is it good or bad news?" I asked quickly, holding my breath.

"Well," he began, "I think it's good. I don't think it's too bad. Two visas have been authorized—but neither is for Julie. The Ambassador is anxious to give you the details himself."

"Don't be discouraged, Tom," the Ambassador told me when I saw him later at Spaso House. "Molotov told me, after informing me that two of the visas had been granted, that the remainder were under consideration. I personally think that Julie will gets hers next shot. Sit tight, relax and don't be worried. That's my advice." These were kind words but I was nevertheless discouraged.

\*    \*    \*    \*    \*

Once more we were in the Banquet Room of the Aragvi Restaurant. Ambassador Bohlen sat at the head of the table. Julie sat on one side and Perle Mesta, a visitor in Moscow that month, on the other. The waiters brought in the steaming and aromatic Karsky shashlyk covered with raw onions. Red Georgian wine flowed freely. The two dozen people who were our guests were enjoying themselves. High-pitched conversation ebbed and flowed along with laughter. The Aragvi orchestra entered and entertained us with a selection of Caucasian melodies including the famous "Suleiko."

It was a farewell which Julie and I were giving for two good friends and for their Russian wives, the lucky girls who had received Molotov's first visas. They were wreathed in befitting smiles. So were we as befitted the hosts. I must admit that our smiles concealed anxiety. Ten days had passed since the first two visas. There had been no further news.

\*    \*    \*    \*    \*

June 17. Julie, Harrison and I had gone out to the dacha. The weather could not decide whether to break out into sunshine or to burst out in a shower. I was restless. I went and worked in the garden but I soon grew tired of that. I wandered around the flower beds and pulled a few weeds, but I soon grew tired of that. I played with Keshka—throwing a rubber ball for her to retrieve. But I soon got tired of that too. Finally I went up to the porch and settled down to read. Harrison and Julie were chatting away in chairs in the yard. And so the day wore slowly on.

From inside the dacha the telephone rang. "I'll answer it," Julie said. She jumped up and ran inside. I heard her talking. Obviously the telephone call was for her, and I paid no further attention.

Suddenly Julie appeared in the doorway of the porch. She had a gleam in her eye. "I've got my visa!" she exclaimed.

Harrison and I both jumped to our feet. "Congratulations!" he said. And I went over and gave her a big kiss.

"All right, now tell me about it," I told her. "Just what were you told?"

"It was Eddy," she said. "He's just been at the Embassy. Foreign Minister Molotov called in the Ambassador today and told him the government had agreed to the Ambassador's request I be given an exit visa to leave the Soviet Union. Permission was granted to three others. Molotov told the Ambassador I could apply for my foreign passport at the OVIR office in the next few days and that it would be issued soon. That's all, but isn't it enough?"

The news was too big to comprehend. So we would be leaving! We would be going to the United States!

We started talking about practical problems. How long would it take for the passport to be issued? What were we going to do about all our books and furniture and other personal possessions—the accumulation of nine years? What were we going to do about the cat, Charley, and the dog, Keshka?

"They are both going to go with us!" said Julie. "I know it's going to be a lot of trouble to take them but I want them both with me. So they are going to go."

That settled that. But there were so many more things left to be decided. Excited and gay, we got in the car and drove back to the city that very evening in order to set to work on the manifold tasks of preparing for departure. It was all too much to believe. One phone call and all our lives were completely changed!

*    *    *    *    *

On the news front June was one more busy month. In foreign affairs there were little things and big. Foreign Minister Molotov attended the British Embassy's Coronation Ball in Moscow and the Soviet cruiser, Sverdlov, went to England to participate in the coronation celebrations. A Soviet communication to Turkey told the Turks that the USSR renounced territorial claims against Turkey. The Press Department took a welcome step by proposing a trip for journalists to Stalingrad and the Volga-Don Canal. It was the first invitation issued to reporters for any trip since 1947. June 23 the Foreign Office announced to foreign embassies in Moscow a significant relaxation in the boundaries of areas into which foreign diplomats were not permitted to travel.

All of these things were in the direction of better relations with foreigners in Russia and with foreign countries.

At the same time it was in this month that the uprising took place in Berlin against the Russians. This was crushed quickly enough—but it caused some bitter explosions indeed of anti-Western and anti-American verbiage in the press.

In domestic affairs the most important development was the up-surge of a campaign against Great Russian chauvinism. June 13 the Party Chieftain of the Ukraine, Leonid Melnikov, was ousted for attempting to impose the Russian language on higher educational institutions in the Western Ukraine. June 18 "serious mistakes" in nationality policy were discovered in Soviet Lithuania. The authoritative magazine *Kommunist,* June 25, attacked "contemptible adventurists" who, the magazine said, had repeatedly tried to arouse hatred among nationalities of the Soviet Union for each other. But then this campaign subsided quite as suddenly as it had begun.

On June 25 the Soviet government got around—six weeks later than usual—to announcing a new State loan, one of the annual features of Soviet economic life, representing in fact a second income tax on all workers and employees. And this year the subscriptions were set at about half of the usual norm.

Yet Soviet citizens were not too certain of the stability of Soviet currency. There were rumors of a currency reform which would involve replacement of existing money with new money allegedly already printed. Long lines of citizens formed at savings banks, many of them putting their money in the bank, but some of them withdrawing deposits so as to purchase goods. And it was necessary for the Finance Minister to make a special statement in order to allay the unrest.

It was on June 28 that the Soviet press announced the attendance of most of the Soviet leaders at an opera. Among the names of those attending that of Police Chief Beria was missing.

\*    \*    \*    \*    \*

The days between June 17, when the news of the exit visa was received, and July 31 when we were to depart, were feverish. So much to be done! So little time to do it!

I had the full burden of the AP Bureau in a period when news stories were sometimes breaking hourly. We had all the problems of red tape involved in getting Julie's passport and visa, plus all the other documents we needed, plus the task of disposing of nine years accumulation of clothes, household goods, books, research materials and every other sort of thing.

Day after day people from the diplomatic corps tracked through our apartment, picking out furniture they wanted. One by one the things we had accumulated with great effort were sold, some of them for a fraction of their value, some for what we had paid, some at a profit. A buyer from a Soviet store came in one day and carefully fingered many remaining pieces. He took most of what was left including a beautiful desk which Julie and Harrison had gotten for me from the United States with tremendous trouble and expense only a few months before.

One day a buyer came from a piano store. He looked over Julie's upright which she had inherited. He bought it. As he filled out the documents he pointed out that he represented the piano store located in the same place as the store which had sold this piano to her mother nearly forty years before.

Julie took some of our clothes to commission stores for sale as used merchandise. Some she gave to friends and to people who had worked for us. Some we packed to take with us.

Day after day I worked in my spare time packing up two dozen wooden boxes with books, newspapers and magazines. Finally these things were ready to be sent off to the Customs House. The customs inspectors looked them over and were going to make me submit a list of every book. But they relented. Everything went off. The chauffeur, Kolya, took my car to the railway station for shipment.

I gave a sigh of relief and so did Julie. We had disposed of nearly every worldly possession except the clothes on our backs.

*     *     *     *     *

July 10. I stood in the room at the telegraph office and looked out the window in the pallid light of the early dawn of the mid-summer morning at a little after three o'clock. I was waiting for the big news story which was about to break. I fingered the telegram I had written several nights before and kept with me to be put in when the announcement came. The censor, of course, had been systematically killing all references to this story for it was a touchy thing.

I took the telegram and looked at it once more. I read: "Bulletin. The Soviet press announced this morning that Lavrenty P. Beria has been dismissed from his post of Minister of Internal Affairs."

That was all I knew up to then. The flood of rumors about Beria's disappearance had begun July 1. It had grown and now it was all over Moscow. There had been no denial. Stories were rife. So and so, who had contact with a Western Embassy, knew a police colonel from his apartment house who had been burning papers all week. The rumors gave details. Beria's residence on the Sadovaya Boulevard had been surrounded on an evening in late June by an armored division of elite guards detailed by the Army. There was panic in police headquarters, some said.

Some journalists and diplomats refused to believe. But I believed. I wrote my telegram and waited. My car pulled up on the street below me as I waited there in the telegraph office, and my chauffeur, Dmitry, got out with a copy of *Pravda* in his hand. I went to meet him. Harrison Salisbury got his copy of the newspaper seconds before I. He glanced at the front page and whispered, "This is it!" I turned back to the counter in the office and handed in my telegram.

This was a story! Lavrenty Beria, purge artist, had been purged. I hurried to my typewriter and began to absorb the details. The announcements were brief. One said the Central Committee had held a meeting, heard a report by Malenkov on "The Criminal Anti-Party and Anti-State Actions of Lavrenty P. Beria," and adopted a decision to expel him from the Party "as an enemy of the Communist Party and the Soviet people."

*Pravda*'s lead editorial went on to elaborate. Beria was described as a "bourgeois degenerate," who had "climbed to leadership by various careerist machinations." He was charged with many things: sabotage of Soviet agriculture; seeking to undermine the "friendship of peoples of the USSR"; "becoming an agent of international imperialism." The principal charge was that he had sought to put the police above the Party and seize "leadership of the Party and the country."

As I dictated my story to London that morning I thought about this development. From the very first days after the death of Stalin I felt that either Beria would run the Soviet Union or that there would have to be some such denouement. I was certain Beria would never permit control by other leaders over his private empire. And it was a vast empire. It included ordinary police, secret police, intelligence, counter-intelligence, border guards, internal security troops, forced labor camps, coal mines and oil wells in the far North, entire cities such as the thriving little Arctic metropolis of Norilsk in Central Siberia, and even all the fire departments. Nor was his empire limited to the Ministry of Internal Affairs. Beria ruled Soviet Georgia, Soviet Armenia and Soviet Azerbaidjan. His police generals played a decisive role in the affairs of Soviet Central Asia. And beyond this Beria controlled the nuclear weapons facilities of the Soviet government.

On the outskirts of the capital there were camps housing well-armed, efficient, tough units of Beria's private police army. These were the same divisions that had taken over the city on the dawn of the day after Stalin's death and held it until his funeral was over. The Commander of the Moscow Military District and the Commandants of the City of Moscow and of the Moscow Kremlin itself, seat of the Soviet government, were officers who had close connections with Beria.

All this power and might was concentrated in the hands of one man who was the most hated and feared man in the Soviet Union. It was not strange that Beria's colleagues had come to the decision that they had to remove this threat. What was interesting was the fact they had succeeded. In this they had on their side the fact Beria was a Georgian and that the Soviet Union had had enough Georgian rule.

No doubt, I thought to myself further, the Soviet leadership in removing Beria had been responding to the overwhelming exigencies of a particular pressing political situation. But now that he had been removed he had to be denounced. And any denunciatory condemnation of Beria made it necessary also to denounce police terror.

This was the single most important thing looming up on July 10, 1953. Now it was really clear that the new era had to become something different from Stalin's. One more thing was clear as well. Premier Malenkov, to the extent that he may have helped pull the rug from under Beria, had undermined his own position. Beria had been the power that put him into office and the power that kept him in office. With Beria gone Malenkov sooner or later would go too.

Who would take his place?

One did not have to look too far . . .

*    *    *    *    *

It was nerve-racking to have such things taking place at a time when the American Ambassador had been told Julie would be allowed to leave the country, but before she left the Soviet government conceivably could, if there were some sort of reversal in policy, decide to go back on its word. It didn't seem likely. But these were nervous days. Fortunately, we were so busy we did not have any time to stop and think.

The days went by, each bringing new repercussions of the Beria arrest, but it became soon apparent there was to be no dramatic turnabout in Soviet foreign affairs.

*    *    *    *    *

I went with Julie one day to the OVIR office where she was to fill out her application for a Soviet foreign passport. They handed her a set of application blanks in triplicate, each resembling in size an examination book of the type used in American universities. There were dozens of questions. They covered every facet of life. "Have you any relatives who live abroad?" "Their names, addresses, occupations?" "Have you relatives who have been arrested?" "Their full names, nature of their crime, length of sentence?" Etc., etc. Where there were questions which could be answered with a simple "yes" the instructions provided that this was unsatisfactory. One had to write out a complete affirmation. I gasped as I watched Julie sit down to work. I was certain it would take her two days, particularly since each of the copies had to be separately handwritten. She set about it. Julie dashed through. She finished them all in an hour. She turned them in to the police officers and we left. Several weeks later Julie was informed that her passport was ready. She was to call for it and pay three-hundred and sixty rubles—equivalent to ninety dollars at the current official exchange rate.

"That's a lot of money for a passport!" I said to her.

"Personally, I think it's pretty cheap," she said. "I might say it's one of the best bargains I ever had."

One day in late July, at the OVIR office, the police officer handed Julie her foreign passport and took from her in exchange her internal passport—a document which all Soviet citizens must have. From the official point of view she was already outside the country.

\*     \*     \*     \*     \*

July 27 at three thirty-five in the morning I hammered out my telegram: "Bulletin. *Pravda* headlined this morning: 'The 27th of June—Signing of the Agreement on the Armistice in Korea.' "

\*     \*     \*     \*     \*

July 30. Julie and I spent this day making farewell visits. Julie stood in the corridor of the old apartment on the Arbat in which she had lived all her life until I came into the picture. She was talking with her neighbor and close friend, Nyura. "Please don't forget us, Yulochka," said Nyura, wiping a tear from the corner of her eye. "Don't forget us way over there in America. Write us. And come back to visit. It's sad to see you go."

Julie went down the still dark hallway to knock on the door of the room in which she and her mother had lived so long. After her mother's death it had been taken over by a family consisting of a husband, wife and six children. They answered and she told them she wanted to take one last look at her old home. They let her in. A little while later we went down the stairway, leaving the familiar apartment building.

"I hope that if I ever come back to visit here that there will be good lights on the landings and that the treads of the stairs will be repaired," she said. We stepped out from the dark hallway into the light of day on the Arbat.

We paid our last visit to the dacha in Saltykovka. We went to see it once more and to fetch Charley, the cat, who had been occupying the residence in solitary splendor during our last month in Moscow.

I wandered about the premises ruefully, thinking of the expenditure of money and labor that we had put into the improvement of that home. I inspected the fine carpentry work done on our glassed-in porch and the orange and blue colored glass which I had obtained with so much effort and negotiation. Who, I wondered, in future years, would get the benefit of that investment? I went and looked with fondness at the bushes and trees I had planted. I looked next door at the Balakiryov household, certain that many of these trees and bushes would manage to migrate next door to that thriving little miniature farm.

We went to say goodbye to Nadya. Julie left her gifts. Perhaps it was imagination, but I rather fancied that Nadya was glad to see us go. I could not blame her. She had a right to her own feelings.

A little later, back in the city again that same day, we stopped at the cemetery. The plot where Mother's body lay was well tended and beautiful. Inside the small fence rosebushes which we had planted grew profusely. The surface of the plot on which there were no plants was carefully sanded. In the enclosure was a small bench where we could, if we wished, sit and contemplate. Julie went in and sat on the bench.

"Why don't you leave me here by myself for a few minutes, Tomochka?" she asked. I went off down the walk, looking at the marble monuments strewn there in such profusion, reading the Russian and foreign names inscribed, and wondering now and then what kind of a person it had been whose body lay under such and such a monument. What kind of a life had he or she led? And—if it was a foreign name—what was it that brought him or her to Moscow, there to live, there to die, there to be buried?

On this day I could at least be happier than I had been on my previous visits. It appeared that I, and Julie too, might have the privilege of dying, not in Moscow, but somewhere else. I interrupted my somewhat morbid thoughts to go back and find Julie. Together we left the cemetery and drove home.

\*     \*     \*     \*     \*

July 31. We got up at five o'clock. It was "D" day for us—the "D" standing for departure. We rattled around, getting dressed, and washed in a barren, empty apartment. Everything—except our bed—had been moved out. In the corner of the dining room stood packed suitcases. In an opposite corner stood a wooden box, resembling in its shape a small doghouse with a handle on top. This was Charley's traveling home.

The problem about it had been how to get him into it. To put him in by main force was risky, since he had claws and knew how to use them. It was Julie who decided on the strategem of luring Charley into the box. He was left hungry and thirsty overnight. In the morning a saucer of milk was put inside the box. Julie peered from behind the door. Charley went in the box to get the milk and Julie popped out and popped the door shut. Charley protested but he was in his box.

We went to Harrison's apartment to have breakfast. Everything was ready. Maria Ivanovna was there and so was the cook, Lena, and the maid, Varya. We ate quickly. I glanced at my watch as we sipped our morning coffee. We were on time but we had none to spare. Kolya, the chauffeur, had been loading our bags into the car. We went upstairs to take one last look. We walked back to Harrison's apartment where Maria Ivanovna, Lena and Varya stood in the front hallway waiting to say goodbye. The little black dog, Keshka, who was going to stay behind with Harrison and come with him to us, when he departed later that year, already sensed that something important was in the wind and jumped up, begging to be taken, but to no avail.

"Well," Julie said, "we're going on a long trip so let's observe the Russian custom." We all sat down in the living room for a moment in silence. Then we got up. Julie kissed Maria Ivanovna and Lena and Varya goodbye. They, of course, like all good-hearted, emotional Russian women at a farewell scene, were crying copiously, but at the same time smiling. I gave nervous little Keshka a final pat on the head and we went out and got in the car.

Fifteen minutes later we were driving along the Kaluga Chaussée on the edge of Moscow. It was a gray, misty summer morning with the sun well hidden. Julie and Harrison and I sat in the back seat of the car and Julie and I looked at the familiar buildings on either side of this highway which we had traveled so many times, going to the airport to say goodbye to our friends. This time there was the realization that this was the last time we would be seeing Moscow for a long time, maybe forever.

"Are you sorry to be leaving?" I asked Julie.

"No, I'm not sorry," she said. "I'm a Russian, and that I shall never forget. I'm proud to be a Russian and always shall be. But for me, this country has been a land of tragedy. It swallowed up my family and now I'm the only one left. I want to begin a new life. And I want to begin it somewhere else. I'm not sorry I'm leaving."

We drove on out the highway to the airport, looking at the little Russian farm villages on either side of the road. Over on the right in the distance there was the old Russian village church with a tall bell tower which I had seen so many times before. Half an hour later at the Vnukovo Airport I stood at the Customs Inspection counter with our suitcases in front of me and also the little wooden traveling box in which Charley, the Siberian cat, was still loudly protesting his confinement. An officious Soviet customs officer was going through my bags.

"What's in here?" the customs officer asked, pointing at Charley's box. I explained that this was our cat, that we had had a difficult time getting him in the box, and that we were taking him to the United States. "Take him out!" said the customs inspector. I protested in vain. I had to let Charley out. He jumped into my arms, angry and at the same time, overjoyed to be out of his cage.

"Now you can put him back in!" said the customs officer.

"That's what you think!" I muttered to myself in English. And I thereupon delivered—inaudibly of course—a string of deeply-felt Russian and English curses on all customs inspectors of all nationalities. Fifteen minutes later with my hands scratched and bleeding, and my face scratched and bleeding, I emerged triumphantly, with Charley back in his box, protesting more loudly than before, to get in line beside Julie in front of the Soviet-made DC-3 which was to take us that day to Helsinki.

The Soviet airlines official called off the names of the passengers, one by one.

"Mr. and Mrs. Whitney." I heard him say as if in a dream.

Julie and I climbed up the ramp to get aboard the plane. At the top we turned around and waved to Harrison. We took one more look around us and climbed into the plane. That was our farewell to Moscow. The motors roared and the plane rushed down the runway and up into the gray Moscow sky.

# 20.    Conclusion

We touched down on Soviet soil once more at the Leningrad Airport. We got out of the plane and sat on a small bench in bright sunlight. Then we got up and went back into the plane. It rose up into the late morning sky and pointed toward the northwest. The motors droned steadily away. I sat motionless, but inside there was still tenseness. We were so near now, it was hard to believe. Julie sat quietly beside me and Charley miaowed plaintively now and then in his wooden box. I looked below. I could see the gray water of the Gulf of Finland and the islands and inlets of the pine-clad, rock-bound Karelian Isthmus. It was still Russia. The heavy-set Russian stewardess announced over the loud-speaker: "Comrade passengers, we have now left the Soviet Union. In a half-hour we will be arriving at Helsinki."

I looked across at Julie. She turned away to look out the window, back behind her. I thought I detected a little sadness in her eyes when she looked back at me.

I relaxed and leaned back in my seat. My mind's eye went back to that other plane trip on May 8, 1944 which had brought me to Russia—nine years, two months and twenty-three days before. I had had so much curiosity about this country I was seeing for the first time! Well, I could say that in some respects, I had satisfied that curiosity. I went back to another plane trip in June, 1937, to California, in order to start my study of Russian. I had certainly not had the slightest inkling of the great adventure into which this new language would eventually launch me.

302

The adventure—this phase of it—was now at an end. It was a happy ending, too. I looked at Julie. A warm feeling crept over me. How big a part of that adventure she had been! I had fallen in love with her. I had sworn to myself a great oath that no matter what came I would stick with her in Russia, protect her to whatever extent I could with my own person, and eventually get her out of Russia. This I had done.

How narrow the margin may have been between success and failure in this, perhaps between life and death! I really did not know. There had been danger all along, and then at the very last the storm clouds had really gathered. The lightning began to flash and strike, hitting one, another, all around us. The whole evil dark thing was about to burst and engulf so many—so many *living people* as the *Pravda* editorials had said with such heavy stress, us perhaps among them.

Then of a sudden the storm clouds had been whisked away and the sun had shone down with a full, clear brilliant glow out of a lovely, blue cloudless sky. And all had been saved—and we with them.

Our fates had been entangled for a time with the fate of a great country. I looked behind me at that country. I thought about it for a bit, what it was, where it was going, what this might mean for it and the rest of the world.

I had come to Russia in 1944, about the time the nation entered a new era—the after-the-war era, the end-of-Stalin's reign era, the era of post-war reconstruction and economic upsurge, the era of deep freeze, cold war, silent terror. I had stayed there throughout this era. I had watched there the ripening of the central contradiction, the dilemma of Soviet life, the conflict between economic growth and the atrophy of the central nervous system of the body politic. The burgeoning and swelling productive machinery of the nation was being artificially confined and pent up by obsolete methods and forms of rule—and warning signs were being ignored.

The crisis had become acute. The nation was shuddering with the premonition and preliminary stages of a great shattering convulsion. But then, suddenly, things had changed overnight. The organism—through luck or through strength—had thrown off the terrible fit and begun to recover. A new leadership had taken over, a leadership which, I was certain, could and would take a new look at things and take measures as far-reaching as necessary to solve urgent problems.

Russia, I knew, had successfully come through its crisis and was now in the midst of a period of reorientation. This would not necessarily go smoothly—but it would be accomplished.

Rule by terror was being discredited. Stalin's style of leadership was being rejected and so now new methods and a new style of rule would have to be worked out for the system. And these would be, I was certain, methods and a style more in harmony with the needs of a modern economy and society than anything Russia had had previously. And this would be the beginning of a new stage of growth and development for Russia.

Out of all this there would come, I felt, gradually and hesitantly at first, but then as time went on, more fully, a release of those enormous creative forces, those unbelievable talents of the Russian peoples and of the Soviet Union which had been, in so many important aspects, suppressed and stifled under Stalin. These would express themselves, I was certain, in the outpouring of a deluge of scientific and artistic creation which would astonish the world and Russia itself. And this would be accompanied by an accelerating upsurge of technological progress and economic productivity which would, in an unbelievably short time, transform the Soviet Union into a tremendously wealthy nation.

And here, I hoped, that for the first time in all of Russia's dark and gloomy history there would perhaps appear the chance for this country, in which tragedy was a member of every family, in which sadness and grief was everyone's boon companion, to become at last a happy land of joyful people.

But the most important thing for the rest of the world that would now take place, I knew, was that Russia would return to the mainstream of international life. Russia would forsake its isolation, knock holes in the Chinese walls which Stalin had erected in order to separate the USSR from the rest of the world, and seek its place not separate from, in isolation from, the other nations of the world, but instead among them.

Yet all of this would take place without abandonment of the Bolshevik Revolution, without retreat from totalitarian socialism, without cessation of vigorous, even occasionally violent, efforts to spread that system.

And all of this would raise as many difficult problems as it would resolve for America and the West. For the first time, getting along with the USSR would become a practical problem which vigor, imagination and determined leadership could hope to solve.

This would be exceedingly difficult. It would involve at one and the same time competing effectively over the whole spectrum of life with the Russians and negotiating and dealing with them with skill and hope.

I was not an optimist about this. I did not see on either their side or ours the wisdom, foresight or patience required. In America, I knew, there were not the beginnings of realization of what a strength their system represented, what an active threat it was about to become, what an effective attack they could launch on our positions. There was no realization of how radical would be the means required to meet and parry this attack—and how many vested interests would have to be stepped on in order for America to compete with them effectively.

But this was not the main point—not at that moment.

The main thing was that Russia had passed its crisis. As a result the world had been given a new chance to work things out, a breathing space, a new opportunity in which the possibilities were infinitely better for a happy outcome than they had been only a few months before. For the time being life had triumphed over death, hope over despair. And what more, after all, could one ask?

As for Julie and me—we too had been given a new chance. We were beginning a new life. I was only thirty-six, and she was much younger, but we had each of us, in joy and anguish, lived already a whole lifetime. Now we were being suddenly, unexpectedly, catapulted into a new life in which everything would be different. I didn't know what each of us, together or separately, might make of our opportunity, but I knew that she and I were glad to have it. We were each glad to be at last free and the masters of our own fates. We could at last go where we pleased.

I looked down at the Finnish countryside below me. Little neat white houses nestled in among pines and birches on neat little farms. And then I looked back over my shoulder to where—already below the horizon—lay Russia. I felt a little pang in my heart. There had been times in Russia when I had felt terribly alien, terribly foreign, when I had been certain that I was as distant from the Russians around me, from their life, as if I had been in a galaxy a million light years away. But I did not have that feeling any more. I had left Russia, maybe for good. But I had left some of myself behind. I had dug in the Russian earth. I had eaten Russian bread. I had experienced Russian hospitality. I had loved and been loved in Russia. I had buried one I loved there. And I had taken some of Russia with me— in my heart. Some of the passion, some of the suffering, and some of the sweeping scope of that broad country and that generous people, even some of its vitality and creativity, had gotten into me and become part of me. Russia was in my life and I wouldn't, of course, ever be the same again. Nor did I want to be. I was glad this was the way things were. And I was also glad to be going home.

The plane began to bank toward the left.

"Comrade passengers!" announced the stewardess over the loud speaker, "We will be landing in five minutes."

The plane began descending fast toward the Helsinki Airport. I looked at Julie. She was staring out of the window. There was excitement in her eyes. She turned back to me and smiled. "Well, Tomochka," she said. "I guess we made it."

\*     \*     \*     \*     \*

Here it is late October, 1961. More than eight years have passed since that summer day when Julie and I left Russia. They have been busy, absorbing, exciting years. And the kind of life each of us lives now is completely different from that we lived in Russia. And as the years go by we talk about that other life in Moscow less and less often. But once in a while we do—like the other day. And when we had finished reminiscing a bit Julie tossed her head and exclaimed:

"It's strange how remote all that seems to me. Sometimes I feel as if it were a dream, as if none of it had ever really happened at all, as if I had lived all my life right here in New York . . ."

We lapsed into silence and I looked at her and thought how quickly and easily she had slipped into her new life in her new country, how she had fallen in love with Manhattan, how she had found new friends, how finally after many hardships and disappointments she had got started again at composing and singing . . . In 1959 she made a long-playing record album of favorite Russian songs entitled *Moscow After Dark*. It was a success. In 1961 she made a different kind of album titled *Twelve Faces of Love*. It contained a dozen new songs all her own—her voice, her music, her lyrics (in English), her orchestrations, her piano, her conducting. And now she is busy working on three or four new record projects, organizing her own music publishing house, up to her neck in problems of promotion and publicity, contemplating the possibility of doing a musical.

I looked at that chic, cosmopolitan, sophisticated New York woman there across from me and I asked myself: "Where has that Russian girl gone—that girl I met in Moscow so long ago wearing that black silk dress with the orange, pink and yellow flower pattern, that girl with whom I fell in love in the Gorky Park of Culture and Rest?" But just at that moment Julie looked at me and there passed across her face a little wistful smile and her eyes grew soft. And I knew that that girl was indeed still there.